TITO'S FLAWED LEGACY

TITO'S FLAWED LEGACY

Yugoslavia & the West since 1939

by

NORA BELOFF

WESTVIEW PRESS
BOULDER, COLORADO

First published in Great Britain 1985 by Victor Gollancz Ltd

First published in the United States in 1985 by
WESTVIEW PRESS
Frederick A. Praeger, Publisher
5500 Central Avenue
Boulder, Colorado 80301

© Nora Beloff 1985

ACKNOWLEDGEMENT
Acknowledgement is due for the following copyright material:
extracts from *Yugoslavia and the Soviet Union 1939–1973* by Stephen
Clissold (OUP for the RIIA, 1975), are reprinted by permission
of Oxford University Press, © Royal Institute of International
Affairs 1975; extracts from *Tony Crosland* by Susan Crosland are
reprinted by permission of Susan Crosland; extracts from
Moscow Diary by Veljko Mićunović translated by David Floyd
are reprinted by permission of the author, Chatto & Windus
and Doubleday & Co. Inc., translations copyright © 1980 by
Doubleday & Co. Inc.; extracts from *Khrushchev Remembers*
(1971) translated by J. Talbot is reprinted by permission of
André Deutsch and Little, Brown and Company; extracts from
Rise and Fall and *Memoirs of a Revolutionary* by M. Djilas are
reprinted by permission of Harcourt Brace Jovanovich Inc.
    The map on pages 8 and 9 is reprinted from *Yugoslavia* by
permission of Stevan K. Pavlowitch, the author, and Ernest
Benn Ltd.

ISBN 0-8133-0322-2
LC 85-51327

Photoset in Great Britain by
Rowland Phototypesetting Ltd, Bury St Edmunds, Suffolk
and printed by St Edmundsbury Press
Bury St Edmunds, Suffolk

CONTENTS

Preface	*page*	11
Introduction: Tito and Seven Myths		15
1 Tito the Latter-Day Patriot		29
2 The Legend of the Liberation		57
3 How Churchill was Hoodwinked		84
4 Tito's Rupture and Reconciliation with Moscow		129
5 Non-Aligned against the West		159
6 Neither Brotherhood nor Unity		190
7 The Holy Grail of Self-Management		218
Conclusion: Pickled Falsehoods		246
Notes and References		267
Select Bibliography		277
Index		281

To my husband,
Clifford Makins

PREFACE

THE REPRESSIVE NATURE of the Communist system in Yugoslavia
debars me from expressing my personal thanks to the large
number of Yugoslavs, particularly the young, who have helped me
during the years I have spent working on this reassessment. If the
book can be smuggled through to them I hope that they will accept
this collective acknowledgement of my debt—all the greater
because they took risks and I took none.

One of the deprivations which the present régime has inflicted
on Yugoslav society is the exodus of many of the ablest and most
uncompromising of its intellectuals: thus qualifying these for the
pejorative label of *émigré* and exposing them to scorn and hatred.
Yugoslavia's loss has been my gain: two scholars, Dr Ljubo Sirc of
the Department of Political Economy at Glasgow University and
Dr Stevan Pavlowitch of the Faculty of History at Southampton fit
into this category. Both have been unstintingly generous with their
time and erudition and this book could not have been written
without their help.

My special thanks are also due to the international lawyer,
Professor Ivo Lapenna, who has helped me to understand why any
Yugolsav who, like himself, respects the independence of the
judiciary, cannot practise his profession in his own country. I have
also been helped and advised by Mr Aleksa Djilas who has
inherited the intransigence of his father Milovan, the only man in a
Communist-led country who after reaching the highest echelons of
the Party and enjoying all the perks of the *nomenklatura*, ever
willingly resigned on a matter of principle. Aleksa has campaigned
steadfastly for human rights and for the observance of the Helsinki
Agreement by Yugoslavia, consequently being forced to seek
political asylum, conceded to him by the British Government in
1983.

I am especially grateful to the Hoover Institution of Stanford
University, California, for inviting me to be a Visiting Scholar
and for giving me access to their fine libraries and archives. I am
personally indebted to its Chief Archivist, Dr Milorad Drachkovitch who allowed me to draw on his encyclopaedic knowledge
of Yugoslav history. I must also thank Mr Irving Kristol, a mem-

ber of the Board of Directors of the Institution for Educational Affairs, through whose good offices I received a grant which covered part of the costs of the frequent visits to Yugoslavia which this work has entailed.

Those of my compatriots who helped me most were the ones who served in Yugoslavia during the war and who opened up a new perspective on the internecine fighting going on between the Yugoslavs themselves and revealed to me for the first time that we had actively intervened in the civil war on the Partisan side. The most important information was from Colonel Hudson who was in Yugoslavia from 1941 to 1944 and from Robert Wade who introduced me to Hudson and who like Hudson was sent to join the anti-Communist Draža Mihailović guerrilla force and then given orders to change sides and join the Partisans.

I am much indebted for useful criticism and suggestions to Sir Alexander Glen, who as junior naval attaché in Belgrade had known Mihailović before Yugoslavia entered the war and who was serving with the Partisans when the Russians arrived in east Serbia in 1944. Another British officer, Mr Vane Ivanović, of Yugoslav extraction, who served with British Intelligence in Cairo and Bari, understood better than most of his colleagues what was really happening in Yugoslavia and has been a valuable critic and adviser.

I would like to pay a special tribute, alas posthumous, to George Waddams who served with the Partisans in Slovenia and, at the end of the war, was appointed British Consul in Ljubljana. Before he died he described to me his unavailing efforts to alert and inform the British government and British opinion of the magnitude of the postwar terror in Yugoslavia, a lot of it directed against friends of Britain.

On the academic side I owe thanks first to the late Professor Hugh Seton-Watson on whose writings and comments I heavily relied. I am also indebted to two scholars with intimate knowledge of Yugoslav cultural and spiritual life, Mrs Celia Hawksworth and Mrs Stella Alexander. My older brother, Professor Max Beloff who, unlike me, is a professional historian, generously read and corrected the chapters as they were written. Neither he nor any of the people I have mentioned in this preface are in any way responsible for the contents of the book—nor for its mistakes.

I owe a special word of thanks to my husband Clifford Makins to whom this book is dedicated and who helped and encouraged me in what has been by far the most arduous and challenging assignment of my professional life. For too long he has had to share my time and attention with the unlaid ghost of Marshal Tito.

This book is in part a penance for unquestioningly accepting the Titoist bias shared by most of my countrymen. I hope it may be regarded in part as the damages I owe to the many victims of Yugoslav police repression, not least the six Belgrade intellectuals who were on trial for their opinion when I was struggling to complete the book. For one of the newspapers which took the lead in sustaining the Titoist myth was *The Observer* on which I spent most of my adult life. Fortunately I had resigned before Tito's funeral when *The Observer*'s editorial staff laid a wreath paying homage to "a great leader". They were as unaware as I used to be that if they had been writers in Yugoslavia and had had the courage of their personal convictions (which presumably include a belief in civil rights), they would either have had to emigrate or to live dangerously outside the law, unemployed and without the dole.

It seems hardly necessary to say, except perhaps for the benefit of the more primitive Yugoslav Communists who believe that the British are their "class enemies", that this book is not officially inspired. On the contrary, it is likely to displease the top people (though not everybody) at the Foreign and Commonwealth Office, the State Department and, perhaps, the Quai d'Orsay.

Finally, I want to thank Miss Livia Gollancz for her moral courage in being willing to publish a book which challenges received opinion on the left as well as on the right.

FEBRUARY 1985   N.B.

Introduction

TITO AND SEVEN MYTHS

THIS BOOK IS written in the belief that the time has come to reassess Titoism: from its Western-sponsored seizure of power and its Western-assisted development, to its present and resented dependence on Westerners who call themselves the "Friends of Yugoslavia".

These are not, as the warm words suggest, an association of scholars or travellers lured by Yugoslavia's unparalleled charms. The name was selected (after some argument) to identify a financial partnership of fifteen capitalist countries, led by the United States and initially inspired by former US Ambassador Lawrence Eagleburger, who have organized the multi-billion-dollar rescue operations, involving governments, international institutions and commercial banks, and so saved Yugoslavia from financial collapse. The participants pride themselves on having warded off the risks of hunger and chaos and perhaps, even, of the reintegration of Yugoslavia into the Soviet bloc.

The contribution of "the friends" has enabled Yugoslavia to honour all its international debts. It has also benefited improvident Western bankers and provided jobs and profits to Western factories short of customers and eager to supply Yugoslavia with equipment, spare parts and finished goods—especially as these have been financed mainly by Western tax-payers.

What it has not provided is any benefit perceptible to ordinary Yugoslavs who are witnessing a remorseless rise in unemployment —90 per cent of it among the under 30-year olds—and the highest inflation rate in Europe. Forty years after the installation of "the dictatorship of the proletariat" (the official euphemism for one-party Communist rule), Yugoslavia is experiencing the curse which Karl Marx predicted would mark the final phases of capitalism: the rich (who keep their bank-accounts in hard currency) are getting richer; the much more numerous poor (for the fifth year running) are getting poorer. Nor are there indications when the "pauperization" will end.

In Europe today, Yugoslavia is the odd-country out. It belongs to neither of the military blocs, yet it is not, like Sweden or Switzerland, one of the recognized neutrals. Its territories, in the heartland of the Balkans, have a long history not only as a meeting-place of many civilizations, which makes it so fascinatingly varied, but also as an area of collision between faiths: Moslem and Christian, Orthodox and Roman Catholic, and, in our time, Marxism–Leninism and Western-style democracy. It has also repeatedly aroused imperial ambitions and suffered invasion and occupation from the Ottoman Empire, Venice, Austria, Hungary and Nazi Germany. Predators have been attracted not only by its natural resources and rich fertile valleys, but even more by its unique strategic importance. Over most of recorded history (though perhaps less in our nuclear and airborne age) what has counted most has been the vital routes between north and south: from Europe to Africa; and between east and west—from the Adriatic to the Bosporus and Asia.

None the less, though the cities and countryside have repeatedly changed hands and big powers have grabbed little princedoms and provinces, none has established lasting and all-embracing control. Each invader brought in new settlers, new languages or dialects, new styles of life, new institutions and political boundaries, all of which intermingled. Yet as the historian Stevan Pavlowitch has pointed out, the multiple nationalities were never completely blended. "Conquerors harassed the populations, mixed or divided them, but never integrated them." And, as he rightly adds: "The geography that attracted intervention from the outside also prevents any single native power from expanding, growing, attracting, unifying and checking foreign intrusion."[1]*

For this reason it is only fairly recently that it has been possible to create Yugoslavia as a single big bloc, now numbering nearly 23 million people. The concept of the unification of the Southern Slavs, and the political passions which the idea aroused, go back more than a century and a half. But it was not until after the First World War that the victors created the new state out of the mainly Slav remnants of the defunct Habsburg and Ottoman empires. Thrown together in haste in the chaotic postwar conditions, the new country, which took the name of Yugoslavia (meaning the country of South Slavs) in 1929, turned out to have greater staying powers than many expected.

As Milan Kundera has shown, the Communist ideologues specialize in the art of historical forgetting: modern Yugoslavs are not allowed to celebrate the birth of their state (1 December 1918).

* Notes and references begin on p. 267.

Yet, it survives today, broadly within the same frontiers (though, after the Second World War, with the addition of Istria and some Adriatic islands taken from Italy), suffering from the same ethnic and religious divergencies and exposed to the same international vulnerability. The familiar old epithet "trouble-in-the-Balkans" still sends shivers down Western spines. And significantly it is here that fighting begins in General Hackett's remarkably successful exercise in futurology *The Third World War*—as indeed it began two wars ago.

According to the official Yugoslav census, the country consists of no less than 17 different national groups, almost all having their own language or dialect and their own distinctive cultures. In Macedonia alone, just one of the eight federal units of which Yugoslavia is composed, there is such a mix-up of races that French cooks have come to describe their fruit salads as *macédoine de fruits*.

Outsiders find it discouragingly difficult to make sense out of such a multifarious community. Millions of tourists visit Yugoslavia every year to enjoy the climate, the scenery and the historical treasures, but most of them very sensibly refuse to allow Yugoslavia's complicated politics to spoil their pleasures. (Admittedly, few people can be quite as successful in putting the whole commotion out of mind as one elderly Manhattan taxi-driver who, in 1978, after being told that two young clients were from Yugoslavia, asked, after a pause: "Say, wasn't that the country where those two guys were fighting it out? Tito and Mihailović, wasn't it? By the way, who won?" Not that anybody seriously concerned with world affairs would underrate Yugoslavia's political and strategic importance. But busy politicians or heads of the big international institutions—the World Bank, the IMF, the EEC, the OECD and others—rarely have the time or patience to look into what seems like a basket of crabs and form their own judgement. Instead, when circumstances require a policy-decision or a political visit, the chiefs allow themselves to be briefed by the small côterie of "experts": men inclined to rely on what Yugoslav officials tell them and on what they tell each other: felicitations all round and nobody is offended.

For since the 1948 Stalin–Tito breach, Western objectives have been modest: to keep Yugoslavia out of trouble and to preserve Titoism intact. In the last years of Tito's life, a former British Ambassador was to recall: "We would have paid any price on earth" to be assured of what turned out to be a remarkably smooth

succession. The few billion dollars, now needed each year to keep
Yugoslavia afloat, seem cheap at the price. A very senior British
mandarin predicted in 1982 that "with economic aid from abroad
. . . Yugoslavia might remain, as we hope it will, a stable member
of the European community of nations."[2]

Not that in Yugoslavia the preservation of a fairly dictatorial
form of government, after the dictator's demise, is without precedent—or as much of a miracle as it seemed to some people at the
time. When Alexander I was murdered in 1934, after suspending
the constitution and assuming emergency powers, many in the
West dreaded the consequences of the political vacuum. In effect,
his highly undictatorial successor, Prince Paul, a personal friend of
the British royal family, who stood in as regent for the child, King
Peter, managed as well as the present-day leaders to keep things
going. He, too, both played off the ethnic and social groups against
each other and, also, relied on the survival of a Yugoslav sense of
solidarity, even after the death of its living symbol. It was only
because of an attack by a far stronger outside enemy that, in 1941,
the state was temporarily destroyed.

Some sense of national identity is apparent to anyone in the
world of sport who has watched a Yugoslav crowd cheering their
own soccer or athletics teams when these are pitted against
foreigners. Indeed, even when Yugoslavs leave their own country,
they tend to seek each other out. As in all big émigré movements,
the outside world hears most about internal rivalries and feuds.
But perhaps we get a more representative sample in the Yugoslav
Club of Glasgow, where a medley of Slovenes, Croats, Serbs,
Macedonians, including shop-keepers and teachers, businessmen
and labourers, enjoy occasional gatherings to talk about home.

After its 60 years of existence, we should perhaps stop thinking
of Yugoslavia as a precariously seated Humpty-Dumpty and
consider it instead as a potentially friendly country, cursed with a
turbulent history. For reasons which will be examined in this book
it is emphatically not, for the time being, "a stable member of the
European community of nations". But there is no intrinsic reason
why one day it might not become one.

There would therefore seem to be a case for asking whether we
are right to dedicate ourselves to the preservation, at any price, of
the present one-party, collectivist system and, in doing so, to
renounce the right to discuss among ourselves and with well-
disposed Yugoslavs any possible alternative.

Has the existing Western policy helped the Yugoslavs to help themselves? And, what is more important from our point of view, has it advanced the political and strategic interests of the Western alliance? Might it not rather be argued that we would have less reason to tremble over "trouble-in-the-Balkans" if the Yugoslavs were free to elect—and where necessary to change—their political leaders? Would the Yugoslavs not have better hopes of freeing themselves from their humiliating dependence on their "friends", if their own leaders, freed from ideological blinkers, were able to make more sensible use of the country's untapped human and material potential? Could we not have greater confidence in Yugoslavia's future if its children were not submitted to a compulsory atheist and Marxist form of education?

Looking further afield, have we been right to suppose that, because Yugoslavia is no longer a Soviet satellite, Tito and his successors have not done anything to forward Soviet ascendancy? Few men have studied the Communist system at such close quarters and so perceptively as the Yugoslav dissident Milovan Djilas, author of the seminal book *Conversations with Stalin*. Djilas now points to the fact that, even though the Communist movement is no longer monolithic, its aggregate strength, and its capacity to damage the West, is far stronger than it was in Stalin's time.[3] In promoting "Movements of National Liberation" (and only anti-Western groups qualify for this title), Yugoslavia within the limits of its potential is at least as active as the USSR. Indeed it could be argued that the mere fact that one of the principal promoters of the anti-Western cause is not officially part of the Soviet empire gives it added respectability.

No Western government or opposition ever raises such questions. In most Western chancelleries and universities the whole topic is virtually taboo. "In intellectual terms", said one independent-minded young diplomat, "Yugoslavia is a no-go area". Though the country is full of articulate anti-Communists, who share Western views and values, these are deliberately kept at arm's length by Western embassies and by visiting officials. A Third Secretary of one of the Western embassies commented: "If you are expelled as *persona non grata* from the Soviet Union or from a satellite country, this could be a professional plus. If you were asked to leave Belgrade you would be professionally finished."

Western willingness to underwrite the Yugoslav system and stubborn refusal to examine possible alternatives, which have now lasted for several decades, can be traced to a curious concatenation of unrelated circumstances. First and foremost has been the readiness to recognize the present leaders as the legitimate heirs of the extraordinarily brave Partisan guerrillas. Certainly, it is difficult to think of any exploits by foot-soldiers on a comparably epic scale since 1915, when the battered remnants of the Serb army fought their way in winter through the Albanian mountains, so that the survivors who reached the Adriatic could participate in the Salonika landings and help liberate Belgrade.

Today few are old enough to remember events of 70 years ago. But this extraordinary feat, with all its horror and heroism, is convincingly recreated in Dobrica Ćosić's four-volume novel *In Times of Death*.[4] During the Second World War, a similar level of dare-devil and superhuman endurance, shown by the Partisans, was witnessed personally by Westerners, parachuted to serve as liaison officers with Tito. Two of these, Brigadier Fitzroy Maclean and Captain William Deakin, by a curious quirk of history, happened to be personal friends of Winston Churchill. Both were young and impressionable and understandably proud of this unique opportunity of demonstrating, to themselves and to the men around them, their rare degree of personal courage in the face of continuous danger. From their arrival, both identified unreservedly with the Communist-controlled Partisans and filed uncritical accounts of what the leadership told them.

Further, Maclean by his unusual gifts as a story-teller, and Deakin, future head of St Antony's College, Oxford, by his teaching gifts, ensured that future generations would carry on the tradition. Deakin remained the unchallenged authority on wartime Yugoslavia and his students included two men who were to rank among leading Yugoslav specialists: Dennison Rusinow, author of the generally accepted textbook *The Yugoslav Experiment*,[5] and Mark Wheeler, the leading Balkan expert at the London University's School of Slavonic and East European Studies.

The wartime enthusiasts could not have known then, as we do now (see Chapter 3), that the briefs received by British liaison officers in Cairo—before they were dropped—were doctored and sieved by an intelligence service infiltrated by the Communists. Nor was it known that the policy-makers in London were being denied field-reports, coming into Cairo, from liaison officers serving with the anti-Communist Chetniks and that these tended to be far less starry-eyed about the scale and nature of Partisan operations.

The second, and, as we shall see (in Chapter 4), largely unrelated event which endeared Titoism to the Western world was the 1948 break with Stalin. This took place at the peak of the Cold War when the enemies of our enemies were automatically our friends: which indeed is the way the Yugoslavs have been seen ever since. The most pro-Titoist are perhaps the American right-wing exponents of *Realpolitik*. They would be inclined anyway to believe that a benevolent dictatorship was just what people as primitive as the Yugoslavs really needed.

The concept of Titoism as a bulwark against the USSR has been ably sustained by the Yugoslav Communists themselves. Tito's blend of charm and cunning (see next chapter) enabled him to present himself as an eager but harassed friend. His followers and successors have been remarkably successful in preserving and embroidering the thesis that, unless the West gives them what they want, they may, reluctantly, find their way back into the Soviet fold.

Visiting diplomats and journalists (including myself, in earlier journalistic forays) have been regaled with reports of Soviet blandishment and threats. But in Western minds the fear of "losing" Yugoslavia has perhaps loomed too large. If the Titoists in Stalin's time had turned back to Moscow, they would have been signing their own death warrants. In the Khrushchev era (see Chapter 4), the Russians no longer felt they needed to insist on identical "paths to socialism". Moscow would be satisfied as long as it could be sure that, in cases where Communism itself was at risk, other Communist countries would line up with the Russians: as, after momentary hesitation, Tito did over the 1956 invasion of Hungary.

Brezhnev's policy of *détente* was manifestly incompatible with any changes in the European balance of power. For the Russians it meant the maximization of exchanges and credits from the West, while limiting the expansion of Soviet power to the areas of the least resistance. The arrival of Soviet troops into Yugoslavia, even if invited by the Communist leaders and with the knowledge that Yugoslavia would be delivered without a fight, would irreparably harm East–West relations.

There are now a million Yugoslavs living temporarily in Western Europe and over half a million permanently settled in the United States: their resentment would have been powerful and highly articulate. For the Russians, it would mean taking over an insolvent and disgruntled country, instead of sitting back as at present and allowing the Yugoslav Marxist leaders, voluntarily and free of charge, to make their own contribution to anti-Western campaigns, as happens now, in any places where the Yugoslavs have a diplomatic or economic presence.

None of these considerations surfaced. Instead, the combination of Western anti-Soviet fears and Yugoslav diplomatic ingenuity managed to convince succeeding generations of Western leaders that the only choice confronting the Yugoslavs was between the Titoist or Soviet versions of one-party Communist rule.

In this predicament, the traditionally right-wing circles—the Republicans in the US and various brands of conservatives in Western Europe—were more than willing to waive any reservations about Communist incompetence and its manifest violation of human rights which, in other parts of Eastern Europe, incurred their displeasure. (The Yugoslav record, on this issue, is not significantly different from the Comecon average.)

It is usual in the Western world that any repressive régime which is defended on the right can expect a corresponding battering on the left. But here Yugoslavia is an exception. For most left-wingers Titoism still qualifies as "progressive". The public ownership of the means of production and verbal commitments to workers' self-management and to the "withering away of the state" have upheld the régime's socialist *imprimatur*.

This has produced a curious anomaly. The Yugoslav Communists themselves seem not to share the Western view that the Yugoslavs have to choose between Titoism or Soviet control. On the contrary, judging by public utterances, party resolutions, and the nature of recent political trials, the most dangerous enemies are those labelled "petty bourgeois" or "anarchic neo-liberals": officialese for critics who favour a politically plural society and who share Western beliefs in an independent judiciary and independent trade unions (the second being impossible without the first). In recent times, the Communist leaders have felt themselves particularly threatened by a tentative coming together of opposition from the three most developed capitals: Belgrade, Zagreb and Ljubljana.

Nor indeed is this the first Yugoslav experience of an inter-ethnic opposition to dictatorship. Everyone knows about the perennial Serbo–Croat quarrels: what has been largely forgotten is that, during the royal dictatorship of the 1930s, the Serb democrats joined forces with the Croat Peasant Party and when its populist leader, Vladko Maček, visited Belgrade, he was received by hundreds of thousands of cheering Serbs and given deafening ovations.[6]

Yet the present-day Yugoslav, who dares to protest against arbitrary rule, receives remarkably little sympathy or help from like-minded Westerners. For propaganda reasons, the Yugoslav Communists, like their Soviet counterparts, always insist that liberalizers are receiving aid and encouragement from the West. In fact this is less true in Yugoslavia than anywhere else in Eastern Europe. The Voice of America and the BBC rarely broadcast anything which might offend the Yugoslav authorities. And there is no Yugoslav service at all from the American-controlled Radio Free Europe.

Nor need the Titoists worry about the bulk of the Western press. Representatives of traditionally liberal newspapers, *The Guardian* and *The Observer* in London and *The New York Times* or *Washington Post* in the US, cherish a vision of themselves as defenders of independent thought and would not consider tying themselves to any party or orthodoxy. If they were citizens of Yugoslavia, the non-belonging itself would debar them from the media and if they persisted in repudiating the prevailing creed, they would be lucky to stay out of jail. Yet in handling Titoism, which (unlike their French and German colleagues) they normally "cover" in quick and sporadic run-arounds, they feel they are demonstrating their broad-mindedness by respecting and believing anything that the Communists tell them. Opponents of the régime are easily dismissed as reactionaries or potential terrorists.

Titoism also benefits in the West from what survives of socialist utopianism. The leading Soviet exiles—Solzhenitsyn, Bukovsky, Zinoviev, and others—however much they differ between themselves, have provided an insight into Soviet life which has sickened even the most ardent fellow-travellers. But Yugoslavia is different: the Yugoslav people are certainly better off and less oppressed than the Russians (they always have been). If they can be shown to have created a free and relatively prosperous society, there would still be a little hope left for those who believe that collectivism is not necessarily incompatible with democracy.

At first, indications to this effect were encouraging: the Communist take-over in Yugoslavia coincided with the early phases of the country's industrial take-off period: this meant, for a time, dazzlingly rapid rates of economic growth. These were paid for, as we shall see, primarily by exploiting the peasants and by inflation rather than savings and they were prolonged by a continued influx of foreign credits. Yet for Westerners disgusted by the blemishes of their own free enterprise society there was a desperate search for any possible alternative. And for believers in workers' co-operatives or co-ownership, Yugoslavia seemed to be providing a fascinating pilot-plant. Few, who went to see, had the intellectual honesty of Professor Harold Lydall, who, having been deeply impressed by the success of the Mondragon Co-operative in Spain, decided to make a detailed analysis of Yugoslavia, which he had supposed "was the world's only predominantly labour-cooperative economy". A closer look induced a reluctant confession: "In view of all the high hopes and instinctive beliefs associated with the idea of self-management, it is disagreeable to have to concede that it has turned out to be not much more than a vast public relations exercise."

What was extraordinary was the degree to which this "public relations exercise" succeeded. Robert Shaplen came to Yugoslavia in 1983 for *The New Yorker*, at a time when living standards were already plummeting and when Yugoslav officials were arranging a private meeting with the Hungarians to find out why their system worked so much better. Yet he still felt able to describe the Yugoslav régime as "a true socialist middle-way" and to predict that "the Yugoslav blue-print will have considerable impact on other nations involved in comparable reform experiments".[7]

But then, as the young representative of a big Yugoslav firm in New York once said: "The world owes us a debt. For anyone who believes in worker control, we have shown the way *not* to do it." All discerning Yugoslavs know, of course, that the blue-print, which so much impressed *The New Yorker*, would never get off the printed page. Nevertheless, in the prevailing goodwill, the International Labour Office sponsored a report on *Yugoslav Self-Management*, written by three Yugoslav specialists, covering 200 printed pages, without once revealing that what was being described was only the theory. The practice was something different.

The Western academic world, too, is sheltered from reality. Teachers on Yugoslav affairs rely on Yugoslav officials, not only for information, but also for invitations, exchanges and sabbatical perks. One case in point is the post-graduate School of Yugoslav Studies at Bradford University. Its founder and now Professor Emeritus, Fred Singleton, is a holder of the highest Yugoslav decoration awarded to foreigners and is currently preparing a book on Yugoslav nature reserves. In March 1983, he and the centre's present director, John B. Allcock, who is preparing a study on the Yugoslav tourist industry, presided at a seminar entitled (misguidedly, as they later admitted): *Open Socialism: A*

Balance Sheet of the Yugoslav Experiment. The meeting was open to all specialists on Yugoslavia and was attended, among others, by two exiled Yugoslavs: Dr Ljubo Sirc, Senior lecturer in Economics at Glasgow University, and Aleksa Djilas (son of the dissident Milovan Djilas), then preparing a D.Phil. dissertation on Croat nationalism at the London School of Economics.

With financial assistance from the Ford Foundation, three professors were flown in from Belgrade, Zagreb and Skopje. When they arrived in Bradford they found a message from their embassy in London forbidding them to talk to "class enemies". The organizers of the "open socialism" seminar promptly accepted the offer of the Yugoslav exiles to leave by the earliest possible train. Arrangements were then made for a special meeting, at a different site, so that the visitors would not have their names listed with the prohibited scholars.

This incident illustrates a manifest violation of basic principles of academic freedom. It is merely an example of the sort of compromise that British academics accept under pressure from the Yugoslav regime.

Given this background, a newly critical look at Tito's record and at the Yugoslavia he left behind him, must run up against adamant opposition from governments, diplomatic chancelleries, most of the academic world and the vast bulk of former journalistic colleagues: institutions which cannot be lightheartedly challenged.

Indeed Yugoslavia presents a particularly difficult problem. Whereas a reassessment of most countries merely requires digging deeper into existing knowledge, on the Yugoslav question it is first necessary to cut through the thickets of misconceptions, created over decades by the stolid and inherited pro-Tito bias. Against the one odd Manhattan taxi-driver, who did not know that Tito had won the civil war, there are millions who know very well he ruled Yugoslavia for a remarkably long time. Further, after the 1948 breach with Stalin, Western textbooks, following the *1066 and All That* tradition, identified him firmly and flatly as "a good thing".

Nor is it just the personality of Tito which is at issue. The purpose of this book is not to point a finger at an emperor who had no clothes (a particularly inappropriate metaphor for a man who paid so much regard to uniforms and sartorial splendour). The results of my inquiry suggest that attitudes towards Titoist Yugoslavia have been shaped by no less than seven separate myths.

Like all myths, each contains a kernel of truth, but these have been so magnified and embroidered that they have become identifiable and damaging misconceptions. Nor can any of the seven be understood without some reference to their historical origins.

Here again, Yugoslavia differs from other countries. For not one of them can be understood without some allusion to its past. All countries cherish legends about their past. But, in Yugoslavia's case, there are additional reasons why this is especially true. First, the various, incompletely integrated peoples tend to be unsure of their identity and therefore particularly anxious to go back to their roots. The result is an all-pervading nostalgia: to understand contemporary Yugoslavia it is necessary to know, for instance, that Croatia already had a kingdom of its own in the tenth century, before the Serbs emerged as a separate entity; and also to be aware that a remarkably civilized Serbian kingdom lasted from the twelfth to the end of the fourteenth century; and that it had its cradle in the province of Kosovo now inhabited mainly by Albanians. It is relevant to current politics that Kosovo's Albanians claim descendence from the shadowy race of Illyrians (see Shakespeare). If so, the Kosovans were there before the seventh century when the Slavs arrived. It is also necessary to know that the separate nationality of Slovenes, who occupy Yugoslavia's north-west corner, boast a singularly long cultural tradition. It was here that the first press to print in any Slavonic language is reported to have been located, and Slovenia was the first territory of what is now Yugoslavia to be industrialized and to allow its workers to organize trade unions.

Yugoslavia's past history, though calculated here in decades rather than in centuries, is no less vital to the present régime. "What right have the Communists to monopolize power?" I asked a young Party official in 1983. The answer was immediate: "We won the revolution." The "we" in question must have included his grandparents. But the fact remains that the legitimacy of the present political system is based, not on elections or inheritance, but on the Partisan war. Further, it was in the course of that civil war that, according to the official history, the peoples of Yugoslavia, without a plebiscite or referendum, made their final and irrevocable decisions to live "in brotherhood and unity" within the confines of a single federation.[8]

For these reasons, though this book does not offer a chronological history of Yugoslavia, the reader must expect frequent references to Yugoslavia's ancient and modern history. And in the latter, whether we like it or not, we cannot shrug off Western responsibility. I am not presuming to suggest that there is any simple ready-made alternative to the policies now being followed by those who call themselves "the friends of Yugoslavia", but who are, more precisely, the friends of the present régime and therefore, implicitly, the opponents of men and women, principally of the younger generation, who are struggling for a more open and less arbitrary society.

Certainly, after 40 years of Communist rule and Communist monopoly of information, Yugoslavia could not be easily transformed into what the West would identify as a democracy. The future of the country must depend primarily on its own people and only peripherally on outsiders.

Yet the country's dependence on continuous Western refinancing itself imposes intrusion. One young bright banker, who has done very well out of the system, warned me that the West should be careful: "We are a young and immature country. We are liable to feel humiliated and react irrationally against any outside interference. . . ." He was, of course, not suggesting that the West should withdraw credits; just that we should go on, as before, providing blank cheques to politicians who were responsible only to their own unelected and intrinsically anti-Western party.

The answers to the Yugoslav problem are not easy: the most this analysis sets out to do is to identify the degree of Western guilt for the distress in which Yugoslavia now finds itself; and so, perhaps, to encourage a radically different Western approach.

Chapter 1

TITO THE LATTER-DAY PATRIOT

JOSIP (CROAT FOR Joseph) Broz, better known in the world as
Marshal Tito, was unquestionably a most remarkable man. He
came to prominence, during the Second World War, as the leader
of what all historians agree was Europe's most effective resistance
movement. He managed to preserve the essentials of the Communist system: collective ownership and one-party rule, even after
Stalin had disavowed and tried to get rid of him. He carved out for
Yugoslavia an international role disproportionately great for such
a small and relatively backward country. And he so much over-
shadowed his compatriots that, several years after his death,
hardly anyone abroad, and probably not too many at home, could
name any other Yugoslav leader.

Indeed this was the way he would have wanted it. The proclamation "The King is dead. Long live the King!" traditionally
announces to the populace that a successor has inherited the
kingship. Josip Broz had no successor. He had arranged that,
when he died, both the role of President and the rank of Marshal
would disappear with him.

The general view of Tito, nurtured by his own party, which has
had a 40-year monopoly of the Yugoslav media, and widely shared
by the outside world, is that the man, who dominated his country
for so long, whatever his faults or errors, was a great Yugoslav
patriot and political visionary. A closer look at his life suggests that
he was neither. Indeed, until he was forty-three years old, there is
no evidence that he ever identified with Yugoslavia at all. His first
military experience was as an NCO in the Austro-Hungarian
army which invaded Serbia in 1914 when the idea of Yugoslavia
was already widely propagated: the first people he killed must
certainly have been those who, had they survived, might have
become his compatriots.

Later in life, he became a paid agent of the Soviet-controlled
Comintern which, until its shift of policy in 1935, required its
Yugoslav employees to engage in agitation and propaganda
directed towards dismantling the Yugoslav state. In obedience to
Stalin's orders, the Yugoslav Communist Party, of which Tito was
a member, declared itself at its 1928 Fourth Congress to be in

favour of the creation of independent states of Croatia and
Slovenia and of the unification, as well as the independence, of
Macedonia and Albania. This would have included the territories
now an integral part of Yugoslavia, which are inhabited mainly by
Macedonians or Albanians. And so, unlike General de Gaulle,
who could affirm of his country: "All my life I have had a certain
conception of France", Tito not only had no conception of Yugoslavia, he was actively committed to wiping it off the map.

As for being a visionary, the record of his speeches and conversations suggests, on the contrary, a sharp but down-to-earth
political shrewdness accompanied by a marked lack of interest in
general ideas. His intellectual baggage included little more than
Marxist–Leninist belief in the concept of class war and a single-
minded adherence to the principle of "the dictatorship of the
proletariat": with the proletariat incarnated in the communist
party, and the party incarnated, first in the person of Stalin and,
after 1948, in Tito himself. The job of working out a different
theoretical version of Marxism–Leninism to distinguish the eras
of the two Josephs (Stalin and Tito) was left to Edvard Kardelj
and other subordinates (see Chapter 7).

There was, of course, an element of chance in the dazzling
ascent of this grandson of a serf, born in 1892 in a farmstead in a
backward province of the Austro-Hungarian Empire, and
escorted to his grave, 88 years later, by kings, presidents and prime
ministers, representing 120 different countries, and mourned by
millions of compatriots along the way.

In reassessing history, there will always be arguments about the
respective importance, on the one hand, of the qualities of an
individual and, on the other, of the circumstances which, at that
particular moment, carried someone of his or her special traits to
international pre-eminence. Most historians would agree, for
example, that if Germany had not been defeated and demoralized
during the First World War, Hitler would have remained a no
doubt troublesome but despised outcast. Churchill did his utmost
to avert the Second World War: its occurrence nevertheless
assured him a place in the Pantheon of British heroes. Tito, like
Hitler and Churchill, was both the creature and creator of his
unquiet times; his glory too was partly fortuitous.

The details of his early life are hard to come by. Most of the
many biographies and studies depend on his own testimony.
Personal recollections are always an inadequate source: partly
because of the human memory's fallibility and partly, too, because

people normally reveal only the part of themselves by which they wish to be remembered. But in Tito's case, a distinct streak of mythomania added to the difficulty. For many practising politicians, deception is a rational choice. Such eminent leaders as President Roosevelt, Harold Macmillan (later Earl of Stockton) and Charles de Gaulle were virtuosos at concealing their thoughts. Indeed they often practised precisely the opposite of what they preached. But many of Tito's tales had no political motivation at all. He was a good story-teller and enjoyed romanticizing his past. The most famous of his stories, and the most frequently retold, relates to his faithful dog Tiger, to whom he said he owed his life. According to Tito, during one enemy offensive in the last war, Tiger threw himself over his master's body and protected him from enemy fire.

According to Tito's former friend and later critic, Milovan Djilas, who was very close to Tito throughout the war, "everyone, except his most slavish toadies, took Tito's self-mythologizing as harmless fun".[1] Aside from "the slavish toadies" however, there were quite a few Western admirers, wartime associates, historians and journalists, who enjoyed what they assumed were his confidences and who circulated the legends around the world.

Vladimir Dedijer, also a wartime associate, who became Tito's official biographer, mentions another problem: Tito was an irascible man and one way he vented his anger was by destroying documents he disapproved of. Dedijer claims that Tito's last wife, Jovanka, was specially good "at getting Tito worked up" and Dedijer attributes to her responsibility for the fact that Tito tore up some valuable reports from his former Ambassador to Moscow, Veljko Mićunović. Tito, says his biographer, would only have destroyed material of this kind "in a burst of rage" and did not behave like this except when he lost his temper. Dedijer asserts that Jovanka, who had keys to all Tito's private safes, goaded him on by accusing the ex-Ambassador of being anti-Soviet.[2]

What we do have, on record, are the broad outlines of Tito's youth. On both sides the future incarnation of the proletariat came from sound kulak stock: the families were poor but one notch better off than the landless labourers who worked in the big estates. His father inherited a half of what was generally thought to be the best farmhouse in the little village of Kumrovec on the Croatian side of the border between Croatia and Slovenia. It had solid foundations, a tiled roof and plastered walls and has now been transformed into a museum and a shrine.

Father Broz had none of his son's stamina, failed to make good, and later in life took to drink. The mother came from a more prosperous family across the Sutla river in Slovenia. When her parents married off their fifteen-year-old daughter, they could afford to provide food and drink for family and friends on both sides for a traditional wedding which lasted several days. But the girl—a pious Catholic—had little to look forward to when she joined the Kumrovec household. She bore fifteen children, of whom eight survived infancy and only four reached adulthood. Josip was the second son and there was no way of telling from which ancestor he may have inherited the genes which so singled him out.

The Broz children spent a good deal of time with their mother's parents and Tito recalled those visits as the happiest times of his childhood: better food, greater comfort, kindlier behaviour. Crossing the river imposed no language problems: literary Croat and Slovene are quite different but in this border area, in the province known as Zagorje, they merged into a curious mongrel dialect. Later, when Tito was in prison in Serbia, he learnt to make Serb his first language. But during the time he was working for Moscow, some of his Serb associates hearing his accent took him for a Russian agent. The truth was that, even at the pinnacle of power, he never lost the Zagorje twang.

Though on both sides of the River Sutla they spoke the same language, the Slovene side was richer and culturally more advanced. When Tito later remembered a gentler form of life, this may have been due as much to the higher Slovene level of development as to his personal preference for his mother's family.

Both Croatia and Slovenia were, of course, still parts of the Habsburg Empire and both were Roman Catholic. But Croatia had belonged to Hungary for some 800 years and at that time formed part of the Hungarian side of the dual Austro-Hungarian monarchy. It was not until the mid-nineteenth century that serfdom was abolished in the region (Tito's grandfather was one of the beneficiaries).

Slovenian lands, on the other hand, were part of the hereditary Austrian territories and in the eighteenth century the peasants were already benefiting from Joseph II's enlightened despotism. To this day, Slovenia remains the most prosperous and the least corrupt part of Yugoslavia (some degree of corruption being inseparable from the present political system).

In the Zagorje, in which Tito grew up, most people were

illiterate, though reform was spreading and, since 1890, elementary schooling had become compulsory. Not that attendance was ever severely enforced: many peasants needed their children to work on the farms. Tito's mother, however, saw to it that between the ages of eight and twelve, Josip did go to class and thanks to the Habsburg tradition of preserving administrative records, Tito's biographers have managed to trace his scholastic record. His teachers noted frequent absences which he said later were caused by illness, including one nearly-fatal attack of diphtheria. In the Broz family, in common to that era, only the fittest survived. As Tito was to show the world, his staying power was remarkable; he was a born survivor.

When he did come to school, he showed himself a good pupil. In his last report, his behaviour was marked excellent and his catechism, reading and arithmetic very good. (He must have retained a happy memory of those days, as he revisited the school with a train of journalists in 1946, by which time he was Yugoslavia's top man. When he learnt that space was inadequate and that teaching had to be in morning and afternoon shifts, he demonstrated princely benevolence by donating the equivalent of £500 from his now bottomless purse.)

His mother also made sure that he was prepared for Confirmation, and he laughingly confessed later that he kept back some of the money she sent to pay the priest. He also served as an acolyte and told biographers that, after being slapped for inattention, he stood on his dignity and withdrew his services. Despite his mother's influence, religion played very little part in his later life, though it was not until he was instructed in Marxism–Leninism that he turned against the church. Later, when he took power, atheism became the established orthodoxy—though he took a little time to get used to it. On 2 June, 1945, when receiving a delegation of Catholic priests in order to complain about their anti-régime attitudes, he let slip the words, "I, as a Catholic . . .". Milovan Djilas, who was at the *Borba* newspaper offices at the time, consulted Edvard Kardelj about how to handle the remark, who exclaimed: "The Secretary of the Party is a Catholic!" "After which", wrote Djilas, "we immediately plucked up courage to remove the word 'Catholic' and replace it by Croat."[3]

The story of Tito's early life shows that, unlike some of his wartime associates, notably the young Montenegrin student, Djilas, he was not a born revolutionary. He did not grow up champing against social injustice nor, as a young man, show himself eager to change society. His career suggests that it was less a rebellious disposition than an accident of history that harnessed his driving ambition to the Communist movement and gave him the pluck to climb to power up the slippery slope of the Communist International. The boy from Kumrovec may have snatched a few pennies from the local priest or had himself slapped in church, but his energies were primarily engaged in breaking out of the vicious circle of poverty and disease.

Indeed, while Tito was making his way through school, Croatia's peasant society was going through rough times. In all of Eastern Europe, the early phases of the industrial revolution were accompanied by the familiar population boom and, in Croatia, there was not enough food to feed growing families. Tito's father, like many of his compatriots, tried to raise enough money to send his brightest son to America to make his own and his family's fortune. When he was about twenty years old he had another chance: a cousin suggested going and Tito told Dedijer that he "agonized" before deciding to stay in Europe. Later in life, he amused himself by imagining the kind of life he might have led in the States. Answering a question from a visiting journalist he joked: "I would have become President of General Motors instead of Yugoslavia."

Indeed, as Tito grew up, he did demonstrate many of the qualities of a successful tycoon: willingness to take risks, unscrupulousness in eliminating rivals, sharpness in negotiations, and an unusual capacity to inspire personal loyalty—a vital attribute before, during and after the war in the fight for power inside the communist party. Further, despite his Marxist–Leninist creed, he was highly acquisitive, coveting property and enjoying luxury. Even though he never emigrated to America, his chosen career in Yugoslavia offered a lavish opportunity to satisfy these cravings. Before he became party leader, he had virtually no personal property. But in 1939, when the Yugoslav communist party, by then under his direction, ceased to depend on Russian subsidies and managed to finance itself out of local contributions, he drew on party funds to buy himself a vineyard. With characteristic stamina and willingness to turn his hand to anything, he proceeded to learn how to make wine: a technique which he later enjoyed describing to his immediate entourage when they were whiling away time during the long interruptions between guerrilla activities.

But the era of grandiose acquisitions started only after the war.

By the time he died, he had accumulated countless residences: castles, palaces, villas and hunting lodges, each of them was full of personal gifts of every imaginable kind, given to him by the vast number of people who wanted—or needed—to please him. When he travelled within the country, as he often did, he let it be known that he preferred to stay at places he owned. Yet unlike his friend Ceauşescu in Romania, he was never a family man and never built up a dynasty or concerned himself about what would happen to his accumulated wealth after he died. Like most of the world's most successful businessmen his work was more important to him than his relatives. The nurses who tended him during his final illness in Ljubljana said that, apart from official visits from family and followers, at the time of his death, he was singularly alone.

If he had emigrated, Tito's taste for conspicuous consumption might have served to improve his credit-rating. In the Balkans, it was a tribute which most of his compatriots were resigned to paying those with political power. Tito never allowed his Marxist beliefs to interfere with his desire to impress not only his country-men but also foreign dignitaries. As he saw it, the proletariat won the class war and, as its rightful representative, he should be seen to be enjoying the same trappings of power as hereditary kings or barons.

Even though his father's insolvency closed the American option, Josip turned his back on the farm. For four years he served his apprenticeship to a locksmith in the town of Sisak, and by the time he qualified, he had earned just enough money to buy himself a smart suit with a tie and handkerchief to match. Unluckily, the new fineries were stolen in his lodgings and he had to wait for better times before his own village (now the location of the High School for Communist Studies) witnessed his splendour.

The story of his first purchases, and the fact he remembered the incident so well, illustrates his lifelong preoccupation with his appearance. He was a strikingly handsome man (though slightly overweight) with considerable sex-appeal and a narcissistic con-cern about how he looked and what he wore. People, who knew him before, during and after the last war, agreed that, even in the most unpromising situations and in the hardships of guerrilla war, he was always immaculately groomed. He told his associates that the diamond ring, that always flashed from his hand, had been paid for with the money he earned in Moscow in 1938, when he and a colleague, Vladimir Ćopić (later liquidated in the Stalinist purges) jointly translated Stalin's *History of the Soviet Communist*

Party. According to Djilas, the original ring was lost during the war but Moscow gave Tito another.

Tito enjoyed not only diamonds, uniforms, medals and the outward show of sartorial splendour but also its more intimate aspects. By the end of the Second World War, his reputation for magnificence was already internationally known. The Albanian leader, Enver Hoxha, later recalled that, having been summoned to Belgrade by Tito in 1946, he realized at once that he would not be able to face up to his host without a ceremonial uniform, non-existent in the Albanian army. As Albania was then short of textiles, material was generously donated by the Soviet Military Attaché at Tirana and Hoxha had himself fitted by the local tailor.

In his book *The Titoists* Hoxha described how, despite these precautions, he felt self-conscious in Tito's regal court and recalled his excruciating embarrassment when he muddied the bottom of his trousers, after being taken out to see Tito's hunting lodge. Then, after a ceremonial banquet, Hoxha said that Tito took him and a small group of other distinguished guests for a privileged tour around his private apartments. Tito's silk pyjamas were already laid out on the vast bed and he opened the cupboard to show his guests the fine array of silk shirts.[4]

Even in his old age, Tito never lost this passion for dressing up. Henry Kissinger in his memoirs described how Tito, then aged seventy-eight, welcomed President Nixon and himself in a marshal's grey-blue uniform with gold-braid epaulettes. The correspondent of *The New Yorker* was impressed by his "dazzling white uniform", worn just a few months before his death, at the Non-Aligned Conference in Havana.

Back in Kumrovec more than 70 years earlier, Tito, though he had lost his only suit, had managed to get his foot on to the first rung of the social ladder. Having completed his apprenticeship, he was now a skilled journeyman and in that long-forgotten Europe without passports or labour permits, such a qualification entitled him to seek work anywhere he pleased. And so, in the Dick Whittington tradition, a penniless seventeen-year-old peasant boy set out to make his fortune in cities which in his primitive society must have seemed paved with gold. He went first to Zagreb, where he worked as a general mechanic in a workshop and then to Kamnik in Slovenia, where he joined the Sokol, a pan-Slav and pro-Yugoslav society. Its political colouration seems not to have marked him and he was soon off to Bohemia, then part of the Austro-Hungarian Empire, earning a good living and having what he later remembered as the merriest time of his life: "The pay was very good. I could buy a new suit every month. Living standards were higher in Bohemia than in Austria. We used to spend our money freely. We went out every Saturday to different places and to other villages. In Bohemia every village had a brass band and we went dancing, drinking, spending. . . ." Even so he did not stay: "Well, you know that at that time I was temperamentally unable to stay in one place for long; when I got fed up with the job and it ceased interesting me, I told them I was going to Germany."[5] He then went on to Munich and worked for a while at Mannheim at the Benz automobile factory before going on to Vienna, where he was employed by Daimler. Here his older brother was already in a job on the railways and when he arrived in October 1912 he found a ready-made home with the family. He acquired a little German (those who knew him said he never mastered any language really well), took up fencing and learnt ballroom dancing.

As his biographer, Phyllis Auty, commented: "He was still a conformist, trying to better himself."[6] Though, during his travels around Europe, he must have witnessed hardship and unrest, his attention was not attracted by the revolutionary movements then gathering force in Central Europe. Far from defying established authority, he obediently went home, when he was twenty-one, and was summoned for military service. He was assigned to a Croat infantry regiment and soon became the youngest NCO in his unit.

At the time Tito joined the Imperial Army, many educated young people in Croatia and Slovenia (though none from the Broz family) were taken up with the idea of the unification of the Southern Slavs: Serbs, Croats and Slovenes to be merged into a single independent state. This sentiment had been openly defied in 1908, when the Habsburgs formally annexed Bosnia and Herzegovina, Slav provinces formerly within the Ottoman Empire. The Dual Monarchy responded to growing Slav restlessness by a mixture of carrot and stick: on the one hand, material and constitutional concessions; on the other, the exploitation of latent differences between its Orthodox and Catholic subjects. (When Tito came to power, he employed similar methods, earning himself the sobriquet "the last of the Habsburgs".)

In 1914, however, he seems to have been a loyal soldier, unaware or uninterested in the gathering storm. The most fanatical wing of the Yugoslav movement was the Serb minority and it was they who recruited, armed and trained the eighteen-year-old

Gavrilo Princip and sent him off in June 1914 to murder the heir to the Habsburg throne. It was on a visit to Sarajevo, then a provincial capital within his uncle's domain, that the Archduke, Franz Ferdinand, was assassinated. In Vienna, the militarists were looking out for an excuse to attack Serbia but it remains just possible that, without the murder, the First World War could still have been averted. In the course of it Serbia lost one quarter of its adult male population: casualties proportionately even heavier than in the whole of the Second World War. It is an illustration of the dominance in the Serb psyche of nationalist sentiment over the respect for human life that in Sarajevo today the site of the murder is marked by a stone honouring Princip's memory and a street in Belgrade carries his name.

It was in the Imperial Army that Tito first experienced warfare and acquired some rudimentary knowledge of military organization. There is no record that he had any misgivings about marching against Serbia but, in any case, a few months later, his regiment was moved to the Russian front. It was by showing initiative and endurance during a reconnaissance mission in the Carpathian mountains that he won the first of what were to be many military medals. The experience of fighting in the Emperor's service may have marked him more than outsiders supposed. A diplomat assigned to Belgrade in the 1960s was astonished at the importance Tito attached to a visit to Vienna: "It seemed that this former Corporal of the Austro-Hungarian army had been deeply moved to be entertained in the Schönbrunn Palace and treated everywhere with tremendous deference."

For Tito's wartime experience, we have to rely almost entirely on his personal testimony. As he recalled, his regiment, having reached a tributary of the Dniestre River, was suddenly attacked and overwhelmed by fierce Circassian warriors. Fighting off one Circassian bayonet, he was pierced in the back by another and left bleeding and unconscious. The Tsarist army, primitive and brutal as it was, seemed to have preserved some concept of military honour and Tito claims he was taken by stages to a little town on the Volga near Kazan, where he spent a year in an Orthodox monastery which had been transformed into a military hospital. He was subsequently employed as a mechanic on the trans-Siberian railways.[7]

The Russians, assuming (wrongly in Tito's case) that they could count on anti-German and pro-Slav sentiment among their Croat prisoners of war, offered to release any soldiers volunteering to fight with the Serbs against the Austro-Hungarians. Curiously, at roughly the same time, the future Cardinal, young Stepinac, was availing himself of just such an offer, made to South Slav prisoners of war in Italy. Yet, 30 years and two wars later, in a famous trial on charges of treachery to Yugoslavia, Tito was the accuser and Stepinac the accused. For what happened after—he was taken prisoner in the First World War—we have only Tito's own word. We do not know whether the offer to fight with the Serbs ever reached him but there is nothing in what he said or wrote to suggest that he would have been attracted by appeals to Slav solidarity. Instead, he remained an exemplary prisoner of war, rising to become foreman of his work-group and staying on the job until the Tsar abdicated and his captors fled.

According to his story, he made his way to Leningrad (then Petrograd), participating in Bolshevik demonstrations against the Kerensky Provisional Government and, like Dostoyevsky before him, was locked up in the fortress of St Peter and St Paul and then sent to Omsk in Siberia. After the Bolsheviks took over he and other prisoners joined the Red Guard and helped protect the railways. When Omsk was recaptured by the Whites, Tito found refuge in the home of a beautiful fifteen-year-old Russian girl, already a member of the Communist party, Pelagea Byelusnova, generally known as Polka.

In flight from the Whites, he said, he found a job as mill operator in the services of Hadj Isaj Djemsembayev, a Kirghiz tribal chieftain who was so pleased with Tito that he offered him a horse and his daughter's hand as inducements to stay on.

Instead, when the Reds got back he returned to Polka, followed her into the Communist party and early in the 1920s married her in the little Orthodox church of Bogoljubskoye near Omsk, where the Marxist message that God is dead had evidently not yet arrived. Today it is inconceivable, either in the USSR or in Tito's Yugoslavia, that party members would be permitted to marry in Church.[8]

Talking of his wartime experiences in later years, Tito evoked the Bolshevik revolution as if indeed to be young in that dawn was "very heaven". In fact, though he and Polka stayed long enough in Siberia to witness the Bolsheviks' final victory, they decided against making their home in this poor and beggar-ridden society. Indeed, there was no outlet for a man of Tito's ambitions and acquisitive instincts. So the young couple packed their few possessions, turned their back on the revolution and made their way slowly, via Petrograd and Vienna, to his childhood home at Kumrovec. It was the same village, though now in a different country, under another dynasty.

For, by then, Princip had achieved his purpose: after the loss of millions of lives, the Austro-Hungarian Empire had collapsed. Several of the returning prisoners of war identified themselves at once with the new Yugoslavia and engaged in skirmishes fought over the Adriatic territories, then being disputed between Italy and their new country. Tito, back home, found himself too poor for politics. During his absence his mother had died and the family had dispersed. For a man with his mechanical skills, jobs were scarce.

From 1921 to 1925, the longest time he ever held down a job outside politics, Tito counted himself lucky to find regular work some 60 miles east of Zagreb, operating a flour-mill belonging to Samuel Polak, "a kind-hearted Jew with a large family".[9] (There was never any indication that Tito shared the anti-semitism, of which there were always some traces in Croatia. It was for quite other reasons that he later backed the PLO and Egyptians in their struggle against Israel.)

While her husband was working at the mill, Polka produced four children of whom only one son survived. The little girls received a Catholic burial and Tito carved a headstone to go in the church cemetery.

The marriage ended badly. Polka returned to Russia in 1929 while Tito was serving a prison sentence. Later he accused her of having dumped their son in an orphanage to free herself for another mate. Like so many of the first generation of Bolsheviks, Polka served a spell in the Gulag and Tito never put in a word on her behalf even when he became a senior member of the communist apparatus. After Stalin's death she was duly rehabilitated but he never saw her again.

The failure of the marriage was a humiliation he was slow to forget. It was not until he was over sixty years old that he brought himself to marry again, though, as all his associates knew, women were still as necessary to him as food and drink. Apart from his unrecorded affairs he had officially recognized liaisons with four beautiful women: two wives and two maîtresses en titre and each time the gap widened between his age and theirs.

In professional life and in private revelry, Tito seems to have been happiest in the company of men. Women had no place in his favourite pastime of big-game hunting. Under his command, during the Second World War, the Partisans exercised no discrimination and women were treated as equals, both killing and being killed. Yet in his personal relations, he stuck by the old-fashioned view of them as mistresses or servants: preferably both. His last wife, Jovanka, whom he married as an old man, seemed, if Dedijer is right, to have manipulated him.[10] But he separated from her several years before his death, refused to see her in the final periods of consciousness during his last illness, and it was only when he was lying in state that she was rehabilitated as his official widow.

Back at Polak's mill, in the early 1920s, Tito's purpose was to make a living rather than to lead a revolution. Indeed, on his return home, the prospects of Sovietizing Yugoslavia seemed hopeless. Before he came back to Yugoslavia, the Communists, benefiting from the Bolshevik success in Russia and from general chaos at home, had done relatively well. In the first parliamentary elections for the Yugoslav assembly, they polled 12.4 per cent of the votes, notably by exploiting the discontent of ethnic minorities not yet adjusted to the new Yugoslavia. But they knew they could never win power by due electoral processes and they tried instead to break up the state by inciting separatism and revolution.

The new state retaliated predictably, placing a ban on any group committed to using violence, and thus making membership of the Communist party a criminal offence. It also neutralized Communist influence by substantial land reforms. Already in Serbia and Slovenia, the small peasant proprietors were the dominant class. The new régime went further and redistributed to the peasants the big estates formerly owned by Austrian, Hungarian and Turkish noblemen. In subsequent years they became the régime's great bulwark against Communist advance.

In their frustration, the Communists resorted to terror. They tried and failed to assassinate the Prince Regent, later King Alexander I (he was murdered fourteen years later, not by them but by the Ustashas, a Croat variant of the Nazi SS). But they did manage to shoot and kill the Yugoslav Minister of the Interior, Milorad Drašković. (His son and namesake fought against the Communists during the 1941–1945 civil war and then emigrated to California, where he re-spelt his name Drachkovitch and distinguished himself as a historian and Chief Archivist at the Hoover Institution.)

After Drašković's murder, the 59 elected Communist deputies

were deprived of their mandate and those caught were arrested. Most of the leadership fled the country, established a Communist Central Committee abroad and involved themselves in esoteric doctrinal disputes, while the membership of the party shrivelled from its peak of 60,000 to a handful of conspirators.

During this time, Tito's talents were hardly stretched by his work at the mill and he had plenty of time to tell nostalgic stories about his role in the Russian revolution. Having allowed his sympathies to be known, he was spotted in 1924 by Stevo Sabić, an educated middle-class Croat and former army officer, first in the Austro-Hungarian and then in the Red Army. Unlike Tito, he had stayed on in Russia to become part of the revolutionary apparatus.[11]

Initially, Lenin and his associates had expected that Communism would spread like a prairie fire to the rest of Europe. When, by January 1919, this manifestly was not happening, the Comintern was set up for the long-term purpose of sustaining the revolutionary impetus by means of propaganda and subversion. Increasingly, as the prospects of world revolution receded, the Soviet leadership came to identify the cause of the international proletariat with the advancement of Russian power. It was the Comintern, as secret arm of Soviet foreign policy, which gave paid employment first to Sabić and, later, to the man who was to present himself as the incarnation of Yugoslav patriotism.

When Comintern agent Sabić returned to Croatia, the Yugoslav Communists desperately needed new cadres. Tito was an ideal recruit: a popular and resourceful young worker, sympathetic to the Soviet cause and seeking an outlet for his personal ambition. He was as ready to take risks and accept discipline from the Soviet Union, as he had been earlier from the Austro-Hungarian Empire. Though by then the party's political wing was banned, the Communists were openly operating in a number of nominally non-political organizations under their own control, of which the most important were the trade unions. It was as a trade-union organizer that Tito, guided and financed by his new friend Sabić, began his thirteen years' ascent from a rank-and-file member of a front organization to being endorsed by Stalin as Secretary General of a reconstituted Yugoslav Communist Party.

Tito's zeal and flair impressed his colleagues. After successfully inciting strikes, first at the Kraljevica shipyard on the Adriatic, then at the railway repair workshop at Smederevo near Belgrade, he was appointed in 1927, legally, local secretary of Zagreb Metal Workers' Union and, illegally, member of the party local Committee.

By now he was a professional revolutionary, living off the Russians until 1939, when he was happy to learn from his associates that the Yugoslav Communist Party was able to finance its operations from its own funds.

During the revolutionary apprenticeship in Yugoslavia, Tito was twice arrested and most of his Western biographers depict the story of his trials and imprisonment as martyrdom. Yet by the standards of the judicial system which he later introduced into modern Yugoslavia, he came off remarkably lightly.

In the royalist era, it was true that judges were bourgeois defenders of the realm and tended to be particularly harsh in cases of violence and turned a blind eye on police brutality. Nevertheless they had been trained, both in the former regions of the Habsburg Empire and in the old Serbia, to respect Western concepts of an independent judiciary.

(In contemporary Yugoslavia they are expected to function as instruments of class war: in other words, to take the side of their political masters against those identified as "class enemies", and the verdicts are fixed in advance of the trials.)

After his first arrest, Tito was charged with inciting violence and, having been manacled, humiliated and beaten up, went on hunger strike to protest against the delay between his arrest and his trial. The waiting period was between May and October (in Yugoslavia today it may last for years), and the judge was a liberal intellectual, Stjepan Bakarić, whose son Vladimir was to become one of Tito's closest followers. He was so distressed by the hunger strike that he let Tito know that his case would not be delayed and meanwhile sent him food from his own kitchen.

After Tito was freed, Judge Bakarić showed him round his own library, well furnished with Marxist books and, with characteristic liberal *naïveté*, urged Tito to keep his politics within the law. In contemporary Yugoslavia, a judge would be in jail himself if he invited an enemy of the régime, or indeed, recognized that such a person could have legitimate grievances.

Tito was out of prison in 1928, when, in the perennial Serbo-Croat quarrel over the centralist Yugoslav state, an extremist Montenegrin deputy took the occasion of a public session of the National Assembly to shoot Stjepan Radić, the popular Croat peasant leader. (To this day, many Croats suspect the secret connivance of the King and his courtiers.) Though sworn enemies of Radić's Peasant Party, the Communists welcomed the public rage, unleashed by Radić's murder. Riots broke out, incited by various political agitators, and Alexander responded by suspending the constitution and assuming dictatorial powers.

In the subsequent round-up, the police found a pile of weapons in Tito's lodgings and he was arrested and this time inculpated in much more serious charges. (In court, he denied the accusation; later he admitted it was true.) In the second trial, a local newspaper reported, the court was packed with his own sympathizers.

> Young workers and students have shown an exceptional interest in his trial, squeezing themselves into the courtroom until it is impossible to move. They are young men, with long curly hair, or young girls with bobbed hair, perhaps the followers of the new gospel, perhaps acquaintances of the defendant. . . . This strange audience listens attentively, stands patiently, drinking in every word, bursting out laughing at every joke made by the defendant.

Although Communism was illegal then, as anti-Communism is illegal now, Tito proudly declared himself a Communist and received an excellent press. (Today, Yugoslav newspapers would not give an anti-Communist a hearing.)

> The defendant, Josip Broz, is undoubtedly the most interesting person in the trial; his face makes you think of steel. His light grey eyes behind his spectacles are cold but alert and calm. Many of those present were doubtlessly aware of the stubbornness, with which he maintained his views, and his cross-examination was listened to attentively and in complete silence. . . .

According to the newspapers of the time, which recorded the story in full, the judge permitted Tito to insult the court and to announce that he would recognize the legality only of a Communist judiciary. With astonishing patience, the bench waited for his final peroration before they stopped him. Responding to this belated interruption, Tito protested: "This shows conclusively that this is a police state." This was only the first of many occasions on which he appealed successfully to liberal values which he privately despised. Looking back on the trial later in life, he commented: "I was trying to overthrow their government and it was only natural that, when they caught me, they would shut me up. I should have done the same in their place. Indeed, I had every intention of doing so, when I *was* in their place."[12] In practice, after his sojourn in Stalinist Russia, he learnt to do very much better.

There was an equally sharp contrast between the way the old and the new régime handled their political prisoners. Tito spent the first part of his five-year sentence in the Lepoglava jail, near his native Zagorje, and the second part in harsher conditions at Maribor in Slovenia. Unlike political prisoners in present-day Yugoslavia, the Communists were allowed to keep themselves apart. They were quartered separately from common criminals and had every opportunity to carry on their subversive activity. (His closest associate, Moša Pijade, and another intellectual prisoner translated the whole of *Das Kapital* while in jail.) The closest modern equivalent was perhaps the H Block of the Maze Prison in Northern Ireland, where liberal British authorities allowed IRA prisoners to train, discipline and organize inmates, so that on release, they would be better revolutionaries.

It was Tito's good luck that one of the fellow prisoners was Moša Pijade, a man two years older than Tito, who made it his business to instruct him in the works of Marx, Engels, Lenin and Stalin, and so provided the ideological grounding necessary for the Party's future leader.[13]

Pijade was from a Sephardic-Jewish family from Serbia who had sent him to be educated in Paris and Vienna. The authorities regarded him as a far more dangerous threat than Tito and he had already served five out of a twenty-year sentence. He was a gifted artist (in prison he produced some excellent likenesses of Tito) and an able dialectician. Intellectual curiosity was not among Tito's qualities but under Pijade's instructions he worked his way through the standard texts and grasped their shatteringly anti-moral implications. He was thus able to rid himself, once and for all, of the "bourgeois" concept of objective truth and of those distinctions between right and wrong on which his mother had reared him.

Even after his training it is true that there were the occasional signs that Tito never quite divested himself of the suspicion that his Marxist–Leninist philosophy might not have answers to everything. Djilas recalled an occasion in 1952, when he and Tito were travelling together in Tito's special Blue Train, escorting to his funeral their friend and wartime companion Boris Kidrič. Djilas expanded the orthodox Marxist view: "There is nothing beyond matter: indestructible and ever-changing. . . ." Tito, perhaps with his mind on the coffin in the next compartment, interrupted him: "Don't dwell on that. Who knows what it's all about, who knows?"[14]

A similar streak of unease led Tito (like Stalin and Hitler) to insist that others than himself put their signature on death warrants. A confessed reluctance to take personal responsibility for capital punishment later commended him to visiting Western liberals. Yet, during and immediately after the War (see Chapter 4) he had no hesitation in ordering and approving mass executions without trial. There is nothing to suggest, however, that, like Stalin, he took pleasure in killing. And though he had accepted Leninist doctrine, he had none of Lenin's revolutionary puritanism. "Thank God he was a *jouisseur*," said one of the few royalists who survived the purges: he was referring to Tito's well-known weakness for sensual pleasures which tended to turn the leader's mind away from class war.

Indeed on some occasions, Tito showed personal compassion for the victims of his own terror. Belgrade society knew all about the beautiful actress whose cousin had been killed in the purge and had left six destitute children. An aide promised to convey her distress to Tito and, after her next appearance, she received an enormous bouquet, enclosing a personal tribute from Tito, to which was pinned a substantial cheque.

Yet in later life, he never showed any signs of regretting the massacres nor of being haunted by his victims' ghosts. Under Pijade's tuition, he had understood and learned to practise Lenin's belief that morality must be subordinate to politics. There is no way, of course, of following the psychological processes, by which Tito was converted from the Catholicism of his childhood to Marxist–Leninist amoralism. Ambition was the driving force of his life. Even though there was a good deal of social mobility in pre-war Yugoslavia, where the Karadjordjević dynasty itself was only a few generations away from pig-farming, the prospects of a skilled but penniless mechanic were unpromising. In those days, in Eastern Europe, for a man of Tito's background and lack of education, Communism was probably one of the few ways forward.

Tito's Western admirers never really came to terms with the sheer amoralism of his attitudes. Indeed his honesty and straightforwardness were often commended by visitors who enjoyed his open-minded hospitality and manifest *joie de vivre*. In some cases Tito seemed genuinely to have enjoyed their company and all his life he retained a soft spot for his wartime backer Fitzroy Maclean. But his Marxist–Leninist training taught him that as a species they remained the class enemy—though he did his histrionic best to play the princely supra-class role into which they cast him.

The harshness with which political prisoners were treated by him and his successors had nothing to do with Tito's personality which could be kind or brutal as circumstances required. He knew from his own pre-war experiences of the severe risks which un-elected rulers would run if they showed any degree of leniency to potential enemies. And by contemporary standards, political prisoners in pre-war Yugoslavia were amazingly free. Tito, as his mentor Pijade, never had the slightest difficulty in obtaining revolutionary literature nor in communicating with the outside world. On leaving the Maribor prison, Tito recalled that his big problem was to find a discreet way of carting out a trunkload of forbidden books.

In the Lepoglava prison Tito, on the basis of the practical skills he had acquired in his pre-revolutionary life, was given the responsibility for running the prison power-station. He chose Pijade, an intellectual-looking, bespectacled little man with a balding head and large moustache, to serve in the improbable role of electrician's mate. The job entitled the two men to move around the prison and also outside it. According to Tito's account, he was allowed to meet his friends in the upper storey of a nearby restaurant. He would have had access to Comintern funds to bribe his jailers to stay downstairs while he and Pijade plotted with party activists behind locked doors.[15] At Maribor there was less freedom of movement, but his fellow prisoners later recalled happy evenings around a stove, which they had managed to acquire, being regaled by Tito's stories of the Bolshevik revolution, after which they would all link arms and sing the International.

By contrast, life for political prisoners in Yugoslavia today is implacably desolate. The case for the defence is rarely reported in the press and once in jail, political detainees are either shut up with hardened criminals or left for prolonged periods in solitary confinement. And whereas in the royalist prisons the Marxist creed was freely taught, in Marxist prisons religion is brutally repressed. The Vatican has repeatedly protested against the prohibition against priests entering Yugoslav prisons, even to visit dying Catholics. And though officials are still eminently bribable, the prison staff today would never dare admit a single text, let alone a trunkload of forbidden texts.

It would be improper, of course, to exaggerate royal benevolence. While Tito was serving his sentence, the King tightened the screws and had 1,000 Communists rounded up. A handful were executed and several were tortured and beaten. But although in his last years Alexander I governed by decree, he had to think of international opinion. Prisoners with good connections, particularly those as internationally well-known as Pijade, were treated respectfully; the brutalities and indignities were reserved for obscure students and trade unionists.[16]

After Tito was freed in 1933, the relative mildness of the royalist régime, which had enabled him to use his trials as a publicity stunt and his imprisonment to further his revolutionary training, also made it easy for him to evade police surveillance. He had been ordered to go back to Kumrovec and report daily at the local police station. True to character, before leaving the city, he had himself smartly attired (presumably drawing on Comintern funds, there being no other source of money at that period) and returned to his village, this time, in upper-class clothes. Here, the local police chief turned out to be an old schoolfellow and, when Tito went back to Zagreb, he could be relied on not to tip off his superiors. Back in Zagreb, Tito's new, forged identity card registered him as a qualified engineer. The neat moustache, pince-nez, dark suit in the official photo suggest the epitome of a successful bourgeois of the kind he was dedicated to destroy.[17]

Tito's effectiveness in court and his subsequent activism in prison had impressed his superiors. Within a few months of his release he was invited to the Party's Vienna headquarters and co-opted into the Central Committee. In the conspiratorial world, in which he operated, he needed several cover-ups. In his communications with the Comintern he was always "Valter", the only name by which Stalin ever referred to him. But it was during this visit to Vienna that, for the first time, he adopted the code-name Tito. The disadvantages of running the Communist Party by remote control were obvious. As soon as Tito had secured the authority bestowed by membership of the Central Committee he hurried home.

Here Tito's job was to canalize public discontent against the state of Yugoslavia. This was not only in line with Stalin's intention of dismantling Yugoslavia, an unacceptable "artefact of

Versailles", but it also happened to respond to a strong current of separatist feeling which was developing inside Yugoslavia during this period. In the early years of the monarchy, the economy had been expanding fast and the people were relatively satisfied, but by the 1930s the country was feeling the consequence of the world slump and some villages were close to starvation. The Communists never had an easy time with the peasantry, partly because of the Party's urban identification and also because information was gradually trickling in about the collectivization of the land in the USSR. But one of the issues on which Tito could expect to draw genuine local sentiments was in playing up the inclinations of the ethnic minorities to blame their wretchedness on the Serb monarchy.

On the nationalities' issue, however, the Communists had no monopoly. The most ardently separatist movement was formed by the Ustashas of Croatia, whose leader Ante Pavelić (later to be Hitler's local Führer) had been exiled in 1929. The Communists saw the Ustashas as their natural allies in the revolutionary struggle and in the early 1930s, the underground Communist paper *Proleter* began calling on Party members to give help and support to Pavelić's followers. In 1932 Communist leaflets were sent out appealing to the whole Croat nation to support the Ustashas and also urging the workers and peasants of Serbia (of whom large numbers were to be massacred by the Ustashas during the war) "to help with all their strength in the Ustasha struggle".[18]

Tito's immediate task was to reconstitute the Party's base, effectively shattered by the King's men after 1928. By kind permission of a sympathizer (brother of the local bishop), in September 1934, he convened a Communist conference in the castle of Gornji Grad, just outside Ljubljana. The hospitality provided not only gilded premises for the meeting but also food and drink for the 30-odd conspirators. The Comintern had already selected two of the younger participants, Edvard Kardelj and Boris Kidrič, for Moscow training, and these were later to rank among Tito's closest collaborators.

Tito's anti-Yugoslav line showed itself in the banners decorating the Gornji Grad hall: "Long live worker-and-peasant states in Croatia, Dalmatia, Slovenia, Serbia, Montenegro, Bosnia, Vojvodina!"—the word Yugoslavia was not mentioned.

While Tito was doing his best to destroy Yugoslavia, King Alexander I was trying to save it, though circumstances were against him. The frontiers of the new state had been recognized by all big powers except the USSR, but Yugoslavia was still surrounded by irredentist claimants: the Italians for Dalmatia; the Hungarians for territories inhabited by Hungarians in Croatia and Vojvodina; the Bulgarians for the Yugoslav part of Macedonia and the Albanians for the mainly Albanian regions of Kosovo. All these threats were more menacing since Hitler and Mussolini were now repudiating as a "scrap of paper" the postwar settlements.

In the period immediately after the First World War, Alexander had lined Yugoslavia up with Czechoslovakia and Romania in the *Little Entente*, a group which the French had sponsored in the hopes of containing Germany. And it was with the intention of strengthening the bonds between France and its East European client states that Alexander set out on an official visit to France. On 9 October 1934, as he set foot in Marseilles, he was murdered by an Ustasha terrorist.

The Communists as well as their Ustasha friends were the targets of the sharply intensified police action which followed the King's murder. Tito decided not to loiter. He left immediately for Vienna and proceeded from there to Moscow, where he arrived with a personal letter of recommendation from the Party Secretary, Milan Gorkić, the man who had to be eliminated before Tito himself could climb to the top. Tito was given a job in the Balkan section of the Comintern and took up lodgings in the lugubrious Hotel Lux, specially reserved for international conspirators and under constant surveillance by the Soviet secret police.[19] As usual, Tito knew how to make himself useful and in 1935 he was appointed Secretary of the Yugoslav delegation to the Comintern's Seventh Congress. It was here that he first set eyes on Stalin. This was the peak of the personality cult and Stalin was heralded as a multi-faceted genius, revered master and glorious fighter; worship that he was particularly in need of at a time when he required his followers to repudiate almost everything they had previously stood for. After the programmed prostration before his God-like presence, he left it to his underlings to give the international Communist movement its new marching orders. Everywhere, since Lenin's time, the Communists had singled out the Social Democrats, liberals and other left-wing defenders of plural societies as the first targets of abuse. Now these "lackeys of imperialism" had to be rehabilitated and embraced as fellow-progressives.

The reasons for Stalin's turn-around were plain: the German Communists had played a significant—perhaps crucial—role in demolishing the Weimar Republic. Hitler, like Lenin and, later, Tito, took help where he could. In taming the trade unions and in inciting mob violence, the Communists had been convenient auxiliaries. But by 1935 Hitler had reached the top and no longer needed them. Using Stalin's own techniques, he was in the process of rounding up and destroying all his opponents, among whom the Communists were now included. And more alarmingly, from Stalin's viewpoint, Hitler was now diverting national energies towards rearmament and preparations for war.

By deciding to divert the full forces of world Communism against the Nazis, Stalin was, somewhat belatedly, closing the stable door. He, like King Alexander, now saw Germany as a serious threat to his country's survival. It was too late to mobilize the German Communists, now in concentration camps, but elsewhere Party members were ordered to organize and join new "Popular Fronts" and given appropriately liberal and patriotic slogans to match the new anti-Fascist line.

Tito, on whom Pijade's training in Communist dialectics had not been wasted, threw himself wholeheartedly into the new campaign. First, the Party had to cooperate with other anti-Fascist political groups, which was far from easy, in view of the peasants' innate anti-Communism. Second, it had to abandon its popular support for ethnic separatism and, instead, promote the defence and unity of Yugoslavia, now to be regarded as a potential ally of the USSR.

It is widely believed in the West that, for cultural and ethnic reasons, the South Slavs feel a natural affinity for the Russians on which the Communists can conveniently rely. British officers going into Yugoslavia during the war were briefed accordingly. One of them, Jasper Rootham, parachuted into Serbia in 1943, has recorded his shock:

When I praised the Russian military achievement, I must truthfully say I was met by a wall of scepticism and something more which was new to me. This was a feeling, which the Serbs apparently have, that they were in a way let down by Tsarist Russia in the Balkan Wars and in the years 1915 to 1917. . . . King Alexander himself had been a student at the Imperial Russian Academy and taken a thoroughly anti-Soviet attitude until the day of his death, and it was only on the eve of war in

1941 that Yugoslavia entered into diplomatic relations with the USSR. This has overlayed the rational friendship of the Slavs for the Russians, and there is no doubt that, among many sections of the Serb population, the prejudice against Soviet Russia was as extreme as was the adulation among the minority of professed Communists.[20]

Jasper Rootham had served with the anti-Communist Chetniks and his opinion might therefore have been dismissed as biased had it not been vehemently endorsed in a letter which in 1948 Tito wrote to Stalin:

> Among many Soviet people, there exists a mistaken idea that the sympathy of the broad masses in Yugoslavia towards the USSR came of itself, on the basis of a tradition which goes back to the time of Tsarist Russia. This is not so. Love for the USSR did not come by itself. It had to be stubbornly inculcated into the masses of the Party and the people by the present leaders of the new Yugoslavia.[21]

In 1948 they were disinculcated remarkably fast.

In later years, Tito tried to disown his early, uncritical Stalin-worship. He could not dodge the fact that, after becoming Party leader in 1937, he was responsible for eleven years of rhapsodic and often inadvertently comic adulation. In Yugoslavia, as everywhere else, glorification of Stalin was spoken, written, chanted or howled, whenever Communists assembled.

After the Comintern conference, Tito returned to his quarrelsome colleagues in Vienna but soon afterwards made his way back to Yugoslavia where he began setting up a nationwide network of loyal subordinates. He also started the process of eliminating "factionalists"—meaning those who disagreed with him—and creating the nucleus of what would become his wartime team. Besides Kardelj and Kidrič, with whom he had worked in Moscow, Tito now met two others: Milovan Djilas, writer and pamphleteer, and Aleksandar Ranković, the clever but largely uneducated son of a Serb peasant. Both were just out of prison and both submitted themselves totally and zealously to his command.

Tito was also quick to appreciate another exploitable loophole in the royalist régime. The traditional respect for the independence and self-government of the universities was never challenged even during the King's dictatorship. Tito saw its political usefulness (when in power, he took care to prevent any reinstatement of academic freedom) and asked Djilas to find him a youth leader capable of mobilizing the students. The man selected was Lola Ribar, son of a well-known middle-class family, whose father had been President of the first Yugoslav Parliament.[22] Later, after losing his sons with the Partisans during the war, the old man helped the Communists produce the facsimile of a parliamentary democracy (see Chapter 4). With their base outside the reach of the royal police, the youth movement expanded more quickly than the party itself. As former students later recalled, they could conduct revolutionary activity behind the university walls undisturbed. Meetings were held, leaflets printed, couriers dispatched and demonstrations prepared. Anyone caught operating outside university premises was at risk, and, if caught, might be beaten up and sometimes tortured. But as long as they stayed inside the academic asylum they were safe. Further, those in trouble could often count on help and support from sympathetic professors. In contemporary Yugoslavia, few teachers with any sense of self-preservation would side with the offenders—though there have been some (in their own interests better left unidentified) who have refused to testify in court against their own students.

As Comintern agent, Tito was also given the task of recruiting as many Yugoslav volunteers as possible for the International Brigade in the Spanish civil war. By 1936, the Fascist grip was tightening in Central Europe and Secretary Gorkić prudently moved his headquarters from Vienna to Paris. Tito joined him there for several months, living in the Hôtel des Bernardins, on the Left Bank, and acquiring a smattering of French, while he organized the international network needed to get his compatriots through Austria, Switzerland, France and across the Pyrenees into Spain.

Some 1,300 Yugoslavs reached their destination: 700 were killed or died in prison and another 300 were wounded. The survivors who managed to make their way home were subsequently to play a valuable and expert role with the Partisans. One project, for which Tito held Gorkić responsible, ended in disaster. A ship-load of 500 volunteers was to have been sent, in 1937, from Budva on the Montenegro coast directly to a Spanish port. The police were tipped off, the ship was seized, most of the men were jailed and Gorkić recalled to Moscow and liquidated in the purge. Between 1937 and 1939 Tito later calculated that about 100 Yugoslav Communist leaders vanished with Gorkić, including almost every member of the Central Committee, past and present, except himself.[23]

Gorkić's elimination must remain a subject of speculation though, as successor, Tito was obviously the principal beneficiary. Despite the fact that he arrived in Moscow with Gorkić's recommendations, Tito coveted his job and distrusted him. Later, in 1952, he told Dedijer that, when he left Moscow after his first visit, Gorkić gave him a forged passport and a pre-arranged route, which Tito carefully avoided: "I got myself another passport and went an entirely different way, because it had frequently happened that comrades, for whom Gorkić obtained passports, were arrested as soon as they reached the Yugoslav frontier. . . . Not long after that, Gorkić was dismissed. He was the one who had been betraying us to the police all these years."[24] That was the last that was heard of him.

As the Sovietologist, David Floyd, has pointed out, Tito never gave any explanation why he was able to say seventeen years later, at the Yugoslav Party's Ninth Congress, that Gorkić had been an innocent victim. Listing a number of early Yugoslav Communists, who now deserved rehabilitation, Tito included his name and said ". . . it is quite clear that Gorkić was not a foreign spy in any sense, as he was accused of being." By that time, Tito had obviously forgotten that he had been the accuser. Perhaps, with the passing of time, he simply recollected the implausibility of the charges and recognized that a dead Gorkić could safely be honoured.

Not that Tito himself was safe from Stalin's lust for destruction. During his visit to Moscow in the second half of 1938, when the purge was reaching its frenzied peak, he claimed that he survived only by remaining prudently inconspicuous. A rather different view has been put forward by another Comintern agent, Josip Kopinič, who stayed much longer in Soviet service. (Indeed, some Croats believed he was still working for the Russians when a book about him was allowed to appear in Belgrade in 1983.)[25]

In the Kopinič version, in Moscow in 1938 Tito had two *liaisons dangereuses*, in the very literal sense: first with a German woman, later accused of being a Gestapo agent; then with a Russian, who worked for the secret police and denounced him for his "capitalist manners". Apart from Tito's sexual frolics, Kopinič and Dedijer recall two particular moments of danger. First, Tito only just cleared himself of charges of "Trotskyism", allegedly detected in his translation of Stalin's *History of the Communist Party*, and for which his co-translator, Vladimir Ćopić, was liquidated. Second, even after 1937, when Stalin had approved Tito as Gorkić's successor, the Bulgarian faction in the Comintern tried to get him eliminated in favour of their own candidate. Kopinič claimed to have saved Tito only by preparing a detailed report on the Yugoslav party personalities, which, he said, he based principally on notes which Tito's old friend Moša Pijade managed to purvey to Moscow from his prison in Serbia.

Two questions are often asked but have never been satisfactorily answered. First, why did Tito keep his head while all about were losing theirs? Second, why did Stalin refrain from dissolving the Yugoslav Communist Party as he dissolved its Polish counterpart? According to Dedijer, there is still in existence a secret report which Tito prepared for the Comintern Control Commission in 1938 but, though Dedijer was allowed to see it, the document has not been made publicly accessible.[26] On the face of it however it seems inconceivable that Tito could have survived had he not made his personal contribution to the Stalinist dossiers, so servicing Stalin's pathological need to expose and exterminate the old Bolsheviks. These could then be replaced by people—like Tito himself—entirely beholden to Stalin. If, as circumstances suggest, Tito was indeed an informer, he could have been motivated not just by fear and ambition, but also by an overriding and probably justified belief that no other man was as capable as himself of reforming the Yugoslav party along Stalinist lines. As we now know, in this *Darkness at Noon* atmosphere, there was no moral barrier against personal betrayal.

Stalin's liquidations were openly applauded by his supporters, including many who were later to become victims themselves, as well as by both Tito and Kardelj. As Kardelj was to write: "The Soviet authorities relieved the Yugoslav Party of the burden of factionalism." In contemporary Communist literature both men used the approved epithets to vilify the victims: Trotskyite, traitor, spy, counter-revolutionary and foreign agent. The open question is whether, as Tito later claimed, he denounced people only after he knew that their names were on the hit-list or whether his own words contributed to their death.

By 1937 Tito had cleared the Moscow hurdle; he had no trouble asserting his personal ascendancy over the formerly divided and cantankerous Party. Even so, looked at dispassionately at the time, the post of General Secretary of the Yugoslav Communist Party had little to commend it. The turn-over among Communist leaders—and the physical liquidation of those turned—might have discouraged a less self-confident man. Tito was taking over a Party in disarray and was being asked to promote the militarily-weak and woefully under-equipped Yugoslav state, formerly the declared enemy, but now to be cultivated as Russia's desired ally. Nor could the Prince Regent be relied on to follow a pro-Soviet line. With some justice he was beginning to see Mussolini as a far more immediate threat than Hitler.

But Tito was soon relieved of the embarrassment of having to make common cause with a Karadjordjević. By the summer of 1939, he was back in Moscow, at the time when Molotov and Ribbentrop were clinking champagne glasses to celebrate the Soviet–German pact. His somersault was performed with exemplary discipline. The guns of the Yugoslav *agitprop*, not yet very formidable, were redeployed away from the "Fascist beasts" and their Yugoslav supporters and against the British and the French. The Party was thus defying most of Yugoslavia's educated élite, whose sympathies were strongly on the Allied side, but could comfortably relapse into its more familiar posture: anti-royalist and anti-war.

Between the outbreak of the Second World War in September 1939 and the German invasion of Yugoslavia, Tito still had another eighteen months left to repair his party's fortunes. He made use of the time to organize a network of cells, covering almost the whole country, which laid the political infrastructure for his future guerrilla army. It was not until Barbarossa (the German invasion of the USSR) on 22 June 1941, that he sent out orders to the party identifying as the enemy the occupiers of Yugoslavia.[27]

In a more open society and in a less turbulent age, Tito's past would have disqualified him from serving as a symbol of Yugoslav patriotism. But he had learnt from Stalin that history is as history is written: all the national archives were taken into custody and the written and spoken word passed under his own and his party's control. The embarrassment of his dubious past—at least during his own lifetime—was thus resolved.

Chapter 2

THE LEGEND OF THE LIBERATION

IT IS PART of the Tito creed, compulsorily dinned into the heads of all Yugoslav children from the age of five and widely accepted by adults in the West, that Yugoslavia, unlike all the rest of Europe, freed itself from Axis occupation by the virtue of its own resistance. Though many wartime legends have been punctured (it took the French 30 years and the memorable film, *Le Chagrin et la Pitié*, before they came to terms with their wartime experience), singularly little has been written or said to pierce the glamour surrounding the Yugoslav Partisans.

"It should not be forgotten that Yugoslavia was the only European country to have been liberated through its own efforts," said John Ennals, chairman of the British–Yugoslav Society on 17 February 1984, on the occasion of receiving the award of the Yugoslav Star with Gold Wreath, to mark the 40th anniversary of his liaison service with the Partisans.[1] The Society, which is partly financed by the British government, includes diplomats, businessmen and others particularly interested in fostering good relations with the present régime.

The conviction is held with equal force on the right as on the left. In his book on Albania, the Conservative peer Lord Bethell wrote: "Yugoslavia's armed force and police were men who fought with Tito in the hills and expelled the German occupation armies themselves without Soviet help."[2] The same view is expressed by Western journalists whenever they visit Yugoslavia. "Yugoslavia emerged from World War Two with a Partisan army that had all but defeated the Germans single-handed", wrote Robert Kaplan in the *Christian Science Monitor* on 4 March 1983.

If "liberated" is taken to describe a territory into which the occupier is no longer able to send his troops, then, as both the German and Italian records reveal, there was no territory in the whole of Yugoslavia to which it applied. The country was held down with relatively small occupation forces and the Germans left the garrison duties primarily to locally recruited or satellite auxiliaries. And if they sent forces into areas which the guerrilla armies had occupied, these often found that their elusive enemy, with the help of the local peoples, had disappeared into the countryside. But, until the final phases of the war, the Yugoslav Partisans, like other resistance movements, did not have the equipment or the firepower to establish fixed lines of defence.

The Partisan harassment of German strongholds was intermittent and peripheral.[3] Stories that they "set the whole of Yugoslavia aflame", as recounted in some of the standard history books, were never remotely true. Further, the occasional acts of sabotage never prevented the Germans from making extensive use of the local economic potential, and indeed Yugoslav oil production was quadrupled during the occupation. Open guerrilla combat was limited to the mountains in the hinterland. The populated parts of Yugoslavia, including the fertile Danube–Sava basin and the two greatest cities, Belgrade and Zagreb, remained as quiescent as the rest of occupied Europe.

After 1941, the Partisan activities were for the most part confined to the Italian occupation zone. It was not until 1978 that the Italian staff published their own full account of Italian wartime operations in Yugoslavia, examining in minutest detail both Italian and insurgent operations. This further confirmed that the Partisans were unusually audacious and bloodthirsty enemies, but it also demonstrated that the Second Army and the XIV corps, assigned to occupation duties, never totally lost control of any of the territories for which they were responsible. Outposts were captured and occupation posts demolished but in all the key areas and in all the important urban centres, including Ljubljana, Split, Zadar, Šibenik, Karlovac, Knin, Dubrovnik, Mostar, Kotor, Podgorica (now Titograd) and Cetinje, the Italian tricolour continued to fly from the time the Italians arrived until they surrendered in September 1943.[4]

The final decision of the German High Command to withdraw its armies from the Balkans was imposed not by the Partisans but by mounting pressure from the Eastern and Western fronts. Indeed from the Allied point of view, the Partisans were disappointingly slack in the employment of hit-and-run tactics which could have been effective in disrupting the German retreat. The route went through the narrow mountain passes of Serbia in which the Axis troops would have been especially vulnerable, but these were areas which the Partisans never controlled. And in the parts of Serbia where the Germans did decide to make a stand, the Partisans needed Soviet help to dislodge them.

The story that the Partisans, with Western help, freed their country continued to be propagated in the West despite a magisterial rebuttal from Oxford's Regius Professor of History, Michael Howard:

> Yugoslavia was liberated neither by the forces of Tito's resistance nor by Anglo-American aid that was channeled to it. Though it is unfashionable to say so it was liberated by Marshal Tolbukhin's Third Ukrainian Army which, by the end of 1944, occupied about one third of Yugoslav territory while the German forces under Field-Marshal von Weichs, were conducting an orderly evacuation in the rest, in order to protect a left flank laid bare by the collapse of Hungary and Rumania. Heroic myths of liberation, whether in Western or Eastern Europe, are all very well, but they don't provide a very sound basis for military planning either today or in the future.[5]

The Yugoslav leaders recognize the mendacious quality of their official version of wartime history and since 1983 have begun denouncing what they perceive as "demystifying" tendencies. Tito's former Prime Minister, now a member of the collective Presidency, Mitja Ribičič, had warned against "alleged historical evidence" used, he said, "to demystify our revolution". Radica Gačić, Secretary of the Central Committee of Serbia, addressing a public meeting of teachers, called on them to struggle against counter-revolutionary messages challenging orthodox history: "We cannot permit people, under the guise of freedom of expression, to raise questions about our recent past and to engage in demystification. . . ."[6]

In the mystified version, which the leaders still cherish, the struggle was a straightforward liberation war against the foreign occupier; the demystifiers saw it instead as part of a many-sided and singularly bloody civil war. It is certainly true that for the rank-and-file of Partisan guerrillas, the objective was to free the country from foreign domination. But Tito was fighting for a Communist Yugoslavia and during most of the fighting the principal enemies were not the Axis troops but his own compatriots. As very few Yugoslavs sympathized with the Axis, the Partisans were often engaged in operation against countrymen who, though they opposed Communist rule, favoured the Allies.

Nothing in this chapter is intended to belittle the epic quality of the Partisan struggle. There is general agreement among historians of the last war that Tito's Partisans were by far the best organized and most combative of all the resistance groups in

Europe. The long, hard fighting was marked by acts of almost superhuman self-sacrifice and endurance and many gave their lives rather than desert the long column of wounded soldiers and civilians who had taken their side. The vast mass of them certainly believed that they were fighting for the liberation of their country. "As long as patriotism aroused the masses, we must be the first of the patriots", Tito had said. But for him and his fellow-conspirators patriotism was never more than the means and the revolution—and the seizure of power—the end. Tito, like Lenin before him, used the defeat of his country and the subsequent chaos to impose Communist rule. But whereas Lenin arrived in a sealed train from Germany, by a curious twist of history, Tito managed to fulfil his revolutionary design with the backing not only of the USSR but also of the British and Americans.

This of course was possible only after the Nazis had invaded the Soviet Union. In 1939 after the signature of the Molotov–Ribbentrop Pact, Tito brought the Yugoslav Communists sharply into line with the new pro-Nazi attitudes and one of the peculiar side-effects of this development was that the Party found itself on better terms with Prince Paul than any of the other centre or left-of-centre political groups. The Prince, though an impenitent anglophile, was at that time painfully conscious of Yugoslavia's vulnerability and was trying, as the British government had done in the previous year, to appease Hitler in order to keep his country out of war. In this shift of Yugoslav foreign policy, he was obstreperously opposed both by political parties of the left and centre and also by a segment of the Yugoslav army. Vituperation against the French and English by the Yugoslav Communists came as a comforting counterblast; as a reward, police harassment against the Party was suddenly and sharply reduced.

The new line was unmistakably set when Tito, alias Valter, writing in the Comintern Journal applauded the invasion of Poland: "The pact for Mutual Aid between the Soviet Union and Germany, and the entry of Soviet troops into Western White Russia [Tito's euphemism for what had been Eastern Poland] have aroused great enthusiasm amongst the broad masses of the Yugoslav population. The Yugoslav people have understood that these events facilitate the struggle for national independence."[7]

The Central Committee, now composed of Tito's own men and acting on his behalf, issued a manifesto blaming "the imperialist war" on Daladier and Chamberlain, though, considering the circumstances, it did manage to strike a cheerful note:

But the Soviet Union, led by the Bolshevik Party and Comrade Stalin, the leader of genius of all progressive humanity, has unmasked the imperialist warmongers' foul trap. German fascism had been compelled to capitulate before the strength of victorious socialism, the USSR, and to conclude a non-aggression pact with it. . . . Through this pact, the Soviet Union has won a great victory and limited the range of the present war."[8]

In accordance with the new policy, the Yugoslav Communists agreed to expel those misguided comrades who were still reluctant to turn against the French and British. On his way home from Moscow Tito got stuck for a few weeks in Turkey waiting for false papers, but as soon as he arrived back in Zagreb he echoed the Stalinist line: "Seven months ago, the English and French imperialists attacked another imperialist power—Germany—in order to conquer her and force her to capitulate and thus to secure their rule and continue without competition their pillage of colonies and semi-colonial peoples. . . . This imperialist war which was begun by the English and French imperialists, heavily affects both you and the entire peoples of Yugoslavia."[9] The anti-Allied campaign was brought up-to-date on 1 May 1940, by a declaration from the Party's Serbian Central Committee: "The crude violation of the Scandinavian countries by England and France forced Germany to move troops into Denmark and to occupy strategic positions in Norway"[10]—material lifted straight from the Soviet press.

For the Yugoslav Communists this era in Party history remains something of an embarrassment. If Tito and the Party were as patriotic as the authorized version claimed, should they not immediately have joined up with other anti-Axis groups? In August 1983 the Communist newspaper *Borba* suggested that they did. A military commentator claimed that Tito and his followers had always been concerned with national independence and upheld the argument by citing an open letter to all members of the Party, 4 March 1939: "The basic task of the Communist Party of Yugoslavia at this moment is to mobilize and organize all the peoples of Yugoslavia to fight and defend the integrity and independence of the country against German and Italian fascist aggressors and their helpers and supporters." The authenticity of this document is beyond doubt; what is significant is the dates. The open letter was issued several months before Stalin came to terms with Hitler; that is to say, at a time when in Yugoslavia, as everywhere else, Communists were committed to popular front and anti-Axis lines. Almost 40 years later, at the College of Communist Cadres Tito gave lectures purporting to show that he had always nurtured secret reservations about the Hitler–Stalin deal. The contemporary evidence of what he and his party were saying and doing during the period of the pact suggests otherwise.

Tito and his men certainly made good use of the relative freedom allowed them in return for their pro-Axis tilt. Their numbers rose to 12,000, they recruited an ever more numerous youth movement and published leaflets and clandestine papers. Most important of all, Tito extended his network over almost the whole country.

At a time when Tito and his men were blasting the British as warmongers, British officers in Belgrade representing all three forces, were getting to know members of the General Staff and examining with them the increasing likelihood that Yugoslavia would be dragged into war. In the summer of 1940, Colonel Clark, the head of the British military mission, and the junior Naval Attaché, Alexander Glen, were told that, in the event of an occupation of Yugoslavia, the planning of internal resistance was being entrusted to staff-officer, Colonel Draža Mihailović.

Glen invited Mihailović to several private dinners and now writes of him with respect: "A man whom I am proud to have known; a man of honour; serious, well-informed, a good listener, articulate when he spoke, and I found him broad in his under-standing with loyalty to the whole of Yugoslavia and not to a narrow Serb hegemony."[11]

Already in 1936, Rebecca West, whose famous book *Grey Lamb and Black Falcon* had earned her a special place in Serb affections, first heard about Mihailović. She was on a British Council lecture tour and visiting the military academy of Niš when she was told that Mihailović was the leading spirit in the anti-Nazi wing of the Yugoslav army. The following year, she was twice shown docu-ments that he had written anticipating a German invasion which urged training for guerrilla warfare.

Others who knew this retiring officer at the time described him as a francophile and occasional reader of prohibited left-wing literature. But Mihailović's well-known anti-Axis sentiments, un-doubtedly sharpened during his term as Military Attaché in the now occupied Czechoslovakia, did not suit Prince Paul's policy of appeasement and his chiefs sent him out to Belgrade. Neither he nor Tito were thus personally involved in the sequence of events which brought Yugoslavia into the war and themselves into world history.

The climax of Paul's appeasement policy was reached in March 1941, after the Germans had lined up Hungary, Romania and Bulgaria, when he reluctantly consented to make Yugoslavia into a non-belligerent member of the Axis Pact. In the West Paul was being denounced for having succumbed to Hitler's flattery or intimidation but the German records show that despite his suave manner he was, on the contrary, a remarkably stubborn negotiator. As Goebbels recorded, the treaty between Yugoslavia and the Germans, signed on 26 March 1941, had "a difficult birth". Against the advice of his military staff, Hitler allowed himself to be persuaded that Yugoslavia should be released from any obligation to make its territory available for the passage of Axis soldiers or supplies. Goebbels noted: "We guaranteed the inviolability of Yugoslav borders and gave an assurance that we would not march through their territory." He added: "All that we want is the right to use Yugoslav airfields." Even this concession was not included in the signed text.[12]

By the time the treaty with Yugoslavia was being negotiated Hitler had already decided to attack Greece. But he was able to dispense with the right to march his troops through Yugoslav territory, as the Germans already commanded access to Greece through the neighbouring states. He therefore agreed that the Germans would respect Yugoslavia's frontiers and that he would content himself only with access to the country's economic resources and an assurance that Paul would not support the Allies.

As the concession might have been interpreted as a sign of weakness Hitler ordered that the clauses restraining German freedom of action should not be included in the published text. None the less, according to the account of Vladko Maček, then deputy Prime Minister, the German negotiators undertook not to disavow these clauses if they were printed in the *Yugoslav Official Gazette*.[13]

Unfortunately for Paul, the publication of the full text was too late to forestall an outburst of public anger and an unresisted military putsch. A small group of officers, recruited mainly from the Air Force and the Belgrade garrison, deposed Prince Paul in favour of his under-age and slow-witted nephew King Peter II (a deed which inspired Terence Rattigan's successful comedy *The Prince's Uncle*, a skit on Balkan politics highly unfair to Paul).

At the critical moment when Peter was needed to broadcast the Royal Proclamation he was having himself driven around his park in the company of his cousin, Prince Paul's son. As the plotters could not lay hands on him, they had an understudy to pronounce the fateful words. After the story broke, the Belgrade crowds threw caution to the winds. The wild enthusiasm took the local Communists by surprise and they decided they had better join in. After a few days they were rebuked by Tito, then in Zagreb, for allowing events to take on a rudely anti-Nazi character. Improving on history, in 1948, Tito told Stalin that it was the Communists who had initiated the *coup*. While the celebrations proceeded, the royal person, later to be welcomed as a hero in London and Washington, was sobbing in his uncle's arms, begging not to be abandoned.[14]

There is no direct evidence that the British and American officials in Belgrade participated directly in the putsch. But the British secret service was operating an anti-Paul local radio station and both helped to create the false impression that an anti-German rising could produce positive results. Hearing the news, Churchill pronounced one of his famous aphorisms: "The Yugoslav nation has found its soul." Unfortunately there was nothing he could do to save its body.

The putschist government, drawn from all the main political groups, including the Croat Peasant Party, was soon aware of Yugoslavia's desperate vulnerability. It promptly reversed the rhetoric and endorsed Paul's deal with Hitler. In Goebbels' crude language: "They are shitting themselves in Belgrade. . . . The provocation will be avenged and they probably realize it. They are being so mild and co-operative that this has the ring of panic in it. . . ." Yet no amount of grovelling could prevent a humiliated Hitler from hurling himself into one of his hysterical rages; the Serbs joined the Jews, Poles and Gypsies, among the peoples to be destroyed.

In his attack on 6 April, Hitler threw in no less than 27 divisions, including seven Panzer divisions, in the view of the British general, Maitland Wilson, "far bigger forces than would have been needed to liquidate Yugoslavia and Greece".[15] Many Serbs afterwards attributed the defeat, as some still do, to Croat or Communist treachery. Indeed, General Velimir Terzić, a former royal officer, who later became Tito's Chief of Staff, confirmed that during the invasion the Croat Communists actively incited desertions.[16] But in any event, the scale of the attack ruled out any prolonged resistance. After a ten-day *blitzkrieg* the Royal Army capitulated.

In the later years, some protagonists of the *coup* claimed that, however terrible the subsequent war, the action was strategically justified as it delayed the German invasion of the USSR. It is certainly true that Nazi failure to reach Moscow before the onset of an unusually early winter, lost them their only hope of winning the war. But the German war records show that this was not a consequence of the Balkan campaign. In fact, Hitler, anxious to preclude a repetition of the Salonika landings of the First World War, had already decided that the Aegean coast of Greece should be occupied as a preliminary to Barbarossa. The British landings in Greece on 7 March compelled him to order his troops to occupy the whole country which required twice the number of troops. After 27 March, however, Hitler felt personally insulted by the anti-Axis *coup* in Belgrade, which he considered relieved him of his promise not to march his troops through Yugoslavia and in practice this facilitated his attack on Greece. The German army, advancing from Belgrade, outflanked the well-defended Metaxas line and the High Command was able to dispatch additional troops through the Monastir Gap, which surprised and destroyed the Anglo-Greek forces.

The German *blitzkrieg* in Yugoslavia ended so quickly that, in a matter of days, the German troops were available for other theatres. By 3 May 1941, the armoured division which had held a victory parade in Belgrade was back in the Berlin region. The records of the military units involved in Barbarossa show that what held them up was not the Balkan campaign but the difficulty of assembling the vehicles required for the invasion of the USSR and which had to be collected from all over occupied Europe.[17]

In his long service with the Comintern Tito had a good training in flexible response, and he was well prepared to keep up with Stalin's zigzagging towards Yugoslavia. It was not until June 1940 that diplomatic relations had been established between the USSR and the royalist Yugoslav government and in 1941 Ambassador Milan Gavrilović joined his Western colleagues in warning Stalin that the Germans were poised to attack. Stalin suspected they were trying to sow dissension between himself and Hitler and stolidly refused to believe them.

Nevertheless he was not happy about Paul's dealings with Hitler, welcomed the putsch and hurriedly negotiated a Soviet –Yugoslav friendship pact. It came into force on the day the Germans bombed Belgrade, and Stalin would have been relieved if the Yugoslav army had put up an effective resistance. Whether or not Tito knew about the friendship pact is not clear (it seems that when Djilas led the first delegation to Stalin during the war, the files of the communications between the Yugoslav Communist Party and the Russians were taken to Moscow for safe-keeping[18]), but in any case he performed the appropriate political somersaults and during the *blitzkrieg*, the Party fleetingly did favour national defence. Most of the Croat Communists failed to get the message in time and went on preaching and practising desertion. Immediately after the defeat Stalin scrapped the friendship pact and on 8 May 1941 expelled the Yugoslav Ambassador.

The Yugoslav Communists were consequently able to shed the patriotic line and Tito dropped any talk of resistance and did nothing to exacerbate the relatively benign Communist–Nazi relationship which continued during the time between the Axis occupation of Yugoslavia and Hitler's attack on the USSR. The pause provided time for the Party to carry through three tasks, which laid the basis for the subsequent revolution. First, they restored the clandestine network, severely shaken up by the defeat. Second, Tito re-established some degree of central control, though this was complicated by Stalin's uncertainty about whether or not Yugoslavia itself should be abolished. The Comintern gave orders to the party's regional Central Committee, notably those in Croatia and Slovenia, to appeal to ethnic separatism. For a time, in those two provinces, the word "Yugoslavia" disappeared from the Party writings. Third, orders were issued for taking possession, whenever possible, of the large stock of weapons which the military collapse had left strewn around the country.

The *sotte voce* Nazi–Communist collaboration did not extend to Croatia. Here, the Nazis immediately set up a nominally independent state and, after Maček had refused a request to govern it on their behalf, they transferred power to the Ustashas, the Croat version of the Nazi SS. These set about executing their political enemies, Communists included.

While Tito, like Stalin, had been cultivating the Nazis, a handful of Serb officers were refusing to accept defeat. They came together at Ravna Gora, a mountainous region south-west of Belgrade, and, in accordance with pre-war plans and, no doubt also because of the absence of any more senior officer, they recognized Colonel Draža Mihailović as their tentative and never very authoritative leader. At this stage their aim was purely military: to organize detachments of guerrillas, to collect intelligence for the Allies, to receive military equipment and to prepare for a general mobilization to coincide with the anticipated arrival of Western liberation armies.[19]

For the next three years, the illusion that the Allies were coming was sustained by memories of the Salonika landings in which many of the officers, including Mihailović himself, had participated. It was purposely fostered from 1942 by a special service known as the British A Force, set up to deceive the enemy and incapable of doing so without its friends.

Though Mihailović named the newly created force "the Home Army", they were, and in historical works still are, known by the sobriquet Chetniks. This was a generic name for guerrillas which was traditionally associated with the Serb struggle against the Turks. Unfortunately for Mihailović, however, the word had other connotations too. Among these was the title adopted by the very right-wing Association of War Veterans, whom the monarchy had used as auxiliary police—particularly in the Croat regions, where the Serbs were a minority. They acquired a reputation for brutality similar to the Black-and-Tans in pre-independent Ireland.

While Mihailović was doing his best to rally as many military men as possible, it was on the support of the local people that he primarily relied. Working on the assumption that all good Serbs would prefer to give assistance to him than to the invader, he regarded not only the peasants but also the *gendarmes* and local officials as his own people. Mihailović has sometimes been accused of being a Serb nationalist: and though there is no indication that in his own mind he distinguished between his loyalty to Serbia and to Yugoslavia, he certainly felt committed to protecting the Serb people against genocide. He frequently refused to take risks which might provoke collective reprisals against them and after May 1941, when destitute refugees flowed in from Croatia and Bosnia to save themselves from the Ustasha massacres, he gave a higher priority to saving Serb lives than to fighting the Germans. His value as a resister was commensurately reduced.

Even before the Communists entered the war, Tito had heard about Mihailović and recognized that he might provide an alternative focus of loyalty for the oppressed and terrorized peasantry. At a party conference in May 1941 Tito therefore ordered operational activities not against the occupiers (this was before Barbarossa) but against the Chetniks and the Ustashas (in that order). Party activists were informed that officers of the Royal Army were now hiding in the mountains and should be denounced.[20] (The Communists seem to have made a regular practice of denouncing Chetniks to the occupiers. One Chetnik commander, Zvonimir Vučković, whose war memoirs are generally accepted as reliable, recalled the capture of Communist files in Gornji Milanovac in the winter of 1942, which included instruction from the District Committee to local cells, ordering individual party members to try and infiltrate the intelligence services of the occupying powers in order to inform against Mihailović's supporters: "The Germans will eventually leave but these people from Ravna Gora will not and we shall be stuck with them."[21]

Tito took the occasion at the same Party conference in May 1941 to look towards the future. According to Milovan Djilas, whose account of the meeting has never been challenged, Tito followed Lenin in repudiating the Marxist postulate of a two-stage revolution: first an alliance of the workers with the bourgeoisie; afterwards the dictatorship of the proletariat. As the Yugoslav state had collapsed and the political parties were discredited, he proposed instead that the party should prepare itself for the immediate seizure of power. As Djilas commented: "All this was clear to us yet someone had to say it. Tito was the first to do so. No one contradicted him." The May 1941 conference seems to have been the first official occasion when Tito stated a position independently of Moscow. Though he seems not to have appreciated it at the time, his power base was already beginning to shift from the Soviet apparatus to his own faithful cadres.

He remained, of course, at Moscow's orders: the Communists were mobilized immediately the USSR was attacked.[22] For Tito and his leadership, resistance and revolution were two sides of the same coin. It took seven years before they perceived that there could be more than a tactical divergence between Moscow's national interests and their own. On practical action, however, the differences surfaced at once. Demanding maximum support for the Soviet war effort Stalin wanted Tito to cooperate with any anti-German elements in Yugoslavia and he objected to an outward manifestation of Communism, which might alienate the peasantry or alarm Russia's Western allies.

After Barbarossa, Soviet and British leaders found they shared a common interest in uniting Yugoslav anti-Axis resistance. Struggling for their countries' survival, Stalin and Churchill were both exasperated by what they saw as Balkan factionalism, which obstructed a united resistance front. Yugoslav terrain was ideal for guerrilla warfare and as the Axis troops were spread out very thinly, it seemed absurd that the full military exploitation of this potential advantage should be stalled—as it was by differences between local politicians.

The Communists later blamed the Chetniks for resisting calls for a common front and this version of history has been widely accepted. What has to be remembered however is that Tito and his men never wavered in their intention of using the collapse of the Yugoslav state as an opportunity for replacing it by a Communist dictatorship and that this inevitably brought them into collision with Mihailović's people who were fighting to preserve precisely what the Partisans were trying to destroy.

Wherever Partisan units operated, they demolished village halls, burnt public records and executed local functionaries, including the mayors, the clerks and the policemen. As these were helping to administer occupied territory they were treated as legitimate targets. The Nazis however had installed an administration of their own, under General Nedić, a former Minister of War of the Pétain type. He and his colleagues in Belgrade frequently asked the Germans to protect them against their common enemy: not the Partisans but the Mihailović men.

Chetnik resistance to the Germans started on 3 May, whereas there was no engagement between the Germans and the Partisans until the late summer. Today the Communist leadership celebrates the anniversary of the insurrection on 7 July, the day on which a Partisan unit shot two Serb *gendarmes*. Both may well have been Mihailović's men, for by this time his people had effectively infiltrated into the Nedić administration and, after the breakdown of the state, the local peasantry had come to depend on "Uncle Draža" to protect their farms from banditry and looting.

None the less, under pressure from their respective backers, Mihailović and Tito did hold two meetings, which revealed that they lived in different worlds and that a meeting of minds would be impossible. After the first held on 17 September 1941, Mihailović expressed astonishment that Tito could favour a general insurrection at a time when there was no hope of Allied aid and nothing to prevent the Germans from exacting fearful reprisals. But needled by London he ordered his followers to join the Partisans in all-out resistance.[23]

As Mihailović had no means of exercising discipline, the order was only partially obeyed, but even so, between them, the Partisans and Chetniks did manage, briefly, to free some 4,500 square miles from enemy control. For the first time, news of effective resistance from the continent of Europe reached the outside world.

Its scale and duration were vastly magnified by Western propaganda and, as the Partisans had not yet emerged into the open, all the credit, in both the Soviet and Western media, went to Mihailović's Chetniks.

Before the second meeting Tito held a top-level conference in the village of Stolica, which agreed on an organizational framework for future political activity and in effect ruled out any possibility of a compromise with Mihailović. The Partisans would set up a "National Committee of Liberation" (or, in the doublespeak of the time, "bearers of the people's authority"), handpicked by the Communists, to replace all existing administrative institutions. Tito then submitted twelve conditions to Mihailović for going into partnership, of which Mihailović accepted six. As an officer, still pledged to the King, he refused to recognize the authority of Tito's committees and rejected the proposal for joint court martials to carry through purges inside the armed forces.[24] On these two meetings only the Chetniks' records survive. (According to Dedijer, the Partisans, during their flight from Serbia, buried the relevant archives in iron chests. A few years before his death, Tito sent helicopters to search the area, but they were never retrieved.[25])

In the autumn of 1941, Bill Hudson, a British mining engineer, selected for his knowledge of the country and language as well as for his physical toughness, was sent into Yugoslavia by SOE, a British organization, set up to collaborate with European resistance movements. Hudson met both Tito and Mihailović and was at first so exasperated by their failure to join forces, that he advised London to suspend further aid until the two sides came together[26] (a proposition which was somewhat academic, as Britain at that time had neither the long-distance aircraft nor conveniently situated airfields to provide significant help).

Before the end of the year, however, Hudson understood the nature of the struggle, and asked urgently to be brought home, so that he could report on what he was already describing as "a state of civil war". In his view eagerness by the SOE to exaggerate the importance of the resistance movements led them to conceal the painful truth that the Yugoslavs were fighting each other far more than they were fighting Axis troops.

By the end of 1941, fighting both between the Yugoslavs and against the occupiers had spread into Bosnia, Montenegro, Dalmatia, Lika and other Serb-inhabited areas all over the country. But it was at Ravna Gora that the Partisans and Mihailović's forces initiated a conflict which was to last until 1947, by which time Mihailović had been shot as a traitor, and the last bands of Chetniks had been rounded up and executed by the Partisans and Communist secret police.

According to the official Yugoslav version, fighting began when the Chetniks unsuccessfully attacked the Partisan-controlled town of Užice (now Titovo Užice). In referring to the occasion M. R. D. Foot, one of the most authoritative Western historians of European wartime resistance, wrote: "The Partisans were sore at heart at having been attacked by fellow-Serbs."[27] But Lucien Karchmar, in his well-authenticated and very detailed study of events, shows that Užice was only one particularly bloody incident in a struggle which had been going on for months.[28] As he claims, both Tito and Mihailović, prompted respectively by Stalin and Churchill, favoured the truce but neither could control their subordinates. Mihailović still regarded the Partisans as dangerous fanatics, but assumed they were on the Yugoslav side. As Karchmar's account reveals, Tito and the Communists, on the other hand, disagreed between themselves not over *where* but *when* Mihailović should be eliminated.

Immediately after the second meeting, on 19 October, fighting resumed. A band of Chetniks, to Mihailović's acute embarrassment, tried on their own initiative to ambush the Partisan delegation on its way home. Two days later, a Partisan group tried to seize Loznica from the Chetniks and soon afterwards drove the Chetnik guerrillas out of the mining town of Zaječar.

By then, the Partisans had established their headquarters at Užice, killed alleged collaborators, installed their own governing committee, removed national and royal emblems and hoisted the red flag. It was then, too, that they adopted the red star, which was later to serve as an identification mark on Partisan berets. The town had a gun factory, and agreement on sharing its output had been reached with the Chetniks. A group of these, claiming they had not received their due, went to Mihailović's headquarters and, in his absence, persuaded his deputy to authorize them to seize the town. The plan of attack, involving several units, was ill-conceived. The Partisans were tipped off, counter-attacked and slaughtered the prospective attackers.

By this time, the Germans had called on an extra division from France and Tito suggested a conditional truce: as a penalty for attacking Užice, the Chetniks were asked to give up Požega, a small town with a usable air-strip. Though Tito seems not to have known it, Mihailović was hoping that this might be used by Allied forces to supply arms, and therefore refused to yield it. As it turned out, Požega was useless: at the time, there was no Allied aid to deliver and the supplies which later materialized came by parachute. In any event, German reinforcements were on their way, and soon both brands of resistance were on the run.

During these initial uprisings, German reprisals had exceeded Mihailović's worst fears. Hitler, as enraged by the rebellion of the Serbs as he had been by the Belgrade putsch, ordered a policy of devastating retaliation: 100 Serbs for every German killed; 50 for a wounded German. The executions began at once. During the month of October 1941, 1,200 hostages were reported killed in Belgrade, 1,175 in Krajlevo and 2,300 in Kragujevac. Here SS men marched out the top two forms of the high school and shot the boys and masters together.

Not surprisingly, there were non-Nazi German officers who favoured conciliation rather than brute force. One of these, Captain Josef Matl, sent a message to Mihailović, indicating that he would be prepared to negotiate. After rejecting Tito's terms and being told that there would be no more help from the British, Mihailović asked for weapons to defend the Serbs against both the Ustashas and the Communists. Matl seems to have been sympathetic but he was overruled[29]—just as other German officers were to be overruled eighteen months later, when they recommended a much more far-reaching deal with the Partisans.

Mihailović withdrew to the mountains and most of the peasants, who had been with him, went back to their villages. The Germans continued executing or deporting any Mihailović supporter they could catch and they were assisted in the task by a group of Serb Fascists led by Dimitrije Ljotić.

At the end of 1941 Tito, with no more than a couple of thousand followers, fled across the mountains into East Bosnia. It was the peasants, left behind in Serbia, who took the punishment for the ill-fated rebellion: some 9,000–10,000 were killed, and according to the British liaison officer, Hudson, who stayed on, it was their angry resentment which kept the Partisans out of Serbia for the next three years.

By this time the Partisans were in total disarray and at a meeting of the Central Committee on 7 December 1941 Tito offered his resignation. It was refused and he continued as unchallenged leader though from this time on most of his activities took place in the remoter regions under Italian occupation, where the administration was both inefficient and less vicious.

In a message to Moscow, on 29 December 1941, Tito admitted that the Partisans had forfeited Serb support: "The Chetniks are rallying all Serb reactionaries, both in Serbia and Bosnia, who are making propaganda against us and are preparing to strike a new blow in Bosnia. They are trying to split the Bosnian Partisans and have partially succeeded, as a number of Partisans and detachments have gone over to the Chetniks."[30]

Stalin remained unimpressed and in February 1942 he reprimanded Tito for conspicuously Sovietizing "liberated" areas (a practice which was later dropped) and also for using the misleading title "proletarian" to denominate the newly formed—and almost entirely rurally recruited—mobile brigades. (Ironically as contemporary diplomatic papers show, while Stalin was trying to hold Tito back, London and Washington were attributing the Partisans' Communist ardour to Soviet influence.) Tito appealed in vain to Stalin's sense of Communist solidarity: "We suspect that a Yugoslav government and England are directly collaborating with the occupiers against the Partisan movement."[31] Moscow sent another rocket: "It is difficult to agree with the view that London and Yugoslav governments are working with the occupiers. There must be some great misunderstanding here." There was indeed. (Yet the proposition, that Churchill and Hitler were collaborating in 1942, still remained part of official Yugoslav history and has been re-asserted recently in three authoritative books: Edvard Kardelj's wartime *Reminiscences*, Vladimir Dedijer's new *Contributions towards a biography of Josip Broz Tito*, and Jovan Marjanović's *Draža Mihailović between Britain and the Germans*.)

What did come through in Tito's message to Stalin was his single-minded preoccupation with the internal enemy. By the end of 1941 the massive eruption against the Germans had petered out. The Germans themselves felt able to move the bulk of their troops away from Yugoslavia to the Eastern Front and, as General Wisshaupt reported to the German High Command, by this time they relied on Bulgarians, Italians, Romanians, Hungarians and Croats to replace German units in maintaining order. And from then on both Tito and Mihailović were to be increasingly engaged in fighting each other.

It was not, as is sometimes supposed, the ferocity of anti-German resistance but the multidimensional civil war between

Yugoslavs, which is the real reason for the appalling wartime casualties, higher proportionately in Yugoslavia than in any other combatant country. Calculations, based on the pre- and postwar censuses of the territories now within Yugoslavia's frontiers, show a negative balance of 2.2 million people: over one-eighth of the population. The figure includes deaths, expulsions, emigration and deportation, as well as losses sustained by the wartime drop in birth rates.[32]

When the Germans dismantled the Yugoslav state they shared out the territories between themselves, the Italians, the Albanians, the Romanians, the Hungarians and the Bulgarians and all of them brutalized the areas they occupied. None the less, the losses which Yugoslavs inflicted on each other in the subsequent internal fighting, aided and abetted by the occupiers, were far higher than numbers killed by foreign enemies.

The Yugoslav holocaust had its origin in the Nazi invasion. Before the war, the various ethnic and social groups had coexisted in peace, if not always in harmony. And the killings really began when the Germans installed the Ustasha puppet régime in Croatia. As Croats today justifiably recall, the Ustashas in the pre-invasion times were no more than a small outlawed minority, no bigger than the Communist group with whom, in the pre-war period as we saw, they occasionally cooperated. Further, unlike the Nazis, the Ustashas were not hoisted into power by their own compatriots: they arrived in the baggage of the enemy. How much they were tolerated or even helped by other Croats during the war cannot be ascertained, any more than we can know how many Germans supported the Nazis. The Ustasha leader, Ante Pavelić, was a homicidal maniac, and hated the Serbs as obsessively as Hitler hated the Jews. Curzio Malaparte reported that Pavelić had shown him a basket filled with human eyes gouged from Serbian bodies "given to me as a present by my dear Ustashas".[33] The Ustasha units attacked isolated and vulnerable Serb communities, massacred entire populations, destroyed whole villages and, in several cases, set the church on fire after locking in all the people. In Bosnia, where, under the Ottoman Empire, the Moslems had been the masters there were some who vengefully joined the Ustashas but others are on record protesting against the massacres, and by all accounts the majority, like the rest of the population, tried to keep clear of the fighting.

The number of Serb victims of Ustasha terror is generally thought to be round half a million. Even German SS generals were shaken. In 1943, the SS Obergruppenführer, Arthur Phleps, Commander of the 5th SS Corps, reported to Himmler: "From the start, the Ustashas' main aim has been to annihilate the Orthodox Christians, to butcher hundreds of thousands of people, including women and children." The same year, General Lothar Rendulic, Commander of the Tank Army II, West Balkans, recalled: "During the time that German troops were stationed in some Croat localities, a barbarous persecution began against the Orthodox Christians. The Croats are said to have killed at least half a million. When I told a high official, close to the Croat Chief of Staff, that I failed to comprehend the murder of half a million Orthodox Christians in that period, I received an answer characteristic of the prevailing mentality: 'Half a million is too high. There weren't more than 200,000. . . .' "[34]

In these horrific circumstances, the indiscriminate nature of Serb retaliation is hardly surprising. Bands of Chetniks, whom Mihailović could not control and dared not disown, hacked to death or cut the throats of men, women and children of Croat and Moslem origin regardless of whether or not they had perpetrated the massacres.

Mihailović himself however was a great deal less ruthless than the Partisans. As we saw, after the 1941 insurrection his chief concern was to save Serb lives. The Partisans, on the contrary, had every interest in maximizing the slaughter: the survivors—and there were always some—provided them with their best recruits: men who had nothing to lose were willing to accept martial discipline and to fight and die wherever they were sent. For the Communist leaders the blood-chilling spectacle of corpses strung up on trees and lamp-posts by the Ustashas or occupiers with the purpose of terrorizing the natives was a positive benefit. It was Tito's closest associate, Edvard Kardelj, also trained in Stalin's Moscow, who suggested that the Partisans should actively encourage enemy reprisals. Writing from Croatia, Kardelj recognized that the Communists there were too unpopular to rally the masses and were indeed being denounced "even by workers". But though the time had not yet come for a large-scale insurrection, Kardelj recommended a policy designed to incite enemy retaliation: "We must at all costs push the Croatian as well as the Serb villages into the struggle. Some comrades are afraid of reprisals, and that fear prevents the mobilization of Croat villages. I consider, the reprisals will have the useful result of throwing Croatian villages on the side of Serb villages. In war, we must not be frightened of the destruction of whole villages. Terror will bring about armed action."[35]

In his letter, Kardelj paid a back-handed compliment to Vladko Maček, the Peasant leader, a declared pacifist, disciple of Tolstoy who spent most of the war under Ustasha detention.[36] Recognizing Maček's enormous popularity among his own people Kardelj suggested to the Partisans, that, if only they could provoke Axis reprisals against Maček's supporters, "this would provoke an uprising in the whole of Croatia." Though Kardelj's premise was wrong and an uprising impossible, his advice about provoking the enemy was duly followed, and enemy retaliation against Partisan hit-and-run attacks was predictably macabre. Indeed, it was the Communists' willingness to sacrifice their own lives, and those of others (during the war the Party lost two-thirds of its original members), which made their guerrilla army so invincible.

For the most part Partisan killing was more selective. As Maček recalled: "The Ustashas and Chetniks had perpetrated their mass executions blinded by hatred. The communists killed with a cool, calculating mind all those who were likely to hinder the ultimate establishment of communism in the country." Those thought "likely to hinder" however, were numerous, and in disposing of them, the Partisans were as implacable as other groups. Dedijer cites a directive from the First Bosnian Partisan Corps, issued in 1943, authorizing mass murder: "Often the confiscation of property is not a sufficient punishment against regions attached to the Chetniks. There are cases when it is necessary to burn whole villages and destroy the populations." According to Dedijer the Partisan leaders, like the Nazis, calculated the killings arithmetically: ten "traitors" (anti-Communists) to be executed for the loss of one Partisan.[37]

Any discussion about the Partisan share in wartime killing is still taboo in the Yugoslav media. During the war the Communists never allowed the retrieval of the corpses or the building of tombs for those they killed. Even now families can be prosecuted for building monuments in memory of Chetnik fighters. The only way of circumventing the prohibition is to retell the story in fictional form. So far the bitterest and most controversial account has been incorporated into a novel, *The Knife* by Vuk Drašković, in which the old Moslem father-figure explains why during the war he never took sides:

All of them: Ustashas, Chetniks, Serbs, Croats and Moslems killed each other and when the knife is used, there is no difference between a cross, a crescent, a tricolour cockade, a letter U or a red star: the pain is the same. . . . The Partisans reacted against ethnic and religious and sectarian massacres. But they too divided us into kulaks and poor peasants, into bourgeois and worker, into progressive and reactionary, and killed accordingly.[38]

Though efforts have been made by both the Partisans and the Chetniks to divide the country into black and white, the angels and the devils, ordinary people caught up in the fighting saw it as a struggle against the invader and in the regions where the guerrillas were active, there are many records of villages which changed sides according to circumstances, sometimes more than once.

The helplessness of the rural communities is vividly brought to life in a book by Louise Rayner, an English woman who fled from Belgrade and was welcomed and sheltered in a very primitive village. She found the people resolutely anti-Axis and they took her in at their own risk and never betrayed her. At first they were pro-Chetnik, flying national flags and singing royalist songs. But as they eked out their living on subsistence farms they had little time or energy for anything else. And as Chetnik action increased and news of massive reprisals trickled in, they did what they could to keep clear of the fighting. In this they failed: the Chetniks forcibly enlisted 100 young men and marched them into the mountains. These later fell into a Partisan ambush. The officers were shot and most of the men were incorporated into Tito's army. In the autumn of 1944, those who survived came back with the now advancing Partisans, wearing red stars in their caps. A few Chetnik prisoners were being marched along with them: "They had been stripped of their boots and outer clothing. One youth had both of his thumbs cut off and was trying to hide his bleeding fists in his underclothes. An old woman offered him a piece of bread. She did not understand civil war. The poor youth was just a child to her. But the Partisans escorting the prisoner shot her dead."[39]

And just as there was no black and white side on the matter of atrocities, so there was no black and white either on the issues of collaboration with the enemy. Both Partisans and Chetniks were primarily concerned with defeating each other and both turned to the Germans when they thought the latter could help. The story of Chetnik collaboration has been widely told though it is not always pointed out that it often took place in defiance of Mihailović, who in order to inflate the scale of his army, tended to exaggerate the range of his authority.

Many of the Chetniks fought under local command and sometimes in close collaboration with the occupiers. The Italian and German commanders in their operational reports (often intercepted by the Western code-breakers) did not trouble to distinguish between the differing groups. But the more detailed Axis analyses, which became available after the war, indicate that both the political and military authorities sharply differentiated between the Chetniks whom they could use as auxiliary troops, and those who were pro-Mihailović and could be assumed to be pro-Allies. (According to British liaison officers the confusion may have been increased as Chetniks, after their own acts of sabotage, generally tried to deflect Axis retribution by leaving around clues suggesting the perpetrators had been Partisans.) Though the Italians were on very close terms with many Chetnik groups, the Italian High Command as late as 28 May was still offering a reward of half a million lire for the capture of Mihailović. The last Italian operation directed specifically against Mihailović Chetniks was not until 29 June 1943, just a few days before Mussolini fell.[40]

By then the British were actively encouraging the Chetniks to link up with the Italians. As Peter Boughey, head of the Yugoslav section of SOE, London, later recalled: "We certainly told Mihailović to be in touch with the Italians. We knew the situation in Montenegro and wanted him to be able to get Italian weapons when the Italians withdrew, collapsed or surrendered."[41]

With all this going on, the Communists had an easy time collating evidence of "Chetnik" collaboration with the Germans which they passed on to Moscow. Until mid-1942 Stalin was too busy to notice and, despite Tito's repeated protests, Soviet propaganda continued to cheer Mihailović. But when the switch did come it was dramatic: Radio Free Yugoslavia, which operated on Soviet territory under Soviet control, suddenly broadcast a vitriolic attack, based on evidence furnished by the Partisans, indicating that Mihailović's Chetniks were on the Axis side.

The accusation was taken up by the world-wide agitprop apparatus and found its way, via the neutral press, to London and Washington. Rebecca West later recalled that it was none other than the Soviet spy, Guy Burgess, who came up to her at the Ivy restaurant in London and asked: "Have you heard the dreadful news? Mihailović is a traitor."[42] There was however no truth in the allegations that Mihailović himself ever supported the Axis against the Allies. As Walter Roberts has written in his masterly account of the civil war:

> What the Chetniks were doing was to prevent the Partisans from entering their territory and in that respect theirs and German aims co-incided. But any direct collaboration between the Chetniks and the Germans must be excluded simply because the objective of the German High Command was the destruction of the Mihailović Chetniks.[43]

Indeed, anticipating an Allied landing in the Balkans, the Germans went on regarding Mihailović as more of a menace than Tito. In his report forwarded in August 1942 by the SS Chief of Police, Meyszner, sent by Hitler to repress Serb resistance, the Partisans were not even mentioned:

> Resistance tendencies exist both inside and outside Serbia. The one being led by Nedić, the other by Draža Mihailović. It can be said that resistance is organized both openly and clandestinely. The Nedić government organizes the resistance openly within the framework of its organization but practises it covertly. On the other hand, Draža Mihailović organizes resistance clandestinely but practises it openly. The Chetnik detachments attached to the Nedić government are unreliable in many ways and are infiltrated by Mihailović elements which carry out military training of the population. In fighting against resistance they have shown little or no value. At the right moment they would probably become the backbone of rebellion. . . . The Mihailović movement covers a whole area of Yugoslavia. In the Serb areas it is enlisting the population, raising detachments. It has infiltrated into all Serb formations. . . .[44]

The links between Britain and the Chetniks were well-known to the Germans and at the beginning of 1943, the German General Staff received a warning from General Reinhardt Gehlen, then head of German military intelligence for Eastern Europe: "Among various resistance movements, which cause increasing troubles for the armed forces in the former Yugoslav state, the movement of General Draža Mihailović is in the first place as regards leadership, armaments, organisation and activities. . . . The followers of

Mihailović come from all classes of the population and at present comprise of about 80 per cent of the Serb people who hope for liberation from 'the alien yoke'. . . . The number is continually increasing. . . ."[45]

This must have impressed Hitler, who, on 16 February 1943, wrote to Mussolini:

> The situation in the Balkans, Duce, preoccupies me greatly. However useful it may seem to play opposition factions against one another, I hold it to be extremely perilous as the parties involved . . . agree unconditionally on one point: their limitless hatred of Italy and Germany. I detect a special danger, Duce, in the way the Mihailović movement has been developing. The great mass of co-ordinated and trustworthy data in my possession reveals clearly that this movement, which is ably and energetically directed from the political point of view, awaits only the moment when it can turn against us. . . . Mihailović seeks to obtain arms and supplies for the execution of these plans by pretending to assist your troops. . . .[46]

The reports from the Axis commanders confirm David Martin's thesis that Mihailović continued his resistance long after the Allies had given him up. In his book *Mihailović: Patriot or Traitor* (1978) Martin compiled an impressive compendium of resistance actions by the Chetniks, all of them witnessed by British or US liaison officers, and based on Allied records for the second half of 1943. Many of the actions were on a relatively small scale and involved blowing up bridges, tearing up railway tracks, wrecking trains and barges. But the list also includes half a dozen large-scale actions, each inflicting enemy casualties of 200 or more. Robert Wade, one of the British officers with Mihailović, remembers interviewing German prisoners who had been captured by the Mihailović Chetniks in the winter of 1943: at a time when Partisan propaganda was churning out "evidence" that Mihailović was fighting on the Axis side.[47]

As late as April 1944 two US liaison officers who travelled widely inside Yugoslavia returned to Washington and claimed that large parts of Serbia and Bosnia were still under Chetnik control and, in the event of an Allied landing, would be able to mobilize substantial forces.[48] Any Chetnik action against the Germans was a source of worry to the Partisans, as it contradicted Tito's reports to Moscow claiming that all the fighting was by them. Indeed Stalin was showing himself much more sceptical than either the British or the Americans about the Partisan communiqués and claims.

Tito's offer to collaborate with the Germans, of which there is now undisputed evidence, demonstrated his very real fear of a Chetnik victory. By 1943 all the Yugoslavs were confident that the Nazis would be defeated, but this only increased the ruthlessness of the struggle for the control of a liberated Yugoslavia.[49] Until very near the end it always seemed likely that if the British and American troops landed anywhere in Yugoslavia—and most Yugoslavs expected their arrival—the number of those rallying to Mihailović would probably have been unbeatable.

It was to fend off this risk that in November 1942 Tito put out his first feelers to discover whether the Germans would accept an arrangement which would allow him to concentrate all his forces on wiping out the Chetniks before the Allies arrived. This particular initiative was ill-timed, as by then Hitler had given orders for a combined operation against both the Chetniks and Partisans to be carried out by Germans, Croats and Italians. In the subsequent action, the Germans drove the Partisans out of Herzegovina across the Neretva River into Montenegro, where they ran up against the Italians and so were surrounded on all sides.[50] It was then that Tito decided to dispatch a high-level delegation, led by General Koča Popović and including Milovan Djilas and Vlatko Velebit, to the German headquarters at Zagreb. The mission submitted three main proposals: first, an exchange of prisoners; second, a truce, to set the Partisans free to fight the common Chetnik foe; and, last, an agreement that the Partisans would be ready to oppose by force any attempted Anglo-American landing on the Adriatic coast; in other words, would fight on Germany's side.

Such a deal went much further than anything which the Chetniks had ever offered the Germans and, in doing so, it demolished the crux of the Communist case against Mihailović, whom they were to execute as a collaborator in the summer of 1946. The discovery of the Partisan dealings with the Germans caused consternation among Western historians, who had committed their reputation to the Partisans. Among these was Phyllis Auty, one of Tito's staunchest defenders, who in a letter to *The Times Literary Supplement* (27 November 1970), said that she had consulted Tito personally about the reported deal and had been told it was untrue: "I see no evidence to doubt Marshal Tito's word on this and know of no credible evidence to refute it." But refuted it was.

The accounts in the German archives were confirmed not only by Milovan Djilas, who was an active participant in the talks,[51] but also, more recently, by another former Partisan, Vladimir Dedijer. The latter not only described the talks but also published documents showing that Tito was already implementing the truce, even before receiving the official German reply.[52]

Dedijer's incriminating evidence is contained in two documents, both dated 30 March 1943. One was an order signed jointly by Tito, Ranković and Sreten Žujović to Arso Jovanović, Secretary of the District Committee for the Bosnia-Herzegovina Communist Party who was told "not to take action against the Germans since this would not serve the interests of our present operations". The orders were unambiguous: "Our most important task is to destroy the Chetniks of Draža Mihailović and to smash their administrative apparatus which represents the greatest danger for the further development of the People's Liberation Struggle."

The other was an extract from instructions which Tito sent to the Commander of the First Bosnian Corps and which, according to Dedijer, was delivered to the Partisan commander by a courier travelling under German protection. The commander was told of an official decision that all Partisan forces should be concentrated against the Chetniks, "the traitorous band which represents the greatest danger not only for the People's Liberation Struggle but also for the future," and was ordered to turn the truce with the Germans to best advantage. "We have split the Germans from the Chetniks and the Italians. You must take this factor into account and direct all your efforts against the Chetniks in Central Bosnia and Krajina." His instructions, which were to stay in force until further order, ruled out the use of force against the Ustashas unless these attacked the Partisans or helped the Chetniks.

On 7 May 1943, Tito realized that the Germans were unlikely to respect the truce and sent a message to all Partisan detachments in Croatia referring to his earlier order for the suspension of anti-Axis acts of sabotage and telling them that these could now be resumed. Once again however he reaffirmed: "The main struggle is for the annihilation of Draža's army." Meanwhile, the German command had submitted the Partisan proposals to Hitler who rejected them with the contempt he had shown for earlier proposals for cooperation with Mihailović. Dedijer indicates that the sudden

German attack took the Partisans by surprise and that the nucleus of the Partisan army and Tito himself were almost captured. His account gives some force to the allegations of Enver Hoxha that while Tito was talking to the Nazis the Partisans slackened their guard and that Tito was therefore responsible for the loss of thousands of Partisan lives.

Acting in line with Hitler's principle that rebels should not be talked to but shot, his commanders assembled five divisions of German and auxiliary troops and sent them into action in what they called Operation *Schwarz* and the Partisans named the Fifth Offensive. Despite the appallingly difficult mountain terrain the Germans almost succeeded and on 10 June 1943 the German commander Rudolf Luther felt able to report: "The last phase of the battle, the hour of the final liquidation of the Tito Army has come."[53]

The Partisan losses were heavy but the last trumpet was premature. With indomitable courage and endurance the kernel of the Partisan forces with their commander and his senior staff broke out of the encirclement and made their way into the relative safety of the mountains of East Bosnia. And it was during this perilous journey that the first British mission was parachuted to Tito's headquarters on Mount Durmitor. It was led by a young academic-turned-soldier Captain William Deakin, a personal friend of the British Prime Minister; Hitler had said "no" just as Churchill was in the process of saying "yes". From being a hunted rebel, Tito became an honoured ally. In return for sporadic and limited support for the military operations which the Middle East Command were conducting against the Axis, Tito would soon be receiving the political recognition and military assistance which he needed to destroy his "principal enemies" and to win the civil war.

Chapter 3

HOW CHURCHILL WAS HOODWINKED

THE STORY OF Western support for the Partisans, which lasted
from 1943 till the end of the war, is primarily one of unrequited
love. In the West the Partisans were perceived as comrades-in-
arms, battling indomitably against the common foe. The Western
leaders were perceived by Partisan leaders as class enemies, intent
on depriving Tito of the fruits of his revolutionary war.

The scale of misapprehension is illustrated in a letter from
Churchill to Roosevelt in August 1944, urging an Allied landing at
the head of the Adriatic: "Tito's people will be waiting for us at
Istria."[1]

All along the coast, the Partisan commanders were indeed
waiting, but for Allied troops whom they regarded as enemies
rather than friends. A Partisan veteran then Lieutenant-Colonel,
later General, Stane Semić-Daki recalled that in the same month
he had received instructions to suspend guerrilla actions against
the Germans in Inner Carniola and rest his units, as they might be
needed to move towards Gorski Kotar and the sea: "This would be
necessary if Anglo-American troops landed on the Yugoslav coast
as the Supreme Commander Marshal Tito was opposed to the
establishment of a second front on Yugoslav territory."[2] This
order was in accordance with the concept which the Partisan
delegation had already discussed the previous year with the
Germans.

Semić-Daki obeyed unquestioningly: "I no longer allowed the
soldiers to become engaged in fighting and told them they should
eat well and have as much rest as possible." He was later ordered
to withhold information from a visiting Allied mission. It was not
until late September that his orders were reversed and he was told
to resume anti-German operations. During his private visit to
Moscow in September 1944 Tito repeated his intention of using
force, if necessary, to prevent Allied intervention. The obsessive
Partisan dread of an Allied landing was evoked by Edvard Kardelj
in his wartime reminiscences. He indicated that Tito had suspected that Western troops might provoke a clash along the Isonzo
River as an excuse to open up an advance towards Vienna.
The Partisans therefore considered blowing up the bridges

and desisted only because they were afraid Stalin might object.[3]

When Field Marshal Alexander came to Belgrade in February 1945, he offered to provide Allied troops to accelerate the German retreat and, according to Kardelj's account, it was only Tito's adamant refusal of this request (which might indeed have speeded up the end of the war and spared tens of thousands of Yugoslav lives lost during the final months) that "saved our revolution".

Yet the belief that the Partisans regarded Western forces as brothers in the common fight was still being put forward twenty years later by a leading British authority on the last War, Professor Michael Howard. Arguing that a less clumsy Allied Command structure might have allowed a bridgehead on the Adriatic, Howard affirmed this would have been useful "in bringing more immediate help to the Partisan armies".[4]

It is certainly true that, as the theatre of war closed in on the Balkans, the Middle East Command took an increasing interest in guerrilla activities in Yugoslavia. Contrary to Tito's assumption, the Allies were concerned only with the fighting potential of the competing resistance groups and not at all with their political coloration.

And in combat terms, the Partisans had unquestionably produced a more effective military machine. They were better organized, more mobile and, above all, far better led. Tito was a natural leader and the commanders he had selected, some of them very young, were of remarkably high quality. Most of the regular officers who refused to accept defeat had indeed joined Mihailović and it might have been expected that it was the Chetniks who would have better professional qualifications. But Tito had over a thousand men with direct guerrilla experience from the Spanish Civil War, with training far more relevant to conditions in occupied Yugoslavia than anything taught in the pre-war Yugoslav military academy.

The surrender of the Italians in September 1943 accentuated the differences in the scale and competence of the rival forces. The Chetniks had expected that the Italians would be defeated by invading Western armies; in fact the collapse took place on the Italian mainland, leaving the Italian occupying troops in Yugoslavia in a vacuum which the Partisans were quick to fill. The Chetnik base was still in German-occupied Serbia and, in the subsequent race for territory and arms, the Partisans benefited from the closer proximity of their troops. But they also displayed

superior drive and flexibility and it was this above all which
enabled them, after Italy's collapse, to seize vast amounts of
equipment. It is still a matter of dispute just how far the British
military commanders, by that time already committed to the
Partisan side, actively encouraged the Italians to surrender to the
Partisans rather than to the Chetniks. We have the direct testimony of British officers that one Italian division, the Venezia, did
surrender to the Chetniks who were told by the British to allow the
Italians to keep their arms as they would from now on be fighting
on the Allied side. Then, while the Chetniks were advancing
elsewhere, the Partisans arrived and captured the whole Italian
unit. This gave the Partisans control over five out of the fifteen
Italian divisions previously engaged in occupation: the rest having
either disintegrated or been captured by the Germans.

Certainly after the Italian surrender the Germans found the
Balkan theatre transformed: "Within three weeks Von Weichs,
the new Commander of the South Eastern Command, reported
that Tito's guerrillas had taken on the aspects of a regular force,
with fully equipped corps and divisions, many of them capable of
holding vast areas and engaging the German occupation troops in
pitched battles."[5]

The Partisans were also well placed to take over formerly
Ustasha-controlled territories as they had already effectively infiltrated into the Pavelić administration. And, in the rallying of huge
numbers of Croats to the Partisan side, they gained more than a
numerical advantage. Previously the Communists had had to rely
for their cadres on Serb peasants living outside Serbia and these
came from primitive regions where the level of education and
literacy was remarkably low. Now they were joined by men of
administrative and technical competence. Further they had no
compunction in recruiting and promoting even Croats with a
Ustasha past: on the contrary, as the East Germans were to find
with the Nazis, such people often proved themselves the easiest to
control and the keenest to demonstrate their zeal.

But even though the offensive capacities of the Partisan guerrillas impressed the Germans in the second half of 1943, the military
value of the Partisan contribution to the war, both quantitatively
and qualitatively, turned out to be much less important than
certain Western officials were leading their political masters to
believe. And in interpreting the gap between what Western political leaders were telling each other about Partisan operations
and what, from Axis sources, we now know they were actually

doing, it is hard to avoid the conclusion that the disinformation was deliberate.

In the European continent, in those days, the words "British Intelligence Service" still evoked a highly coordinated network of professional agents, masterminded undeviatingly in the higher interests of the British Empire. The reality, as Graham Greene, Malcolm Muggeridge and many others personally involved have told us, was very different. The miscellaneous bunch who staffed the *ad hoc* special services tended to spend as much time fighting each other as fighting the enemy. And as Andrew Boyle has shown, the intrigue, secrecy and unaccountability of these proliferating bodies provided ideal conditions for subversive activities.[6]

In the crucial decisions, taken during 1943 and finalized in 1944, to concentrate all Allied material and moral support behind Tito and to help him to destroy Mihailović (later shot as a traitor), there can be little doubt that the Communists and pro-Communists working within the Western intelligence apparatus made a crucial contribution.

The opportunity of the Westerners dedicated to the Partisan cause came in 1943 primarily because of the changed military situation. Responsibility for contacts with the resistance movements in Yugoslavia consequently shifted from London to Cairo and whereas the personnel in the London office was stolidly anti-Communist and consistently underestimated both the fighting strength and the internal discipline of the Partisans, the key people in Cairo were ideologically and, at least in one case operationally, committed to the Communist cause. As these were in control of British and, until 1944, also of American intelligence-gathering, they were in an unchallengeable position to select, direct and repress material coming from the field. Any incriminating evidence showing that they tampered with reports or that they eliminated deviating agents, if it ever was in written form, would by now certainly have been destroyed. But in the view of many of the British officers who served with Mihailović, any material they sent in, if it seemed to favour a more helpful attitude towards Mihailović's Chetniks, was quietly shelved.

Lieutenant-Commander A. R. Glen, DSC, RNVR (now Sir Alexander Glen) was a witness of what seemed, retrospectively, like a politically-motivated suppression of evidence which could have been damaging to the Partisans—although he did not see the political implications at the time. Glen who, as we saw, served as

Assistant Naval Attaché in Belgrade in 1940/41, was sent by the Navy in 1944 to lead an aerial mining operation on the Danube. Though never part of SOE, he had to send his messages through SOE channels, as there was no other communications route to his naval commander, Admiral Sir John Cunningham. Most of his signals were on operational matters and, as he reported, he was impressed by the fighting quality of the Partisan unit which assisted him on his mission. But he also sent reports of a political nature which were less reassuring and which reflected his doubts and anxieties about the Partisans' intentions. After accomplishing his task, Glen stayed on with the Red Army in Sofia and it was not until December 1944 that he was brought back to Allied Headquarters at Caserta where he took the occasion to try and collate the signal log for a more complete analysis. In the general confusion he was not surprised that some of his reports had gone astray but it did strike him as remarkable that all the signals which had contained any political reservations about the Partisans turned out to be missing from the files.[7]

One Communist, well-placed to serve Party interests in Cairo, was James Klugmann, a senior member of the British Communist Party, and correctly identified as such by General Vlatko Velebit, Tito's first delegate to the West. Klugmann served as a staff officer, first in Cairo and later in Bari, handling the traffic of men and materials in and out of Yugoslavia. He was a popular figure, known to be hardworking, and his Communism was so widely known that it seemed unlikely he was a spy in the usual sense of the word. But he would have been disloyal to his own convictions if, in this highly sensitive job, he had not placed his loyalty to the Soviet Union above his loyalty to Britain. (After the war, when Stalin expelled Tito from the Soviet bloc, he wrote a book taking Stalin's side.) Klugmann's importance in relation to other Communists inside the intelligence edifice must remain a matter of guesswork. As Glen later commented: "One can only be astounded that Klugmann was left installed in a key position in Bari. But I would guess there were many more little creatures with sharp noses and long strong claws digging away for the new red dawn that obsessed them in the East."

James Klugmann was at school and college with Donald Maclean and certainly formed part of the old-boy network comprehensively exposed by Andrew Boyle, of which the most famous members, besides Donald Maclean at the Foreign Office, were

Anthony Blunt at MI5, Kim Philby at MI6 and Burgess in political warfare. This group operated in comfort at a time when reformist intellectuals tended to regard the Communists as left-wing members of their common progressive family.

Recalling the intellectual atmosphere of the time, Professor Hugh Seton Watson, a leading specialist on Eastern Europe, later evoked his personal reaction to the discovery that Kim Philby was working at MI6: "My own view, like that of my contemporaries, was that our superiors were lunatic in their anticommunism. . . . We were therefore pleased that at least one communist should have broken through and that the social prejudices of our superiors had, on this occasion, triumphed over their political prejudices."[8]

In American intellectual circles, the concept of the Communists as friendly progressives was equally prevalent. In 1942 one fellow-traveller, Louis Adamic, having written a book favouring a more "progressive" policy towards liberated Europe, was invited to a dinner with Winston Churchill at the White House. During a private conversation after the meal, Mrs Roosevelt expressed the view that, in Europe as elsewhere, Churchill was more of a threat to freedom than Stalin.[9]

As his immediate superior Klugmann was fortunate in having Basil Davidson, a man whom I later came to know and who never concealed his sympathies for what he saw, at that time, as the forces of progress in the East, against the Western capitalist world.

The task Klugmann and Davidson set themselves was facilitated by the fact that C. M. Keble, the head of Cairo SOE, was a not very clever Brigadier, whose importance and rank were in direct relation to the military significance of Yugoslav resistance. Though himself a conservative he had an entirely non-ideological need to maximize Partisan activity. Davidson described how, on one occasion, to avoid security checks, Keble hid his Communist assistant Klugmann in the lavatory.[10]

The flabbiness of Western security is illustrated by the fact that it took the Partisans themselves by surprise. At the end of 1943 when Tito sent out his first delegation to the West, General Velebit later confessed that he and his colleagues had expected an icy reception from personnel whom they had assumed would have been recruited "from banks and big business". Instead they were received with open arms and Velebit commented on SOE's "interesting" staffing policy, in which "people were accepted who did not conceal their left-wing and even communist affiliations".[11]

The fervently pro-Partisan reports which SOE were sending back to London intrigued one of the recipients, the novelist Anthony Powell, who was then working in a branch of military intelligence. In his memoirs Powell attributed the abandonment of Mihailović to "deviously reliable evidence sent in by some of the British elements in the structure at work on the spot" and comments: "I have myself read reports circulating on the situation applauding the Yugoslav communist irregulars in a tone more suitable to an adventure story in the *Boys Own Paper* than a sober appreciation of what was happening."[12]

War maps, suggesting that the Partisans had already "liberated" most of Yugoslavia were kept in secret operational rooms, first in Cairo and later in Bari, but on closer inspection most of the areas on which the little flags had been pinned, turn out to consist of impenetrable mountains and forests. Several officers remaining from the Chetnik side protested that they could testify from personal knowledge that the territory claimed by the Partisans was in fact controlled by Mihailović's men. After a few skirmishes in which, on one occasion, the protagonists came to blows, liaison officers returning from Mihailović's side found the map room permanently barred.

Claims put forward about the number of men serving in Tito's army were also wildly exaggerated and though SOE figures were used to brief the press, the Foreign Office seems to have shared Powell's inherent scepticism. In September 1943 (before the Italian surrender) Premier Purić asked a senior Foreign Office official whether he really believed that Tito disposed of 300,000 men; information reaching the royalists suggested a much lower figure. The FO man agreed that the claim was excessive, though he said he personally did believe that Tito had more than 60,000 men. "But 60,000 is not 300,000" said Purić, but his informant declined to discuss the discrepancy.[13]

The complete turn-about in Allied policy took more than a year. Between 1943 and 1944 the Communists and pro-Communists in SOE Cairo, assisted by friends in the propaganda and auxiliary agencies, fully fulfilled their objectives. They could not have done so, of course, unless the Partisans had been able to chalk up some impressive military operations of sufficient importance to impress the Allied high command.

On the negative side of the operation, already by the summer of

1942, as we saw in the last chapter, the Communists had started work on the discrediting of Mihailović. This may have run into some difficulty as the intercepts of German intelligence messages during the last months of 1942, according to F. H. Hinsley, the official historian of British Intelligence, "cast some doubt on arguments that Draža Mihailović's forces were doing no fighting at all".[14] None the less, as he says, already in March 1943 Cairo began its campaign for the dumping of Mihailović. It repeated that demand in August, though according to Hinsley, Bletchley, the office breaking the top-level German cypher, in the same month "left no doubt that at least at the highest level, the Germans remained set on Mihailović's destruction".

SOE's resolve that the Partisans must be seen to be the only resisters was the reason Hudson gave for the failure of a Chetnik sabotage operation against Axis communications planned in September 1943. Hudson had sent a request for explosives but these were withheld and he was told that operations must be delayed until SOE could parachute a sapper from the British engineers to provide the necessary expertise. Hudson said this was totally superfluous as he already had at his disposal a highly competent sapper from Slovenia.[15]

Though, in the second half of 1943, Mihailović's forces were engaged in a series of anti-Axis actions (see page 80), aid was cut off completely in November and British liaison officers accredited to Mihailović were instructed to try and join the Partisans. Nearly all the historians of the period repeat the same story that, before abandoning Mihailović, the Middle East command had given him one last chance to prove himself: he was told that aid would only continue if, before the end of the year, his men carried out two sabotage operations against well-defended bridges on the Morava River. Mihailović had no difficulty persuading the British mission that for this purpose he would need heavy weapons including mortars and anti-tank guns, and Brigadier Armstrong consequently sent the request on to Cairo with the comment:

> I would strongly advise that if we take the big and long view, it will pay us in the end. Mihailović undoubtedly commands superiority in the areas of vital North and South Command. In months ahead you will not want these constantly under attack. The Partisans will not, repeat not, command sufficient support to be able to do this, Mihailović does and will. At present he is

committed to cooperation. If you seize the opportunity and support with sorties, the dividends you gather will be greatly increased. If you hesitate to provide material support and continue propaganda attacks you will relapse to the old spirit of the preservation of Serb blood—the British want all but will give nothing in return. As a result the work of the BLOs [British Liaison Officers] out here will be wasted and useless.[16]

And wasted and useless it was. For as Hinsley divulges, the ultimatum to Mihailović was a fake. Indeed, if Mihailović had received the necessary equipment, the whole purpose of the exercise, which was designed to induce King Peter to disavow Mihailović, would have been foiled. As Hinsley explained, the decision to abandon Mihailović had already been taken but there was the remaining problem of how to induce Peter to dissociate himself from the resistance leader he had appointed as his Chief of Staff and later as his Minister of War. Mihailović's failure to fulfil the orders of the Allied commanders was intended to clinch the argument. Hinsley tells us that the plot ran into difficulties in London "where the test was not accepted as realistic or indeed even responsible".[17]

Those BLOs who did manage, at enormous peril to themselves, to join up with the Partisans found themselves in a very different relationship with the local inhabitants. Mihailović's commanders left them free to move around the villages and make their own local contacts. With the Partisans they were under constant supervision. Hudson later recalled taking out his gun when a young Partisan guard tried physically to constrain him from leaving Partisan premises. When SOE Cairo heard of the fight, they took the Partisan side and ordered him to surrender his transmitter to another British officer of the same rank but more deferential to Tito's men. He filed a furious message reminding the SOE of all the promises of material they had made and broken and concluded: "At least refrain from treachery towards your officers in the field. Such conduct is unworthy of a prostitute let alone an SOE officer."[18]

When in April 1944 Hudson did manage to extricate himself, after more than three years of uninterrupted service, his chiefs in Cairo refused to see him. As he discovered, rumours were circulating that, as a result of his ordeals, he was mentally deranged. At the BBC most of the staff were more than willing to switch from the

Chetniks to the Partisan side. Initially, the BBC, had been ordered to attribute all resistance activity in Yugoslavia to Mihailović and until the beginning of 1943, the Partisans were designated only as unspecified "patriots". Within a year the U-turn was complete and Mihailović could not be mentioned without the epithet "collaborator".

On several occasions both British and American liaison officers witnessed Chetnik actions and subsequently heard these attributed by the BBC to the Partisans. In Serbia, where the Germans systematically presented all resistance as Communist, the BBC, both in giving to the Partisans all credit for operations and in denigrating the Chetniks, seemed to be echoing the Nazi line. Jasper Rootham reported in early 1944: "The BBC service in Yugoslavia over the last nine months has steadily contributed to weakening British prestige in the part of the country where I was serving. To put it shortly and brutally, I was ashamed that people who were protecting me and who were my companions should have been by implication almost always, and sometimes explicitly, accused of treachery to the Allied cause. The Serbs are not a nation of Quislings".

Faulty intelligence from SOE would not have been enough to lead the BBC to these excesses unless it had been carried along by the prevailing pro-Soviet euphoria. British and Soviet views on the future of Europe were "fundamentally identical", said the European Editor of the BBC in his "man-in-the-street" commentary, in which the outside world was told that Britain would welcome "the final liquidation of the forces of political reaction" and would be happy to see the European democracies "adopt what they have learnt to admire and respect in the Soviet system".[19]

For the pro-Partisans at Cairo the demolition of Mihailović was not enough. In order to justify maximizing military and political support to their friends it was also necessary to convince Western governments of the indispensability of the Partisans in the war effort. And as soon as the German and Italian war archives became available the scale of the exaggerations made on the Partisans' behalf became apparent—though only a few scholars troubled to examine the evidence, which did little to dent the world-wide reputation of the Communist-led guerrillas. By the summer of 1943 Churchill, briefed by SOE Cairo, felt able to inform Roosevelt that the Partisans were "pinning down" 33 Axis divisions. In reality Axis troops in Yugoslavia never exceeded 30 divisions of which at that time only seven were German and most of these were battered and diminished units back from the Russian Front or youngsters in training.

One of the seven was an SS division composed of locally recruited volunteers under German cadres, most of them Yugoslavs of German ethnic origin. The Italians never had more than sixteen divisions in Yugoslavia, all qualitatively below average strength, and the rest of the occupation force was recruited, either voluntarily or forcibly, from the native communities. Some Moslems preferred to serve in an SS division rather than join the Pavelić Croat army. In October 1943, that is after the Italian collapse, the occupation troops in Yugoslavia consisted of fifteen German and eight Bulgarian and Croat divisions, nothing like enough to make up for the units lost by the Italian withdrawal. By June 1944 the Germans had no more than eighteen divisions of their own in the whole Balkan theatre.

But besides the inaccuracy of the figures, there was a second and even more important fallacy in the image presented of Partisan strength. For what is also clear from the Axis archives is that it was not the Partisans alone who were responsible for pinning down Axis units. "The Axis divisions, all of low strength, some of poor quality and most of bad morale were held down in Yugoslavia not only by the Partisans but also by the Mihailović Chetniks; even more by the distrust of one another [particularly true before the autumn of 1943 when the Germans and Italians were locked in incessant rivalries]; and even more by the fear of an allied invasion."[20] As Seaton has recalled in his book on the German army: "Hitler had always been sure that the British intended to land in the Balkans in order to free the Dardanelles and Bosphorus sea routes to Russia and to deny the Germans the Balkan mineral resources. . . . Yet the Germans' strength in the Balkans was never sufficient to do more than keep open the main lines of communication."[21]

The vast Yugoslav hinterland was never occupied at all and the local communities were largely left to fend for themselves. The guerrillas did present a problem: both in 1943 and 1944 the German High Command launched several large forays to try and clear both Partisans and Chetniks from their forest and mountain lairs from which they organized assaults against military targets. Some of these sporadic operations engaged several German divisions fighting in such inclement conditions and such brutal forms of combat—hardly any prisoners were taken on either side and bodies were often mutilated—that some German soldiers asked in preference to be posted to the Eastern Front.[22]

But within the general framework of the war the number of Germans involved with the Partisans was negligible and indeed the desperate shortage of German manpower was a grievance of which local commanders constantly complained. On 24 September 1943 the Commander-in-Chief of the German forces visited Hitler to protest that he was expected to hold down a front of 5,000 kilometres with ten poor-quality divisions; both he and other professional soldiers tried vainly to persuade Hitler to evacuate the Balkans altogether. Hitler was obdurate, perhaps deceived by the elaborate spectacle mounted by the British A Force in order to divert attention from the Normandy invasion. In his book *Dudley Clarke: Master of Deception*, David Muir, who served under Clarke, claims that in the expectation of a 1944 spring invasion three German armies were immobilized and that bogus orders of battle held back two SS Panzer divisions which might otherwise have tipped the balance in Overlord.[23]

After the Italians left, a large part of Yugoslav territory remained unoccupied though, as Muir points out, most of it consisted of mountains and forests of no particular consequence to the Germans. It was in these areas that the final battles of the Yugoslav civil war were fought, by which time the Allies were totally committed to the Partisans.

But though the Communists and pro-Communists in Cairo played an important role in turning Allied policy around, it is doubtful whether they could have succeeded so completely without the help of two British officers, Captain William Deakin and Brigadier Fitzroy Maclean, neither of them in the least Communist but both coming to commit themselves totally to the Partisan side. The two men were quite accidentally caught up in the affairs of Yugoslavia, having had no previous knowledge of either the country or its languages and, by the strangest of coincidences, both happened to be friends of Winston Churchill. For this personal reason their military and political evaluations found their way directly to the Prime Minister's office. For the rest of the war all decisions taken by the British Cabinet regarding Yugoslavia were to depend on recommendations from Maclean.

Neither Deakin nor Maclean ever seem to have recognized "the substantially defective nature" of Allied intelligence gathering about the Partisans though it was already emphasized at the time by an OSS officer, Major Richard Weil. As he reported back to headquarters: "We do not know whether the Partisan reports about action are accurate, exaggerated or utterly untrue. This is because for the most part we have taken the Partisan word for what went on since we seldom had our own observer with them. . . ."[24]

Deakin, who arrived in Cairo at the end of 1942 and eagerly assimilated the Cairo material, had been Churchill's literary secretary while Churchill was writing his life of the Duke of Marlborough. And it was to the great Duke of Marlborough that Basil Davidson later attributed Churchill's willingness to take in an SOE briefing on the Partisans, when he came through Cairo on his way to Turkey in January 1943. The epic story of the gallant guerrillas fired the Prime Minister's imagination and it took him more than a year before he realized that the gallantry was being expended in another cause.

In May 1944, when the choice for the Partisans and against the Chetniks had already been made, Churchill invited Hudson, the man who had served with both Mihailović and Tito, to Chequers for a private chat. Hudson, after having been cold-shouldered in Cairo, was amazed to find that his distrust of his superiors was shared by the Prime Minister. Hudson recalled that Churchill said that he knew that Cairo had cooked the books, destroyed records and that the SOE office was "a nest of intrigue".[25]

By then, the military commitment to Tito was irreversible. After Churchill's visit at the beginning of 1943, followed by a more positive attitude by British and American authorities towards the Partisans, the SOE set out to establish direct contacts. The first batch of emissaries to be dropped by parachute, were Canadians of Croat origin, recruited from the Canadian Communist party: "Our information about Partisan groups was meagre," Eden wrote to Churchill on 24 June 1943. "As a first step therefore we agreed that SOE should send in agents to various Partisan and Croat groups. The object was to obtain detailed information regarding various organizations, to decide how far military support was desirable and finally to bring about, if possible the unity of all the resistance movements."[26] No one, apparently, drew Eden's attention to the political provenance of the agents on whom Allied policy would depend.

Arriving in Cairo, Davidson later recalled asking what Klugmann was doing, and being told that he was "looking after the Canadians": he did not mention who these Canadians were. Certainly, no one told Tito, who was so surprised to learn of the

arrival of a Communist contingent from Canada that he had their
authenticity checked in the Comintern files.

The Communist reports from Croatia may have contributed to
a change in the Western attitude towards the Croat Peasant
leader, Vladko Maček, then under Ustasha detention. Previously
it has been assumed that he was the truest representative of Croat
opinion, a view shared, as we have seen, by Edvard Kardelj. Now
PWE Cairo (the Political Warfare Executive, which handled
British propaganda to wartime Europe) dismissed him as "a
reactionary" and suggested that members of his Peasant Party
should be encouraged to join Tito: "This would be to our advantage as they may exercise a moderating influence and thereby
weaken the communist element among the Partisans."[27]

On joining Tito on Mount Durmitor, Deakin was bowled over
by what he saw of the Partisans' courage, discipline and human
endurance and by their self-sacrificing concern for their leader.
The experience, as he later wrote, made him feel part of their
struggle: "I had taken on by stages a binding and absolute
identification with those around me."[28] And binding and absolute
it remained. As we know from Partisan literature, his devotion was
not reciprocated. Though he was later decorated by the Yugoslav
government his intentions always remained suspect. "The Partisans felt they were fighting another war," he was later to write.
Indeed they were though Deakin never saw why. Though during
his first three months' assignment, all he could see for himself were
Partisan skills in evading Axis troops, he believed and reported
back all the stories he was told of Partisan exploits in harassing
the enemy and in uniting the people behind them. And he sent
back plentiful "evidence" of Mihailović's treachery, apparently
oblivious that all of it came from men intent on Mihailović's
destruction.

But it was above all by Tito himself that Deakin was enthralled.
Knowing nothing of the Partisan discussions with the Germans
earlier that year, in which Tito had proposed joint resistance to
a prospective Western landing, Deakin expressed unreserved
admiration for a leader at whose side he had endured such fearful
hardships. Indeed, on several occasions he was at Tito's side when
they both narrowly escaped death.

Everything Tito said had to be true: Deakin listed *The Economist*
among the favourite reading of this former Comintern agent,
educated in Stalin's Moscow and who knew no more than a few
words of English. Unaware that merely by joining the Partisans he

was already heavily engaged in a civil war, Deakin felt able to report: "The Partisan leadership has *no* [his italic] plan or intention of immediate social revolution. The prime object is the construction of the country after the war and it is realized that revolutionary action will cause internal struggles which will fatally weaken the country."[29] Initially Deakin's brief had been exclusively military. The man sent to gather political intelligence was an officer, fluent in Serbo-Croat, Colonel Stewart, who was killed in an air attack shortly after the mission arrived. Deakin then took both assignments and in subsequent decades has remained Britain's most widely recognized expert on wartime Yugoslavia.

In a valuable study of British propaganda towards Yugoslavia during the war, M. M. Stenton has placed Deakin's epic *The Embattled Mountain* within the wider context of what is now known about the Yugoslav civil war: "Deakin was able to observe the remarkable fighting qualities of the Partisans. But inevitably did so without reference to simultaneous anti-Chetnik operations which the Germans deemed of great importance, or to the larger framework in which it could be said that the Partisans were not so much fighting the Germans as trying to escape from them at a time when they preferred to be hunting Chetniks"—an aspect of the war which the Communists most needed to conceal.[30]

The deception of Deakin was witnessed by Bill Hudson who, at the end of 1943, had been ordered to leave the Chetniks and join the Partisans. Having been in the country since 1941 he was by this time widely known and trusted by the local people. Hudson recalled that, on a number of occasions, Partisan communiqués depicting aggressive and heroic deeds and duly sent back to Cairo, were sheer inventions: the peasants from the localities were able to tell him that nothing whatever had happened in the areas mentioned.

(A later witness of the unreliability of Partisan communiqués was Ljubo Sirc, who participated in the Partisan advance from Split to Ljubljana. At one resting-place, the Partisans came within earshot of German guns and the local commander and his staff were the first to flee. Within a few hours foreign radios were reporting intrepid Partisan resistance from the same locality.)

Throughout the summer of 1943 Cairo's main preoccupation was to get as much aid as possible to the Partisans and as little as possible to the Mihailović Chetniks: "Poor old Mihailović depends for his supplies on what his forces could capture", wrote the head of the British mission, Brigadier Armstrong: "I remember particularly two drops at my headquarters: one consisted of gumboots and the other of office equipment. . . ."[31]

Mihailović still saw himself as the King's Minister of War but officers sent in by SOE were encouraged to treat him as a wilful subordinate. Missions to Tito were on the other hand expected to show the deference appropriate to an allied Commander-in-Chief. Further, whereas on the Partisan side, the chief of mission at Tito's headquarters was in command of all the submissions, each of the liaison officers in the Chetnik area reported directly back to Cairo, leaving Brigadier Armstrong complaining that he was working in the dark.

At first the regular air-drops to the Partisans, which started soon after Deakin's arrival, were only conditional: they would be delivered only on the assurance that they would not be used against the Chetniks. Tito never for a moment hesitated either in making or breaking the promise: as he told Maclean soon after the Italian surrender his first objective must now be "to overrun the Chetniks" and by October it was generally known that the Partisans were using Allied weapons against their internal enemies. Yet within two and a half months the Partisans received more aid than the Chetniks had done since the beginning of hostilities. By the turn of the year 1943–44 as much as 6,000 tons of arms and ammunition a month were being dropped and by the summer of 1944, according to OSS (Office of Strategic Services and the US equivalent of SOE) officers, half the Partisan military equipment came from Allies' sources.[32]

And whereas in June 1943 Allied aid had started out conditionally, within a few months it was Tito himself who was setting the conditions. Hinsley recalls that the real reason for the final decision, taken in February 1944, to send no more missions to Mihailović was that Tito had insisted on institutionalizing the rupture as a *sine qua non* for allowing the Allies to send their officers to Partisan units, in order to facilitate further arms deliveries to the Partisans themselves.

During the crucial turn-around period, the US missions to Yugoslav resistance were part of General Donovan's OSS, and served under British command. Though Donovan was a dedicated anti-Communist, his quandary was the same as Keble's: his own status and the importance of his organization were directly related to the military significance of the various European resistance movements and, of these, the Partisans were by far the most active.

SOE was thus well placed to feed him with disinformation to justify building up American support behind Tito's forces.

It would be hard to find any other explanation for Donovan's letter to Roosevelt in September 1943 (by which time every Partisan unit had its Communist political commissar) in which he asserted: "There is no factual foundation for the allegations of communism being made against the Partisans. Such influences are to be found only among a small set out of the rank-and-file and some of the leaders."[34] It was thus OSS officers who, after the Italian collapse, organized a secret sea-ferry which, for several weeks, delivered to the Partisans not only light weapons, notably machine-guns, but also armoured vehicles.

The change of sides by the Western powers during the Yugoslav civil war, in which Roosevelt willingly followed the British lead, is often attributed by non-Communist Yugoslavs to Churchill's heartless indifference. Yet, as his correspondence shows, considering the pressures on the British Prime Minister during 1943 he spent a remarkable amount of time and emotional energy trying to sort out the affairs of a small and relatively minor ally.

Churchill had taken the young king under his protection when he arrived in 1941, had installed the exiled government in London and endorsed the choice of Mihailović as Minister of War. What shocked not only the Prime Minister but all those around him were the quarrels among the London Yugoslavs themselves. These were primarily between Serb and Croat, both civilian and military, which started immediately after they arrived and got very much worse with the news of the Ustasha massacres. Theoretically, after the *coup*, as the Yugoslav Parliament had been dissolved and a state of emergency declared, all power lay with the King. But Peter proved totally incapable of exercising it, except on the one personal matter which really concerned him: his resolution to marry the woman of his choice, a Greek princess, which meant the dismissal of any of his ministers who disapproved.

According to Sir George Rendell, British Ambassador to the exiled government, it was the squabbles between the exiles in London and which later spread to Cairo "which made it possible for Britain to abandon the royal government with hardly a qualm and to acquiesce in Tito's anti-monarchical revolution."[35]

By March 1943, Mihailović had already fallen from grace. Normally field-despatches from his headquarters would never reach London but Cairo made sure that Churchill's attention was drawn to a report of an anti-British diatribe by Mihailović, which had been personally witnessed by liaison officer, Colonel Bailey. The occasion was a Christening ceremony at the home of the Mayor of Lipovo in Montenegro, where Mihailović had his temporary headquarters, and before the speech, as Bailey noted, "a great deal of plum brandy had been consumed by all present except the baby". Bailey paraphrased the relevant passages: "Mihailović accused the British of keeping the King and government as virtual prisoners. The Allies' lust for blood was satisfied by the untimely, hypocritical and anti-Yugoslav activities on behalf of the Partisans. But let the Allies know that nothing they could do or threaten would turn the Serbs from their vows and sacred duty of exterminating the Partisans. As long as the Italians remained his sole adequate source of benefit and assistance, nothing the Allies could do could change his attitude towards them. His enemies were the Partisans, the Ustashas, the Moslems in that order and when he had dealt with them he would turn to the Italians and Germans."[36]

Churchill's roar of fury was both understandable and self-serving: it cleared his conscience before doing what he had been told was operationally sensible. The Lipovo scandal and Deakin's ecstatic reports were no doubt in his mind when in August 1943 he wrote to General Alexander of "the marvellous resistance being put up by the so-called Partisans, followers of Tito in Bosnia", contrasting it with "the powerful and cold-blooded manoeuvre of Draža Mihailović in Serbia."[37]

It was then that Churchill arranged to have his friend Fitzroy Maclean, Tory MP and intrepid adventurer, promoted to Brigadier and assigned to lead Britain's mission to the Partisans. In a letter to Tito, Churchill expressed his regret that he was too old and too fat to be parachuted himself into Yugoslavia. But he could hardly have expressed his personal concern better than by acceding to Maclean's request that his son Randolph would join the mission.

Maclean was even more uncritically committed to the Partisans than Deakin. In his wartime diaries, Harold Macmillan, who as Resident Minister in the Middle East had frequent encounters with both, described Maclean as one of Tito's fans and noted that Deakin was "not so prejudiced as I feel Fitzroy to be." The Tito–Maclean special relationship survived the war and Maclean was rewarded by becoming the only foreigner whom Tito allowed to acquire real estate on Yugoslav territory. Maclean chose a seventeenth-century nobleman's house in the little town of

Korčula on an Adriatic Island not far from Dubrovnik and dating from the same period. The house was well-preserved and had been lived in previously by a Count Boschi whose fate is not recorded and whose family fled.

It was a report sent out by Maclean on 16 November 1943, which finally clinched the case for the Partisans and against the Chetniks. Later described by insiders as "a blockbuster", it recommended the dumping of Mihailović; massive aid to the Partisans; and the redirection of the BBC and other propaganda organs accordingly.[38]

In view of the importance of the document, it is worth reassessing it in the light of what we now know was going on inside Yugoslavia at the time it was written. The report opens by endorsing the Partisans' most extravagant claim: that they were killing five Germans and ten Chetniks for every man they lost. As we know, from the German archives, German casualties were less than one-tenth of those suffered by the Partisans. The Partisans claimed losses of 305,000 killed and 425,000 wounded. According to the official German war records, the German losses between 22 June 1941 and 1 April 1945 for the entire Balkan theatre, both killed and missing, were 20,256 men including 394 officers. These included casualties incurred in Albania, Bulgaria and Greece as well as Yugoslavia (against both Mihailović's and Tito's forces). Most of the losses were sustained not against the Partisans but during the Soviet and Bulgarian attacks on the retreating German army in 1944/1945.[39]

Without knowing the language or having access to anyone not vetted by the Partisans, Maclean felt able to report that his hosts had "the wholehearted support of the civil population". To make this proposition credible, he presented the leadership as pink rather than red. "Their only concern," he wrote, "is to remain true to the traditional love of liberty of the peoples of Yugoslavia." He declared himself unable, he said, "to find any evidence of mass arrests or executions, similar to those perpetrated by the Ustashas and Chetniks." His inability was hardly surprising as he never travelled except under Partisan control. In fact, as we saw in the last chapter, the Partisans killed extensively and systematically, until the middle of 1945, when Tito himself called for an end to the slaughter on the grounds that "nobody is afraid of death any more".

By asserting that "the Yugoslav communists have profited by the experience of others and have not found it necessary to

persecute and thereby alienate whole sections of the population"
he claimed that the Partisans practised religious toleration. Evidence to the contrary was supplied by the Catholic novelist,
Evelyn Waugh, who joined the British mission and was asked a
few months later to file a detailed report on the state of the Catholic
church in Croatia. Waugh listed incidents of which he knew,
involving the slaughter of priests, the closing down of churches
and the compulsory indoctrination of Marxist–Leninist atheism
in all the cities for which evidence was available.[40]

On the future of the monarchy, Maclean claimed that the
Partisans agreed that "this must in due course be freely decided by
the peoples of Yugoslavia". Meanwhile, "partisan propaganda
has scrupulously refrained from attacking His Majesty" (meaning
Peter). He was evidently unfamiliar with the words of one Partisan
familiar marching song:

> Give me a rifle
> three metres long
> to kill King Peter . . .

Less than a fortnight after the dispatch of the Maclean report,
Tito assembled his Communist and fellow-travelling supporters at
Jajce in Bosnia and, on 29 November, the monarchy was repudiated. The text of the resolution, on which the present régime has
been founded, set up a provisional government and affirmed:
"King Peter was, from the very beginning, the centre round which
gathered all the reactionaries who had ruined the country. . . . In
the light of this, only by a republican, democratic form of government can we ensure that similar misfortunes never again overtake
our peoples."[41] Tito had already sent a message to Stalin six weeks
before Jajce telling him that the Partisans "acknowledge neither
the Yugoslav government nor the king. We will not allow them to
return to Yugoslavia because that would mean civil war."[42]

But Maclean's chief error, as the Allied commanders were to
learn to their cost, was the proposition that the more aid they sent
to Tito, the more willingly he would cooperate in their military
plans. "I have no doubt [Maclean was not of the doubting kind]
that Tito's readiness to accept our guidance and suit his strategy to
our plans will be in direct proportion to the amount of material
help we are able to give him." The reverse turned out to be true. As
soon as Tito had ensured a regular flow of aid, he stepped up the
fight against his principal enemies, the Chetniks, ordered his

commanders to obstruct any Allied action inside Yugoslavia, and
became increasingly reluctant to fall in with Allied strategy.

The shift from the Chetniks to the Partisans was officially
endorsed at the Big Three meeting at Teheran at the end of
November. In the preliminaries, both Churchill and Roosevelt
received briefings exclusively from the Partisan side. Some officials suggested that British officers accredited to Mihailović
should also be summoned but, though these were asking to come
home and report, SOE Cairo withheld the available transport. For
this reason the Teheran conference produced some curious
anomalies. It was at a time when Stalin could still dread that the
British and Americans might make a separate peace with the Axis
and he had scolded Tito for the anti-monarchist stance adopted at
the Jajce Assembly, as no less than "a stab in the back" sure to give
him trouble with his allies. He must have been amazed to discover
that Churchill now favoured abandoning Mihailović and gave far
greater credence than he did himself to Partisan military claims.

Maclean was always to defend himself against charges that he
misled Churchill by pointing to evidence that he had warned
Churchill from the start that Tito was a Communist and would
probably try and establish a Soviet type system. On the first
occasion, before Maclean was dropped with Tito, Churchill had
told him that his task was no more than "to find out who was
killing the most Germans and suggest means by which we could
help them to kill more."[43] A few days before Teheran, Maclean
saw Churchill again and was this time told that as neither he nor
Churchill intended to live in Yugoslavia they need not worry
about its future form of government. Yet in Maclean's own
account, Churchill did add an important proviso: "That [i.e. the
future form of government] is for the Yugoslav people to decide."
As things turned out, in Yugoslavia as in other parts of Communized Europe, the people had no part in the decision.

What emerges from the official records of discussion in London
and in Washington on the future of Yugoslavia is that both
Churchill and Roosevelt were seriously misinformed and, as a
consequence, both failed to perceive that their policies contained
an inherent contradiction: on the one hand, arms and equipment
were to be provided for only one side in a raging civil war, while, on
the other, they would respect the rights of the people to determine
their own political future. The restoration of the monarchy was not
regarded by either Churchill or Roosevelt as a firm commitment,
though Churchill would have been happy to have "the little king",

as he called him, restored. But through a combination of mis-information and disinformation, both wrongly supposed that Tito would be willing to leave his compatriots a freedom of choice. And it was on this assumption that the Allies decided to betray Mihailović.

As Churchill wrote to Eden on 3 January: "I have been con-vinced by the arguments of the men I know and trust that Mihailović is a millstone tied round the neck of the little king and he has no chance until he gets rid of him." (By this time Churchill had already received a note from his son Randolph, now part of the Maclean mission, telling him that Mihailović should be aban-doned without demanding any *quid pro quo* from Tito as "such a gesture might create an atmosphere in which the King's future could be advanced". Churchill had annotated in the margin: "It seems sound". Soon afterwards the Prime Minister sent Eden another note: "My unchanging objective is to get Tito to let the King come out and share his luck with him and thus unite Yugoslavia and bring in the old Serb core. I believe the dismissal of Mihailović is an essential preliminary."[44]

Plainly Churchill had more urgent matters to worry about than Yugoslav policies, but it is curious that the men he said he knew and could trust never told him that, after what had already happened at Jajce, his "unchanging objective" was meaningless nonsense. As we now know, London was shielded from the full impact of Jajce by receiving an earlier version of the resolution which conveyed a meaning precisely the opposite of what the Assembly had decided. Elizabeth Barker, a Balkan specialist and, like most of her associates, totally committed to the Partisan side, was given a badly blurred text of the transmission of the Jajce broadcast. Working on the assumption that the Partisans were as committed to freedom as they claimed, she felt able to report: "There appeared to be a sentence saying that our people desire, in what concerns the King and the monarchy, that steps should be taken to ensure that the King joins in the struggle for national liberation."[45]

The full text of the document was forwarded to London by the British Embassy in Cairo on 28 December 1943, but the mistrans-lation seems to have circulated long enough to implant itself in the official minds. A Cassandra was occasionally heard: "It seems to me", wrote Sir Alexander Cadogan of the Foreign Office, "that we may be a bit rash in urging the King to throw over Draža Mihailović, until we know whether the Partisans will have anything to do with him. If they won't [and they didn't], what do we do then: acclaim Tito as Führer of Yugoslavia?"[46] But Anthony Eden paid no attention. On 3 January 1944 he wrote to Churchill of a still unidentified secret report "which seems to us to ring true and which we have heard that both [Ambassador] George Stephenson and Brigadier Maclean consider to be true," which alleged that "many of Tito's followers were royalist but believed that the cause of Yugoslav unity could be best served if the King broke with Draža Mihailović."

Accepting the Communist identification of Mihailović with Greater Serb nationalism (a view repudiated, as we have seen, by those who knew him personally), Eden concluded that if the King were to join the Partisans "thereby demonstrating that he did not start from a policy of Serb hegemony, but from the Yugoslav idea", then "that might be well received by many of Tito's followers who might be naturally loyal to the King."

Churchill, now wholly committed to Tito, remonstrated with Eden against any policy which might split the Partisans. Eden wrote back reassuring him: "If we were to succeed in bringing the King and Tito together, it ought to increase the effectiveness of the whole resistance movement [a 'movement' existing only in Foreign Office files] which is at present dissipating part of its strength in internecine fighting."[47]

Six days later, on 9 January, Churchill went some of the way with Eden by sending Tito a personal plea: "Can you not assure me that, after King Peter has freed himself from Mihailović and other advisers, he will be invited by you to join his countrymen in the field, provided always that the Yugoslav nation is free to settle its own constitution after the war? If I judge the boy right, he has no dearer wish than to stand at your side against the common foe."[48]

Knowing from Velebit's mission in Cairo that the West had already decided to abandon Mihailović, Tito declined to reply. Churchill remained undaunted: "No doubt Tito is sufficiently Oriental to be a keen bargainer."

But the principal misinformer was still Maclean. On 6 February he sent an urgent message to Churchill, claiming that Tito's chief concern "was to enable his country to become strong, united, democratic and independent." It followed logically from this that "the King's willingness to disown Draža Mihailović is the only repeat only chance for the monarchy."[49] As the King's advisers told him, this was rubbish, but Churchill, without waiting for the royal approval, announced to the House of Commons on 21 February that aid for Mihailović was to be cut off and that the Partisans were lucky to have found in Tito "an outstanding leader, glorious in the fight for freedom".

Having got this over with, Churchill now turned all his attention towards D-Day while Tito was able to turn most of his towards winning the civil war. In the subsequent months Partisan conflicts with the Axis troops, though enough to justify continued aid, were primarily defensive. In Bosnia, Herzegovina and Montenegro the Chetniks were still the principal targets and in Serbia they were effectively barring Partisan penetration.

On his side, Mihailović was reluctant to believe that the British and Americans could be backing the Communists against him and went on behaving as if he were part of the alliance. In the second half of 1943 he stepped up anti-German sabotage (see page 80) and tried to establish his democratic credentials by convening an assembly of Yugoslav politicians, both royalist and republican, to agree on their war aims.

Those with Mihailović claimed afterwards that the meeting was delayed by the enormous difficulty of ironing out differences between the disparate delegates. It did not take place until January 1944 and was perceived in the West as a belated effort to rival Tito's assembly at Jajce. Its prestige was further diminished among Westerners by the fact that it was named after the village where it met "the Ba Congress". Very little attention was therefore paid to its repudiation of the charges of Serb "hegemonism" and its call for a federal state, a freely elected constituent assembly and negotiations with all anti-Axis groups, including the Partisans. The only Western observer was George Musulin of the OSS and the only authorities who took it seriously were the Germans who later executed or deported several of the participating politicians.

Meanwhile in the spring of 1944, after a hazardous and costly escape from Montenegro, the Partisans set up their headquarters at Drvar in East Bosnia and it was here that they received their first Soviet mission headed by General Korneyev. Soviet arms for which Tito had been pleading since 1941 were unavailable, but the Partisans now enjoyed important additional support of a special Balkan Air Force set up at Bari. It is still a matter of dispute whether without it they would have survived.

The nearest Tito ever came to being captured was in May 1944, when the Germans mounted their fiercest attack on the Partisans, the only one in which they deployed paratroops. Tito escaped with his hysterical mistress only by climbing out of the back of a building while the Germans were coming into the front. He and his followers clambered up the dry run of a mountain waterfall and hid in thick forest. At the same time the Balkan Air Force mounted a massive assault against the Axis attacks engaging 300 light bombers and 200 fighter aircraft. Transport planes were sent to evacuate the leading Partisans and the Allied mission, though an aircraft allocated to the Soviet mission at Bari got there first and it was a Soviet pilot who rescued Tito and Korneyev.[50]

The whole group flew first to Italy but, for political reasons, Tito preferred to operate from Yugoslav soil and the British, eager to accommodate him, flew him to the island of Vis, which remained Partisan headquarters for the next four months. It was thus under the protection of the British Army, Navy and Air Force that Tito was able to issue orders to his commanders in his own civil war.

With the King and Tito now both under Allied control, the British thought the time had come to bring the two together. Their remoteness from Yugoslav realities was reflected when Churchill's son, Randolph, at a private audience with the Pope in June 1944, expressed the view that the Communists in Yugoslavia were "regressing".[51]

In negotiations sponsored by the British in Vis, Tito agreed to join in a coalition government within a royalist framework, to be set up in partnership with the King's representative, Ivan Šubašić, the former Ban (i.e. the King's Governor) in Croatia, though anyone familiar with Communist practice should have known that the discussions were a waste of time. As Tito later told his own people, he felt he was negotiating under duress and never had the faintest intention of keeping his word. Šubašić was a vain and stupid Croatian lawyer who had been sent by the exiled government to the United States and had persuaded those around him that he was the only man who could reconcile Tito and Peter, the Serbs and Croats, the Catholics and Orthodox, and all the other squabbling Yugoslavs. Under British and American pressure, King Peter was forced to dismiss his Serb supporters and name Šubašić head of a new government in which, as it soon became clear, no other Yugoslavs were willing to serve. He therefore became Minister of Everything and was sent to Vis to reach an agreement with Tito on any terms Tito would accept.

Neither the British nor the Americans knew that their chosen negotiator was in an especially weak position, as the Communists were able to remind him that they held him responsible for the death of most of the Communist leaders in Croatia. These had been in prison at the time of the Axis invasion and he had failed to release them before fleeing himself. Tito had no difficulty in forcing Šubašić to recognize the Communist-appointed Committees of National Liberation as the only legitimate authorities operating on Yugoslav soil and the Partisan army as the only legitimate military force.

In dealings with Western diplomats and journalists at Vis, Tito promised he would never use force to impose Communism on Yugoslavia—even going as far as to declare himself pained and insulted over the constant demands that he repeat that pledge. In the talks he not only got the better of the Ban—but also of Churchill. The two men met at Caserta on 12 and 13 August —days of sweltering heat in which Churchill was dressed informally, in the lightest possible clothes and was surprised to see Tito in a tight-fitting ceremonial Marshal's gold and blue uniform, decorated with golden lace. (The Jajce conference had endorsed his military promotion and when Djilas was sent on his mission to Moscow, in March 1944, he took with him Tito's body measurements; the Russians would be more familiar with what a Marshal was supposed to wear.) But it was the over-dressed guerrilla who had the last laugh. Few documents better reveal the Western failure to understand what the Communists were fighting for than the memorandum which Churchill submitted between his two meetings with Tito and which set out the British position:

They [the British Government] expect that Marshal Tito will make a positive contribution to the unification of Yugoslavia by including in the declaration on which he had already agreed with the Yugoslav Prime Minister [Šubašić] to make, not only a statement regarding his intention not to impose communism on the country, but also a statement to the effect that he will not use the armed strength of the movement to influence the free expression of the will of the people on the future régime of the country. . . . Another contribution which Marshal Tito could make to the common cause [the cause, of course, was not common] is to agree to meet King Peter, preferably on Yugoslav soil [an encounter which Tito carefully evaded]. If it should turn out [as it did] that any large quantities of ammunition sent by HMG are used for fratricidal strife or other than in self-defence, it would affect the whole question of Allied supplies, because we do not wish to be involved in Yugoslav political affairs. [By now both Britain and the United States were deeply engaged in the Yugoslav civil war.][52]

As Churchill later recalled, Tito had taken exception to his assertion that the Partisans were "divorced from the Serbian people," a view fully in accord with the reports from British liaison officers with Mihailović, though not true of the Serb minorities outside Serbia who, as refugees from Ustasha atrocities, had been the first to rally to the Partisans. But Churchill decided he would not press this point: "particularly as Tito had said he was prepared later to make a public statement about not introducing communism into Yugoslavia after the war."[53]

Churchill came away from this meeting quite pleased with himself and felt able to tell Roosevelt: "I've had a meeting with Tito and with the Yugoslav Prime Minister (Šubašić) and told them both that they should combine their resources so as to wield the Yugoslav peoples into one instrument in the struggle against the Germans. . . ." and commented: "This agreement between the Yugoslav Prime Minister and Tito will enable us with more confidence to increase our supply of war materials to the Yugoslavs"—a term which by then was used as synonymous with the Partisan leadership.

Tito's success was partly personal. Macmillan recorded in his diary "on the whole a favourable impression" after meeting him in Caserta on 9 August 1944. "He is quiet, well-behaved, interesting and seemed reasonable. I think he is very much on his best behaviour. . . . It is difficult to form an estimate of his quality. He obviously has character and power of command. He is shorter, stockier and even fatter than I expected but he has a certain dignity which is impressive." The US representatives, as Macmillan recalled, were completely won over: "The Americans cannot resist any social figure and in spite of their natural leaning to General Mihailović have taken Tito to their bosom. An immense dinner was given with bands playing and drink flowing freely. The Marshal seemed duly impressed by the wealth and magnificence of the American display."

Tito took the occasion of this goodwill for approved purposes of disinformation. Robert Murphy, the US Political Adviser to the Allied Mediterranean High Command, spent a whole afternoon at Tito's residence at Vis on 31 August, 1944 and found him "in excellent spirits". As he reported back to Washington, "I took the opportunity to ask him a few questions. Among them were whether in his opinion the Soviet Union would invade Serbia and attack Mihailović's forces. He spoke with great assurance on this point, stating that he was convinced that the Russians would not enter Serbia but would confine their activities along the Danube in Hungary leaving Marshal Tito to deal with Serbian matters. . . ."[54]

For Tito the sojourn in Vis, which started in such precarious conditions, ended in triumph. Without giving anything away, he had achieved two vital objectives. First, Churchill was now ready to dragoon the young King into making a broadcast to all Yugoslavs telling them to back Tito's Partisans, and explicitly denouncing all Tito's opponents, including the royalist Chetniks, as traitors to their country—and this time unlike in March 1941 Peter himself read the royal proclamation. According to the reports of OSS officers still serving with the Chetniks, the declaration damaged the King's prestige even more than Mihailović's but it nevertheless severely weakened Chetnik morale and drove uncommitted or divided villages scurrying into Communist arms.[55]

Tito's second triumph was to induce the Allied military command to recognize the authority of his own military and civilian institutions set up by the Communists in Yugoslavia and consequently not to undertake military operations on Yugoslav soil without Tito's permission. According to Milovan Djilas, political recognition was even more important to the Partisans than material aid. Yet even with this bonanza of concessions Tito did not think that the Partisans could take Serbia on their own and, as we know from documents published in Moscow but never in Belgrade, Tito wrote a letter from Vis on 5 July 1944—two months before his conversation with Murphy—imploring Stalin for help. After thanking him for diplomatic and material aid, Tito expressed the hope that this assistance would continue "as in these decisive days Soviet help is needed more than ever". After stressing the difficulties which still confronted the Partisans he ended his letter with the plea: "The strongest support you could possibly give would consist in the Red Army crossing the Carpathians, advancing across Rumania and moving South."[56]

This was indeed the route which Stalin had chosen. On the eve of flying off to arrange with Stalin for the entry of Soviet troops into Serbia, Tito called in the trusting Maclean and repeated his assurances that the Russians had no intention of coming into

Yugoslavia: the message was conveyed to Murphy who sent it on to Washington. What we shall never know is whether or not the Partisans could have reached Belgrade without Soviet intervention. Some Serbs who remember the period still insist that the Serb anti-communists could have stopped them; most historians agree however that, even without external aid, Tito's men were militarily strong enough to have bull-dozered their way into the capital.

When Tito left Vis on 18 September for his projected meeting with Stalin he did his best to conceal his intentions. A Soviet-flown Dakota had been observed leaving Bari the previous day and, once Tito was on his way, his staff announced that he had departed for an unknown destination. Hoping to mislead the British and Americans for as long as possible into thinking he was still in Vis, he ordered the guards to remain posted outside his residence for several hours after he had gone.

Eager as ever to defend Tito from unfavourable judgements, Maclean reported to the Americans that he was not unduly alarmed over the suddenness and manner of Tito's departure from Vis. He added that it was perfectly natural for Tito to want to meet the Russians to discuss military matters and that undoubtedly some word would come from Tito in three or four days.

Maclean went on to say that he thought "Tito would endeavour to persuade the Russians not to enter Yugoslavia; that he would attempt to convince Soviets that Partisans with some Russian heavy equipment could complete the liberation of the country". He added that in his opinion if the Russians should insist on participating in the liberation of Yugoslavia, Tito would urge them not to do so until after the Partisans had captured Belgrade. Maclean commented that if the Russians were as shrewd as he thought they would be, they would follow Tito's counsel. Maclean was as wrong about Soviet action as he was about Tito's counsel.[57]

This did not deflect the Brigadier from his fidelity to the Marshal. When he visited the headquarters at Caserta on 25 September 1944 Macmillan found him "in a very good mood" and arguing that Tito's power would now be very strong "with the Russian army by his side [it was the day when, contrary to Maclean's predictions, the Soviet armies crossed into Yugoslavia] and the splendid equipment which we have given him". Maclean concluded that if Britain hesitated in recognizing Tito, "we would deprive ourselves of all the goodwill we have built up painfully over a long period and of course drive Tito into the arms of the Russian bear".

At the time Macmillan commented, "I am bound to say that I find his [Maclean's] thesis convincing." But the Resident Minister was impressed two months later by "the good sense" of an OSS Colonel, Robert MacDowell, a man who had known Yugoslavia before the war and had just come out of Serbia with a very different message. Macdowell told Macmillan, who was evidently inclined to believe him, that the Serb peasants, though not particularly keen on the King or on Belgrade politicians, were staunchly anti-Communist, anti-collectivist, and eager to exercise control over their own agricultural cooperatives.

Macmillan recorded that Maclean and "all the rest of the Tito fans" regarded Macdowell's mission as a sinister anti-Titoist plot. But though Roosevelt had indeed promised Churchill in August 1944 not to send any more missions to Mihailović, Macmillan believed that Macdowell's prolonged stay was not a conspiracy but the result, partly of a failure of the authorities to find him and, partly, of his own desire to stay in Serbia and hear the other side of the argument.

While Tito had every interest in using Maclean to persuade the British and Americans that he had virtually already won the civil war, he and his men were manifestly far from sure. Nor could he have been reassured by his meeting with Stalin. Though he received the standard welcome he could not fail to observe that Stalin's principal preoccupation at the time was Poland. During the long drawn-out Warsaw insurrection the British and Americans had watched impotently while Stalin held back his own advancing armies to allow the retreating Nazis time to wipe out the city. He may well have calculated that to follow this with a military action which would extend Communism to Yugoslavia might provoke the Allies into a separate peace. This seems the likeliest reason why he counselled Tito to bring back King Peter and to wait for a more convenient moment "to stick a knife into the royal back". It was a risk which Tito dared not take. In the existing circumstances he could not know whether, at some future date, he would be any better placed to get rid of the King's men than they might be to get rid of him. According to the Yugoslav historian, Vjomir Kljaković, Tito told Stalin that an interim deal with the monarchy was "not in keeping with the prevailing circumstances". He expressed suspicion at Allied intentions and informed Stalin that the Allies knew (though there is no record that he ever told them) that the National Liberation Army was ready to fight against any attempt to impose a royalist solution.

Further "the Yugoslav people [and Stalin would know what that
meant] would feel that their three-year-long struggle had been
betrayed. The return of the King would imply the return of the
bourgeoisie to power regardless of anything the Partisans could
do, and eventually lead to civil war."[58]

Stalin fell in with Tito's plea and when the Russians penetrated
into Yugoslavia from Romania on 28 September 1944 they came
with instructions to give the Partisans the help they needed. Tito's
units were allowed to share in the glories of liberating Belgrade: a
job which German resistance made much more costly than anyone
expected. The Russians stayed in Yugoslavia for only a few weeks
and once the Partisans were safely installed in Belgrade, Tito no
longer needed them. Indeed their presence there would justify the
dreaded arrival of a balancing Allied force from the West.

Soon after seeing off Tito, Stalin was receiving Churchill mainly
to discuss their respective plans for the newly liberated territories.
It was on this occasion that Churchill informally proposed a
provisional share-out of countries of Eastern Europe, marking
Yugoslavia as 50:50. Stalin's secret concession to Tito nullified the
proposition in advance but the rumour of a share-out got around
and exiled ministers in London began receiving messages from
Croats asking into which of the 50 per cent they would belong.

Before leaving Moscow Churchill drafted a note to his colleagues interpreting the deal:

> Coming to the case of Yugoslavia, the numerical symbol 50:50
> is intended to be the foundation of joint action and an agreed
> policy between the two powers now closely involved, so as to
> favour the creation of a united Yugoslavia after all the elements
> there have been joined together to the utmost in driving out the
> Nazi invaders. It is intended to prevent for instance armed strife
> between Croats and Slovenes on the one side and powerful and
> numerous elements in Serbia on the other, and also to produce a
> joint and friendly policy towards Marshal Tito, while ensuring
> that weapons furnished to him are used against the common
> Nazi foe rather than for internal purposes. Such a policy,
> proposed in common by British and Russians, without any
> thought of any advantage to themselves, would be of real
> benefit.[59]

The benefit needless to say never materialized. Yet in the minds
of many Yugoslavs even today the 50:50 deal is remembered as

evidence of Churchill's cynical inhumanity. For Tito the 50:50
arrangement would be out of the question and, to avert it, he
needed not only to get the Russians in, as he had already succeeded in doing, but also to keep the Western Allies out. For, as he
knew, many of his countrymen not only expected Western troops
but relied on them as a protection against a Communist take-over.
Retrospectively such hopes may seem absurd but those who
entertained them might have derived some encouragement from
Churchill's own speech to the House of Commons, on 28 December 1944. Democracy, he said, "could not be treated as if it were
merely grabbing power and shooting those who do not agree with
you and was based not on violence and terror but on reason, on fair
play, freedom and respecting the rights of other people." He
openly urged resistance against attempts "to introduce a totalitarian régime which clamours to shoot whoever is politically in-
convenient, as part of a purge of those who are said to have
collaborated with the Germans during the occupation".

The Allied aim, Churchill said, was to "give the liberated
countries the right by universal vote to decide on the government
of their country and whether that government shall be of the Left
or of the Right. . . ." Though the speech referred to Greece and not
to Yugoslavia, the case against their respective Communist parties
was identical. And the incompatibility between Churchill's declared war aims and Partisan practice was as obvious to Tito as to
his enemies. For this reason, as the Allied victory became increasingly certain, Tito felt the necessity to disregard and defy
Western commanders and to concentrate instead on beating his
enemies and completing his revolution. Even before leaving Vis,
on 5 September 1944 Tito sent out a secret order to his commanders for an all-out effort to establish themselves in Serbia:
"Keep in mind that the basic aim of this operation is to liquidate the Chetnik forces of Mihailović and the Nedić forces as
well as their people and administrative apparatus. Do not allow
Mihailović to carry out his mobilization and to take his people
with him."[60] The reference here was to a mobilization order
issued at the beginning of September 1944 by Mihailović, in the
King's name.

Crossing the frontier from Bulgaria the Soviet troops first
assumed that the long-haired guerrillas (sworn not to shave until
the King came home) must be allies. Partisan liaison officers were
rapidly sent in and the Chetnik troops were handed over to their
executioners. Mihailović himself and a few thousand of his follow-

ers fled from Serbia and took refuge in the Bosnian mountains, as Tito had done three years before.

In Karchmar's view, the political impact of the brief Soviet occupation may have been underrated by the historians of the period. "The Soviet penetration into Yugoslavia, although of short duration, was decisive for the fortunes of Mihailović, since it compelled him to abandon without further fighting his principal base of popular support where he might otherwise be expected to put up a prolonged, if doomed, struggle against the encroaching Partisans. The retreat into Bosnia finished his movement as a major factor on the Yugoslav scene."[61]

And whereas in 1941 Tito had found the region occupied only by widely scattered Italian garrisons, the Chetniks were having to operate in an area where the roads and communications were under what, for them, was enemy control. The last contribution of the Chetniks to the Allied cause was the rescue of over a thousand of the US airmen, parachuted into Yugoslavia after losing their aircraft in raids against the Romanian oil-fields. A large contingent of OSS agents went in to help and sent out messages protesting that Chetnik units were being bombed by the Balkan airforce at the very time that they were engaged in saving American lives.[62] Many of these were to describe their experiences under oath to the Commission of Inquiry of the Committee for a Fair Trial for Draja Mihailovich (American spelling) set up under private auspices in Washington DC after the war.

Truman's only concession was to award to Mihailović posthumously the Legion of Merit in the Degree of Supreme Commander. To avoid trouble, the decision was kept secret for another twenty years.

At the end of 1944 the exiled government in London received Mihailović's last desperate message:

> The Partisans have instituted a ruthless terror in which the best among the leaders of the community and the heads of the old established families are being indiscriminately killed. Concentration camps are being set up and filled with the flower of the Serbian people. In the hopes of bare survival, people are fleeing to the mountains like animals. There they are exposed to cold and hunger. We entreat you to send a delegation to the country to inform the Allies of our tragic situation. Our appeal is urgent for tomorrow may be too late. Help us to find a way out of this hell![63]

The full story of the final phase of the Yugoslav civil war has never been documented nor have the casualty figures been published. As we know from the instructions sent out by the Partisan leaders and from the testimony of those who managed to escape, it was common practice for Partisan units to kill not only individuals, but whole communities which showed themselves actively recalcitrant to Communist rule. In these operations Tito drew no distinction between those who had fought with the Germans and those who had fought with the Allies. On 13 May 1945 he sent the following messages to his First Army:

> A group of Ustashas and some Chetniks, a total of over 50,000 men, is reported by Third Army in the Konjice–Sotanj area towards Dravograd. It includes Pavelić, Maček, the Croatian Government and a huge number of criminals. They are attempting to cross at Dravograd and give themselves up to the British. . . . You must move your forces most urgently from the Celje area in the direction of Sotanj–Slovenjgradec in order to concentrate for an attack aimed at the annihilation of this group.—(signed:) Tito.[64]

(It was characteristic of Partisan propaganda to link Maček, the leader of the popular Peasant Party, with the war-criminal Pavelić, whose Ustashas detained Maček throughout the war.)

The discovery that non-Communists were being exterminated came as a shock to the Slovene poet Edvard Kocbek, initially a Christian fellow-traveller and co-founder of the Communist-controlled National Liberation Front. He later described how he had been assigned to Partisan headquarters, where he was paraded as a symbol of patriotic unity and not been allowed to return home to check what was happening. Djilas described how the Communists handled him:

> One of our leading "allies" in the war time "National Liberation Front" [Djilas' own quotation marks] was Edvard Kocbek, a distinguished Christian Socialist, a fine upright man, imbued with a sense of asceticism and utterly honourable in his thoughts and actions. He was also a writer whose talent we all acclaimed. He had been on our side from the beginning, thinking that there would somehow be room for Catholic spirituality under a communist system. One day rumour reached him that we were shooting thousands of Slovenian Home Guards ("White

Guards" as we used to call them in those days). Kocbek was worried. As a head of the Christian Socialist Party in the Liberation Front, he rushed off to see the leaders of our Slovenian Central Committee to ask them whether these rumours were true.

Our comrades in the Central government pooh-poohed the idea to reassure Kocbek. "No, no, Mr Kocbek", they said. "Of course these rumours are absolutely untrue. The Home Guards are in camps and they are being well looked after. Every case is being conscientiously investigated and will eventually come before the courts if there is a case to answer. . . ."

So Kocbek came back, visibly relieved, to tell us that he had received perfect satisfaction and was at peace with his conscience. We of course knew that he had been told a pack of lies because those Home Guards had been shot to the last man. But Kocbek *wanted* [his italic] to believe that we would give the repatriates a fair hearing. . . .[65]

Later Kocbek discovered what had happened and his inquiries into the wartime and postwar killing brought him into constant conflict with the authorities.

A bleak account of the massacres in Slovenia reached the Foreign Office in 1944, through the British delegation to the Vatican. The pre-war political parties had sent on four declarations, expressing hopes for an Allied victory and protesting against Partisan atrocities. Thousands of people were listed as killed, including 27 Catholic priests, and 70 churches were reported desecrated. As these reports showed, the destruction was indiscriminate. Many clerics, though more in Croatia than in Slovenia, certainly did collaborate with the Germans and some Croat Franciscans actively involved themselves in the Ustasha policy for the compulsory conversion of Orthodox Serbs to Catholicism, but the Communists made no effort to ascertain whether or not their victims were guilty. One of the four statements came from the Slovene Socialist Party, dated 17 December 1943, and intended for the British Labour Party. It declared Tito's movement "neither democratic nor socialist, only communist" and cautioned the Labour Party against the credentials of a man sent to England by the Partisans. He claimed to represent the Slovene Socialists but had been expelled for approving the Hitler–Stalin pact and the Soviet attack on Finland. The Slovene Socialists defended the peasants for seeking Italian arms to protect themselves and their families: "If you are assaulted by a thief you do not ask who is the owner of the stick you use to protect yourself. . . ."[66]

It was against this background of terror that at the end of the war a large number of Yugoslavs—Serbs, Croat and Slovene —sought sanctuary with the Allies. The flood of the refugees had started in 1944 when the Adriatic was reopened to traffic and thousands of anti-Communists including many Chetniks found their way to the Allied headquarters at Bari. Glen remembers that a left-winger who was later to be prominent in Anglo-Yugoslav affairs (but whom Glen prefers not to name) suggested that the Chetniks should be handed to the Partisans. "Over our dead bodies", said Glen and his friends and, on this occasion, none was repatriated.[67] Early in 1945 some of the Serbs, with Mihailović's approval, decided to make their way across the mountains to link up with the Allies in Austria. A large proportion of them were killed by the Partisans, Ustashas or Germans along the way, but 12,000 did manage to reach Istria and give themselves up to Allied forces. Their lives were saved only by the prompt and resolute action of British officers working on their own initiative. Their story is told in a letter to a friend by Anthony Crosland, future Foreign Secretary, then an intelligence officer with the units advancing towards the Isonzo River:

> On our side of the river, an army of no less than 12,000 Chetniks (a figure later confirmed by General Horatius Murray, commanding the Six Armoured Division) were moving slowly west. The tents are struck and the caravan of humanity is on the move with a vengeance. It was a sight so medieval, so unreal, so Hollywood almost, that one could hardly credit one's eyes. Of the men many were giant bearded figures, others wore their hair long, so that it fell over their shoulders, Elizabethan fashion, and no-one could tell from behind whether they were men or girls. Among them were old men of sixty and young boys of fifteen . . . drawn wagons piled with baggage and riding on them the sick and older women. Behind the wagons marched more women looking very strong and wiry. Their uniforms appeared mostly German save for those who wore the brown uniforms of the Serb regular army. I had come to look on them as Fascists: whereas the people, or at least the rank-and-file, were peasants and worker-types, kindly and cheerful and anything but a collection of mercenary thugs.

Crosland himself visited a locality near Gorizia, where the Chetniks had camped, and recalled: "They freely and in fact proudly admitted that since 1942 they had been fighting only Tito. When one pointed out to these people that we were bound to treat them as enemies they could not see it at all. They are genuinely pro-British and seemed to think we shall help them against Tito." (What Crosland did not know was that many Partisans had spent the war exclusively fighting the Chetniks: as they told OSS officers who interrogated them when they fell into Chetnik hands.)

"Well what could we do with this army?" Crosland wrote: "Clearly we have no alternative to treating them as POWs or at least internees. Tomorrow they will be concentrated south of the Udine and disarmed. Their sick and wounded are being looked after and eventually the whole lot will be evacuated south in our transport. After that, who knows? At least the British Army on the spot having no warning had shown its usual gift for improvisation and— more important—for humanity in action."

A Tito battalion marched into the town with orders to take it over while the Chetniks were still there: "The British Commander on the spot wirelessed frantically for orders and was told to keep the Tito forces out until the Chetniks were clear and then let them into the town, which he did, thus avoiding a massacre."[68]

Tito and his men did their utmost to keep the wholesale massacres out of Western sight. One week before the Soviet troops crossed into Yugoslavia, General Arso Jovanović, Tito's Chief of Staff, issued orders that all SOE and OSS personnel be strictly forbidden to leave the headquarters to which they were attached except under supervision. The tussles were predictable. General Lloyd-Owen, BLO with Tito, found it "incredible" that after all the aid that Britain had delivered, "British patrols should be put under arrest and sometimes thrown into squalid jails and deprived of means of communication with their base." Evelyn Waugh, reporting from Split in December 1944, was less surprised: "They [the Partisans] are ill at ease in Dalmatia, where the cultured townsmen dislike them heartily. The Partisans react by a régime of suspicion, arrests by the secret police and discourtesy to the BLOs. A British cruiser is moored in the harbour and greatly resented." Waugh blamed English politicians and newspapers for their failure to recognize the Partisans as a homogeneous revolutionary army. "Instead we have called them patriots and resistance groups or armies of liberation and put the word communist, when used at all, in inverted commas as a German propaganda lie."[69]

By the end of 1944, the Partisan determination to keep the Westerners out at all costs went to the length of turning away UNRRA supplies. Although the peoples of Dalmatia were starving, Tito refused to allow the delivery of food unless the distribution was carried out by his own men. Instead the shipment was sent to India.[70]

Joint operations between Partisans and Allied troops became virtually impossible. In November 1944 an operation under Sir Henry Floyd, intended to harass the German retreat, had to be suspended in mid-action when Tito objected to Western forces operating under their own command on Yugoslav soil.

Churchill sent a plaintive message to Tito via Maclean: "You view with suspicion and dislike every military operation on your coast that we are making against the Germans." And with very good reason, Tito did.

The British Commander-in-Chief in the Mediterranean, General Wilson, tried in vain to fit the Partisans into his battle plan. Maclean was told "to explain to Tito that now was the time to strike, with the German troops withdrawing through the mountains from Albania and Macedonia." He was to stress "the importance of closing the bottle-neck on the roads from Sarajevo and to make Tito understand that a successful battle there would prevent the Germans from stabilizing their front in the northwest" (which indeed was what they did). Tito was offered full air support for this operation. But at that period Tito was busy linking his troops with the Russians for the capture of Belgrade, an operation which, as Wilson pointed out, "from the military point of view was unnecessary, as the Russians would take Belgrade anyway". As a result: "Whereas planning and cooperation were really wanted to bring off a major success in the Bosnian mountains, this was allowed to go by default."[71] The Germans were themselves amazed that their troops were able to retreat unscathed through narrow and vulnerable mountain passes.[72]

Tito's first priority was not to precipitate the now inevitable German departure, but to consolidate his domestic power; in consequence he repeatedly refused Allied requests to bring in their own troops to fight at his side. On 19 November 1944, he turned down a personal request from Wilson to allow a British armoured regiment with field artillery to be sent to help the Partisans reported to be in difficulty in Zadar. When he went as far as to demand that the additional equipment intended for the British landing be handed to his own troops, Wilson called the operation off.

In February 1945 General Alexander, who had succeeded General Wilson, came to Belgrade and Tito once again refused to authorize Allied landings and so, as Kardelj was later to claim, "saved the revolution". The West by that time was convinced that the Partisans were unassailable; Kardelj was not so sure.

As Wilson had predicted, the failure of the Partisans to assault the Germans during their retreat enabled the latter to build themselves powerful defence lines, on the Srem front, further north. In Belgrade all men from the age of sixteen were mobilized and untrained boys were pitted against strong German fortifications. Trench-warfare, reminiscent of the 1914–18 battles, cost over 25,000 lives and some Serbs still suspect that the Partisans were retaliating against those who had failed to join them and who might constitute an anti-Communist opposition.

Once the Russians had secured Serbia Tito knew that Yugoslavia was his and directed his ambitions towards consolidating and enlarging his domain. The Yugoslavs had ethnic claims to the Istrian peninsula, which many of them believed had been unfairly restored to Italy at the end of the First World War. Tito ordered the Partisans to speed along the Adriatic coast and to grab Trieste before the Eighth Army arrived from Italy. The Partisans won a neck-and-neck race, arriving on the morning of 1 May 1945 while the Germans were still defending some of their positions, and it was not until later on the same day that a New Zealander unit advanced into the city from the other side.[73]

Alexander immediately informed Churchill that the Partisans were now occupying Trieste, adding that it would be difficult to eject them by force as his troops "have a profound admiration for Tito's Partisans and a great sympathy for them".

In his diary on 14 May Macmillan also predicted that there would be a problem in getting British opinion to accept the need to fight the Partisans and felt that there must be no repetition of the divisions which had shown themselves over Greece. But he rightly thought that time was on Alexander's side: "The troops in the area will get to know and dislike the Yugoslavs. They will see the so-called Yugoslav administration thieving, raping and killing and they will not like it."

Indeed by 19 May Alexander was able to report to Churchill that the goodwill towards the Partisans had disappeared and that a strong line was now possible. Unlike in Yugoslavia itself,

Western troops had been able to observe at first hand Partisan behaviour towards the local population and see for themselves (or be told by those they met) arbitrary executions and deportations. "The feeling against the Partisans is strong and getting stronger," Alexander reported, and he concluded that there could be no question of any joint administration of the city by Western and Partisan authorities.[74]

Given a green light from London, Alexander announced that the future of Trieste would be decided at the Peace Conference: "Marshal Tito's apparent intention is to establish his claim by force of arms and military occupation. Action of this kind would be all too reminiscent of Hitler and Mussolini and Japan. It is to prevent such actions that we have been fighting this war."

Tito's self-righteous indignation was predictable: "Such an accusation cannot be thrown against a tortured Ally, who has been bled white and has been recognised by all freedom-loving people as an example of patriotism and self-sacrifice in the great war of liberation. . . ." Few people in the West knew that the only Yugoslavs being bled white by May 1945 were the victims of Tito's own Partisans. In Trieste alone 6,000 were arrested, of whom over 1,000 were executed. All over the country the Communists were liquidating their internal enemies: quite accidentally Trieste happened to be the only patch of land where the process was visible.[75]

A massive show of allied force proved enough. Stalin refused to intervene on Tito's behalf and the Partisan troops were withdrawn. Trieste was to become an Italian city, to which future generations of well-to-do Yugoslavs flocked to buy the things which their own régime was incapable of producing.

Tito similarly sent his troops in to stake a claim on the Austrian province of Carinthia, which also had a Slovene minority. But on this occasion it was not by a show of force that they were induced to leave but by a deal—incomprehensible except in the prevailing chaos—in which territory was exchanged for human flesh.

In Carinthia, in May 1945 the Allied troops and the Partisans combined were easily outnumbered by the columns of anti-Communist refugees, who regarded the Allied occupation zone as a sanctuary. There has been some controversy over the number of Yugoslavs involved. In his book *The War Ended Seven Days Later*, former Partisan General Milan Basta recalled that the Partisans had at first thought that the Ustashas were exaggerating the figures but that, in fact, as many as 100,000 "Croat soldiers, sundry Chetniks, as well as civilian refugees" did reach Carinthia.

In General Basta's view, the British commander was so eager to get the Partisans out of the zone that he was willing to let them leave "at the cost of taking with them the remainder of Pavelić's army."[76]

The provenance of the Yugoslav escapees is also in dispute, though there is no doubt that the large majority were Croat soldiers in uniform. Western historians have been inclined unjustly to regard all these as Quisling. In reality the Ustasha government had been imposed on Croatia by the invaders and if a Croat peasant had refused military service he would have been shot. Nor would he see the wearing of the Croat army uniform as treachery to his people: he would still identify himself with Croatia rather than the new-fangled state of Yugoslavia. Though by the time the Croats reached Carinthia the war with Germany was over, the British made frantic efforts to force the refugees back into Yugoslavia. For this purpose, on 15 May Colonel Denys Worrel, commander of a battalion of the Durham Light Infantry, was ordered to move his men to the Drava river near Bleiburg:

> I immediately put platoon posts and in some cases company posts along the part of the Drava where they might cross. . . . I remember that I went down with my driver in a jeep to look around and make certain that everything was alright. In the evening this tremendous flood of chaps came down the road, some of them mounted. I didn't know what to do. I went up to the chap and eventually persuaded him to get them to sit down which they did. There were thousands of them; they weren't hostile at all but they were armed. They just wanted to surrender to us but our instructions were that they weren't to. Of course if they had really taken a dislike to me I couldn't have stopped them at all. Anyway they agreed to go back into Yugoslavia.[77]

Some tried to resist. According to Crosland, whose division had now moved up from Istria into Carinthia, "the armed lot south of the Drava were dealt with thus: our troops withdrew north of the river and behind them took out the centre section of the bridge; after we had gone, firing broke out and a number of Croats swam back across the river and more tried to repair the broken bridge; so we put up wire and other obstacles to stop them getting back to safety. . . ."

The man in charge of dealing with those Croats who did break through was Brigadier T. D. Scott, whose first task was to stop the fighting which began at once between them and the Partisans. In accordance with Allied policy, the Brigadier accepted the Partisans as allies and warned the Croats that the British would side with their enemies unless they allowed themselves to be disarmed. He offered them what in his innocence seemed a fair deal: they would return to Yugoslavia and would be treated as prisoners of war with the exception of political criminals, who would be tried by an Allied Tribunal.[78]

What happened to those who went back has been described in lurid terms by the few who survived. The vast majority were either shot or else died from beatings, torture, exhaustion or hunger during long marches to undisclosed destinations. Brigadier Scott however felt satisfied. He had been told that he should on no account allow the Croats to surrender to the British and was very proud of the conduct of his troops: "By some unerring instinct the British soldier always seems to do the right thing. The chaps have supreme confidence in themselves and it never occurs to them that any of these scallywags, who had cut each other's throat without a moment's hesitation, would dare to interfere with them." The Brigadier's chronicle ends with a cheerful post-script: General Alexander visited the Brigade headquarters "where he was received with drums and pipes and treated to a good old-fashioned blow-up with sticky cakes and strawberries and cream."

A group of some 18,500, which included Slovenes and Serbs as well as Croats, were repatriated by an action which one British officer, Colonel Robin Price of the Welsh Guards, described as "of most sinister duplicity".[79] To avoid resistance the men being sent back to Yugoslavia were put on to trains and told their destination was Italy. According to Robin Price, Tito's men were in the guard's van of the departing trains.

"Among the officers here", wrote Crosland, "there is a great deal of anger and resentment against the deception and dishonesty involved." His letter, evidently written soon after the event, betrays his own frustration: "They [the disarmed prisoners] crowded on to the trains in the best of spirits and were driven off under a British guard to the entrance of a tunnel at the frontier; there the guards left them and the train drove off to Yugoslavia."[80]

The operation, which shocked the British officers compelled to carry it out, was directed from Klagenfurt by General Keightley and his staff-officer Brigadier Low, later Lord Aldington. On 13 May shortly before issuing the orders, Keightley received a visit from Harold Macmillan, whose diary reveals that many of the refugees were known to be innocent of war crimes or of collabora- tion: "They included anything, from guerrilla forces raised by the Germans from Slovene, Croat and Serb to fight Tito and armed and maintained by the Germans, to people who, either because they were Catholics or conservative in politics or for whatever other cause, are out of sympathy with revolutionary communism and therefore labelled Fascist or Nazi." Macmillan observed, in parenthesis, that "this is being tried, I observe, in English politics."[81]

For Tito and his men, the intellectual climate in which anti- Communism was identified with Fascism was to prove of inestim- able value. It took nearly 40 years before the British public learnt, through the programme *Time Watch* on BBC Channel Two, 2 October 1984, of the crime committed by British officers.

According to the British archives, the number of Yugoslavs sent home by trickery was 18,500 and, as Milovan Djilas later wrote: "They had no murder on their hands. Their only crime was fear of communism and the reputation of the communists. Their sole motive was panic."[82] The same view was taken by Captain F. Waddams, who had been a liaison officer with the Partisans and remained to become British consul in Ljubljana. Waddams agreed with Djilas that the Domobranci were "simple peasants" and though he conceded that "towards the end of the war they came under German control", in his view "their concept of right and wrong did not extend beyond protecting their lives and prop- erties". Waddams went further and claimed they were "fun- damentally anti-German and pro-Allied and some of them helped to save Allied airmen".[83]

In commenting on repatriation orders, Lord Aldington (ex- Brigadier Low) told the author that neither he nor General Keightley had the slightest idea that these men were being sent to their death. The destination of the trains was concealed, Lord Aldington said, only because the British Commander supposed that, as the men were wearing German uniform, they were afraid of being treated as prisoners of war: "We assumed that the Yugoslav soldiers should go back to Yugoslavia, just as British soldiers should go back to Britain."[84]

By the time the men were sent back the war was over and the Commander in Carinthia may not have known what was happen- ing in territories which were indeed outside his field of operations. What does seem strange is that the British diplomatic mission in

Belgrade failed to alert him about the hopelessness of negotiating with Tito's representatives. The man best placed to know was Deakin, by then deputy *chargé d'affaires*, who was well aware that the Partisans were inclined to murder those Yugoslavs known to be anti-Communist, whether they were patriotic or not. Indeed, Deakin's friend, Vane Ivanović, a Yugoslav who had worked in London and was then serving in the British army, said later that it was Deakin's knowledge of Partisan practices that saved his life. Ivanović had been so inspired by the reports of Partisan heroism that he had suggested to Deakin that, as an experienced officer and man of exceptional physical strength (he had represented Yugoslavia in the Olympics), he felt he should be parachuted to fight on Tito's side. "You would not last long," Deakin warned him.[85]

Yet, knowing what he did, Deakin's "binding and absolute identification" with the Partisan cause seems to have prevented him from alerting the military command and he must share in the responsibility for what Nikolai Tolstoy later named *The Klagenfurt Conspiracy*.

Circumstances rule out the possibility that the killings were carried out in the spontaneous frenzy of civil war. According to the survivors, mass graves were prepared and reception centres organized before the train loads arrived. Prisoners were tied together by wire and marched in couples to be mown down. In the massacre of the repatriated prisoners, Tito's personal responsibility can be no more in doubt than Stalin's. In neither case is there any documentary evidence and the orders were probably verbal. But by the time the killings took place, Tito, like Stalin, was in full control of his Party and police and none of his well-disciplined subordinates would have dared to operate on this scale without his approval. (Not, of course, that he necessarily knew or favoured the sadism practised by some of the men and women who volunteered to be the executioners.)

Though the Yugoslav officials have never publicly admitted that tens of thousands were massacred, Dedijer's history takes the knowledge for granted.[86] He recalls that he was himself in San Francisco at the time and after he returned he asked Djilas why the men had been killed. Djilas replied that the leadership feared the men might otherwise be used for anti-revolutionary purposes by the Western Allies. Djilas who in May 1945 was in Montenegro says he cannot remember giving this explanation "but it was certainly in accordance with Partisan mentality at that time".

Partly, as we have seen, because of Tito's defiance of Western strategists, the war lasted longer in Yugoslavia than anywhere else in Europe. But by the time it ended Tito had fulfilled his war aims. Any physical resistance against Communist one-party rule was smashed.

Chapter 4

TITO'S RUPTURE AND RECONCILIATION
WITH MOSCOW

WHEN ON 28 JUNE 1948 the Western world learnt that Yugoslavia had been expelled from the Communist bloc, Tito, the man who led Europe's most effective resistance force, was cast in the role of David defying the Soviet Goliath. At closer range things looked different. As a true believer, Tito was appalled by his excommunication and later likened the experience to being hit by a thunderbolt. Some of his associates believed that the trauma induced the first of his gall-bladder attacks.

Stalin, for his part, had no reason to doubt Tito's fidelity to the Communist cause. But as he had shown over the royal question and over Trieste, he did not always approve his disciple's over-eager, anti-Western thrusts. By 1948 it was most probably the nervousness about the risks of an East–West collision which induced him to try and have Tito replaced by a more biddable Yugoslav satrap—which was all he initially intended.

In the unreal world of diplomacy, Yugoslavia's future had been decided in February 1945 at Yalta, where the Big Three agreed the country should have a coalition government and free elections. Stalin certainly supported Tito's avoidance of either. Everywhere in Eastern Europe he was urging Communist leaders to liquidate potential enemies and when he scolded the Poles for being dilatory, he told them they should take Yugoslavia's example: "Tito is a tower of strength. He wiped them all out."[1]

At the end of the war, while Tito was primarily concerned with wiping out the remains of internal resistance, his friend Maclean was pleading his cause with the Americans as well as with the British. As the US political adviser Kirk wrote to the Secretary of State, "In Maclean's opinion it is extremely urgent that an early agreement be reached with the Russians and Americans and a firm offer of equipment and training facilities be given to Tito as soon as possible. Otherwise the Russians will inevitably get the contract and all it implies. . . ."[2]

Acting on similar advice, Churchill was doing his utmost to give Tito's seizure of power an internationally respectable cover. After Teheran, at which the Big Three approved the Vis agreement on a coalition government, King Peter accepted the proposition that it should contain twelve of Tito's men and six of his own. But before the prospective coalition government could legally take over in Belgrade, it was necessary to get the King to surrender his rights and convey his royal prerogative to regents acceptable to Tito. Not surprisingly Peter demurred and Churchill, busy as he was, took Eden along to overcome the well-founded royal reluctance. The Prime Minister told the King that he could rely on the Tito –Šubašić deal, as it had been approved by Stalin: "Mr Churchill said that he had always found Stalin a man of his word". Peter's choice he was told was either to submit "and so retain his position" or to refuse and "be bypassed and left isolated and impotent". When the King suggested going home Churchill warned: "Your Majesty, if you should go back to Yugoslavia you would be compelled to sign many death warrants at Tito's request and if you should refuse to sign them, you would find that within 24 hours your own name would be added to the list."[3] Eden added his own word of comfort: "If Tito were clever he would not try and introduce communism into the country."

Immediately after Yalta it was therefore to the figureheads exercising the royal prerogative that the ministers of the prospective coalition government took their oath. Tito, the effective dictator, absented himself from the occasion, the ministers never held a single meeting, and the phantom government faded away. This did not prevent the British and American governments from promptly accrediting diplomats to Belgrade. A few weeks previously the State Department had insisted that it would only be represented "on the assumption that arrangements will be made for the establishment of a truly representative administration, with provisions for free elections as set forth in the agreement, with such assurances being fundamental to the whole agreement."[4] Verbal assurances were given but nobody complained when they were disregarded.

For it was not on elections that the Communists intended to rely to seize and sustain a monopoly of power but on two trumps they already held: the euphoria inspired by the liberation from the Axis and the terror imposed by OZNA, the Communist secret police. Seen from outside the liberation aspect was the more apparent. Tito's image burnt bright and his opponents were willingly branded collaborators and reactionaries (at that time the epithets were synonymous). His Partisan forces were a genuine people's army; few of the older fighters had survived the ordeal and it consisted largely of dispossessed peasants, many recruited from the most primitive parts of the country. After appalling struggles and unimaginable hardship, the troops were only too eager to celebrate in any way the leadership saw fit. Boys and girls chanted slogans, waved banners for Stalin and Tito and were ready to throw themselves into the work of rebuilding their new Yugoslavia.

As hostilities ended, volunteers arrived from the West to help them. The young enthusiasts were kept within the confines of their tireless work-brigades and at a careful distance from the columns of forced labour, "class enemies" or prisoners of war, employed to do the most back-breaking jobs. Later the foreigners went home recalling with pride how they had voluntarily accepted the long hours and discipline and many became lifelong propagators of the Tito cult.

In the big cities, however, where few people identified with the liberation struggle, the terror counted more than the euphoria. The Partisans arrived in Belgrade with the Russians in October 1944 and as Djilas recalled, could not find a single Party member who had survived. This created difficulties: they were bound to destroy vestiges of the past yet needed experts to help operate the new administration. A former official of the royal government was offered a big job in the National Bank but wrote declining to serve unless he could be told what had happened to the 103 citizens personally known to him, who had vanished without trace. He got no reply, did not take the job and looking back on it nearly 40 years afterwards one of his children marvelled that he escaped with his life.

Reports of terror deriving "from unofficial contacts in Belgrade" were conveyed by the US Political Adviser at Caserta to the US Secretary of State. Claiming that this was not the sort of liberation that the people had expected, the despatch affirmed: "Propaganda and organised 'spontaneous' demonstrations, forced labour, high-handed and summary requisitioning, arrests and punishment, a sense of intimidation are too reminiscent of occupation. Fear and dislike of Communism and Communists, excesses of Croats and Montenegrins in the army and police, the presence of Bulgar troops as allies, interference with the religious education of youth are other factors."[5]

On his arrival in Belgrade, Milan Grol, one of the King's men who had joined the coalition as Vice-Premier (which he soon discovered was an empty title), was shattered: "This is not a state;

it is a slaughterhouse," he wrote to his friends in London.[6] As the US Ambassador Patterson reported to Washington, Grol told him that the Communists were ruthlessly eliminating their opponents and that Mihailović's men were being killed and having their property confiscated. The Ambassador said he had faith in Grol's honesty, though as Grol was being assailed by the victims' families, he might be seeing only the dark side of the picture.

A visiting envoy from the State department to Belgrade expressed American anxieties about the reported terror: "Edvard Kardelj (now unofficially Tito's deputy) told us we must understand that Belgrade is not Yugoslavia but a city of disgruntled functionaries and financial interests, bent on recovering their old positions and exploiting the masses."[7]

It was seven months later that the Partisans arrived in Zagreb and Ljubljana and the bulk of the Catholic population went on hoping that the Allies would get there first. In Zagreb "liberation" started, according to a reliable witness, with the arrival of some very unkempt guerrillas, whose task was to ferret out members of the royal army and shoot them on sight. One of the royal officers, an eminent international lawyer who later resumed his practice, attributed his survival to a friendly concierge with good Communist connexions who pretended not to know where he was. After a few days of free-lance killing, the official administration arrived and repression became more systematic and orderly.

In Ljubljana the non-Communist groups made a frantic last-minute effort to organize themselves into a National Resistance Council and appealed for Allied support; no one was listening. When the Partisan units arrived they were held outside the city for several hours while the Communist activists went in to round up remaining opponents and to line up the populace with banners, flowers and refreshments for a triumphal welcome. The proposition that, now that the war was over, the secret police could be disbanded was denounced by Tito at a public meeting on 19 June 1945. "The People's Defence is an organ of security which has sprung from the people. If it strikes fear into the bones of some of those gentry abroad, that is not our fault. But certainly, I think it an advantage if OZNA strikes fear into those who do not like the new Yugoslavia. . . ."[8]

The following month the British embassy in Belgrade expressed the opinion that the terror was not Tito's fault: "British assessments claim Tito as relatively moderate, open to reason and anxious to preserve some ties with the West, increasingly bypassed by more militant subordinates who might end by manipulating him altogether. In our opinion Tito puts Yugoslavia first and his subordinates put communism first. . . ."[9]

And in August 1945 the US Ambassador Patterson had forgotten all about Grol and fallen under Tito's celebrated charm. During a visit to Washington he reported that he had been able to tell President Truman that Tito and he were "good friends", that he was seeing a great deal of the Yugoslav leader and would be returning to Belgrade with 5,000 cartridges so that he could go hunting at his invitation. "I said, Mr President, Tito is colourful, dynamic, hospitable, a military genius, but a thorough communist and his economic and political philosophy is not ours. Nevertheless, since he is intelligent, I would suggest that I be permitted to bring him back to America for a month of indoctrination provided that the elections [for the constituent assembly, held in November 1945] go reasonably well."[10]

Living outside the hubbub of cosmopolitan Belgrade one British representative Frank Waddams gave a first-hand account of what he had seen or been able to piece together about the postwar terror though in the prevailing climate it elicited very little response.

In 1946 Waddams returned to England and published a report printed privately and anonymously describing what he had seen:[11]

> The most unpleasant feature of life in Yugoslavia today is the existence of the all-powerful OZNA, the political police. This body is responsible for the murder of thousands of Yugoslavs, for the maltreatment in concentration camps of thousands more and for the permanent terror in which the vast bulk of the population lives. It possesses its agents in every block of flats, in every street, in every village and in every barrack room. These agents report on the conduct of the inhabitants of their flat, street, village or barrack to the OZNA section of their local council or military unit. On the results of these reports is built up the *karakteristka* or conduct-sheet of every citizen, which assesses each man's reliability (or lack of reliability) from the Communist point of view. OZNA has complete control over the life, liberty and property of all citizens and if it chooses to arrest, to imprison without trial, to deport or "to liquidate" anybody, no one may protest or ask the reason why. That is why the populace is in such a state of terror.
>
> The only way that an ordinary citizen can be confident about keeping his freedom is to say nothing, hear nothing and see

nothing which can possibly be interpreted as critical of the present state of affairs. . . . Even so, he cannot be safe against the common informer, who may invent tales against him in order to pay off a personal grudge. He must attend street meetings regularly for the "street agents" keep a careful record of his attendance and want to know the reason if someone fails to come at least once or twice a week.

At these meetings he is taught the glories of Soviet Russia and the Red Army, the evils of the degenerate capitalist world of Britain and America, and that anyone who harbours sympathy for these Western powers is a traitor to his country. He is taught that it is the mission of Communist Russia to set up communist "people's democracies" throughout the world. Woe betide the person who questions these principles or who dares to suggest that Britain and America have had any share in winning the war and are, in fact, generously trying to help war devastated countries such as Yugoslavia by the gifts from UNRRA, the Red Cross, Yugoslav societies of the USA and so on. It would all go onto his *karateristka* and when a man is classified as unreliable he can get no work and he and his family are left to starve or live precariously from his friends' generosity or by selling his goods. If he is classified as dangerous, he is a candidate for night arrest, deportation, concentration camp or "liquidation."

(Commenting on this account Milovan Djilas questioned whether "concentration camp", suggesting orderly emplacements behind barbed wire, was the right designation for the barns, stables, barracks, cellars and any location available into which the Communists installed their prisoners and from which they organized them into labour battalions.)

Waddams claimed that he knew at first hand of ten such camps, and had spoken himself to former inmates of nearly all of them: "the tale is always the same: starvation, overcrowding, brutality and death-conditions, which make Dachau and Buchenwald mild by comparison. Many Slovenes who were released from Dachau at the end of the war came home only to find themselves in a Slovene camp within a few days. It is from these people that the news has come that the camps are worse than Dachau. . . ." He believed that between 20,000 and 30,000 were in prison out of a total Slovene population of 1,200,000.

The number of victims of the terror has never been ascertained. The Communist newspaper *Borba* gave figures for "criminal" trials of which the overwhelming majority appear to have been political: for 1947 260,000; for 1948 220,000; and for 1949 160,000. Ljubo Sirc, a former political prisoner at Ljubljana, has estimated in his own unpublished autobiography that during the postwar period some one million Yugoslavs must have gone through OZNA prisons—though some, like his own mother and fiancée, were kept for only 24 hours.

Having been personally involved in delivering Western supplies to the Partisan units, Waddams was enraged to find that the Communists gave all the credit for food and arms to the Russians. He also described the misappropriation by the Yugoslav authorities of UNRRA aid for political use. He did not know at the time that the British Communist James Klugmann, formerly of SOE, had become the Deputy Director of UNRRA's Yugoslav section.

Many witnesses in Croatia as well as Slovenia corroborate Waddams's account of religious persecution, though here again the number of priests executed or imprisoned is still at least publicly unrecorded. One incident which Waddams reported could have come from many other cities:

> Before Christmas last year [1945] a group of about 200 children gave a "spontaneous" demonstration of "the people's will" outside a nursery school run by nuns. They shouted "these whores should leave the place within twenty-four hours or be hanged!" Similar "spontaneous" children's demonstrations took place at other convent schools during the same evening. The women who accompanied the children at these disgraceful episodes were bribed to do so with permits to buy stockings —probably originally a free gift of a Yugoslav society in America. All the Sisters of Mercy were expelled from Ljubljana hospitals in December and their places taken by demobilized Partisan girls, who possessed neither the medical training nor the experience.

Tito knowing the power of the church in his native Croatia did his best to neutralize its opposition and to win over as many priests as possible. He benefited from the fact that, unlike in Poland, the Catholic church had not openly identified itself with patriotic anti-Axis resistance, and many priests had positively welcomed the installation of the German-sponsored separate state of Croatia.[12] Some Franciscan friars had even officiated at the compulsory conversions of Serbs whom the Ustashas forced to choose between life and religion.

The head of the hierarchy was Archbishop Stepinac who enjoyed widespread respect and who had always tried to keep the Church out of politics. He had conducted a *Te Deum* service after the 1941 putsch in which Serb nationalists ousted the Prince Regent and another one a few weeks later when the Germans installed the puppet government of Ante Pavelić to run his nominally independent state. During the repression Stepinac had privately signified his disapproval of the massacres of Serbs, Jews and gypsies and denied the validity of conversions under duress. But he had never used his pulpit to denounce Ustasha atrocities.

Tito tried to tame him: he would be allowed to continue in his job if he would break with the Vatican and lead an independent Croatian church. Stepinac's refusal was implacable and in September 1945 he was arrested and put on trial together with easily identifiable war criminals. Before his arrest Stepinac had privately informed the British Ambassador that the Church had files on 150,000 Croats reported to have disappeared during the terror. The British Ambassador reported this information to Tito and the communication was used during the trial as evidence that the Church was plotting with foreigners against the state.

Though predictably the verdict (seventeen years' imprisonment) was settled in advance of the trial, and the public galleries were reserved for the claque, international concern prevented the Communists from following their usual practice and silencing the defence. Stepinac's lawyer had a long record of defending political prisoners and counted Marshal Tito himself among his pre-war clients.

Found guilty of war atrocities for which lesser priests would have been hanged, Stepinac was kept in prison for seven years and lived out the rest of his life under house arrest. His prestige today is probably higher than it has ever been and the Party has weakened its case by confiscating his personal diaries. Extracts of these are leaked to suit Party purposes and the concealment of the rest suggests that, if published, it would have demolished the prosecution case.

The elimination of all opposition on the political side has been well chronicled in a short book, *Party Pluralism and Monism*, written by two young Yugoslavs, Vojislav Koštunica and Kosta Čavoški, and sponsored by the Belgrade Institute of the Centre of Philosophy and Social Theory. One thousand copies slipped through the censorship while officials were on vacation during the summer of 1983 and, though it was subsequently trounced by party historians, the facts have never been disputed.

The Stalinist era of Yugoslav history, roughly from 1945 to 1952, lasting well after the break with Stalin, is still scrubbed out of Yugoslav text-books and it is largely unknown in the West as it took place at a time when Yugoslavs could be—and often were —prosecuted for having contacts with "imperialist powers". Koš-tunica and Čavoški steered clear of the physical aspects of the terror but tell, with remarkable clarity the story, from the summer of 1944 at Vis, when Tito agreed to a coalition government and a plural society, until 1947 by which time the Communist dictatorship was total.

The only pre-war politician of whom Tito was afraid, as he once confided to Deakin, was Vladko Maček, leader of the Croat Peasant Party, interned by the Ustashas during the war and thus preserving intact his very considerable prestige and popularity. But for Tito this problem resolved itself as, at the end of the war, Ustasha leader Ante Pavelić, anxious to save his skin, ordered Maček to be brought in to him so that he could propose a deal through which they could both be under Allied protection. The meeting alone enabled the Communists to pin charges that Maček had collaborated with the Ustashas and Maček's friends warned him that if he stayed in Croatia he would certainly be shot. His flight decapitated the most effective of the pre-war political parties.

For the rest, very few of the pre-war political leaders had survived. Many had fled to London and these had followers who had stayed in Yugoslavia and sought Axis—mainly Italian— protection from the Ustashas and the Communists—often from both. Their leaders could thus be charged with condoning treachery and very few took the risk of coming back.

Those who had accepted posts in the phantom coalition government were deprived of any way of popularizing their views or of rallying support. The (nominally) Vice-Premier, Milan Grol, fought a last ditch defence round the one surviving opposition newspaper *Demokratija* which was frequently grabbed by party thugs who beat up its distributors. Reporting that his paper was being burnt in the streets, Grol described this as "an honour accorded to all documents of truth, from the Holy Inquisition to Josef Goebbels". One eighteen-year-old student had the audacity to try and distribute *Demokratija* within the premises of the

Belgrade University. She was brought before the assembled and petrified university, submitted to a kangaroo trial and expelled "by unanimous acclaim".

Justifying the suppression of the last of the non-Communist papers, Tito told foreign journalists that the printers' trade union were refusing to produce *Demokratija* and "in our country there is freedom to strike." The party responded to Grol's arguments by blackening his character. "Peeping from the intellect of Milan Grol are Draža Mihailović, the Ljotić and Nedić ideologists, who are awaiting salvation from the Grols of democracy", wrote Djilas. "The people cannot stand idly by and remain indifferent."

With no possibility of campaigning and with systematic intimidation of their supporters, the opposition parties decided to boycott the constituent elections, on which Churchill and Roosevelt had pinned their hopes: "For elections to be free", Grol wrote, "voters should be able to choose between several viewpoints. This they cannot do if only one viewpoint is presented to them"—and only one viewpoint was.

The violence of the election campaign and the irregularities of the voting procedures were later described by a witness, Josef Korbel, then Czech Ambassador to Belgrade.[13] Korbel said that the authorities preserved a semblance of free choice by installing an alternative ballot-box, nicknamed "the black urn", which voters were given to understand they had better not use. (In some areas, I was later told, voting was in secret, but the opposition box was made of tin and the police could hear when anyone voted wrongly.) Korbel also observed that soldiers were particularly active on election-day, as each voted in several constituencies, and he commented: "Communist leaders knew it was all a gigantic deception, but no one ever said so. Wild enthusiasm was organised for all Tito's appearances".

It was not until after the elections were over and the official opposition had been hounded out and imprisoned, that Tito turned his attention towards his flabbier political associates who had tried to evade Party wrath by actively participating in the "All Yugoslav National Front" set up earlier in the year. Kardelj had announced that it contained "all freedom-loving elements of the population" and dismissed as "malicious" reports that it was Communist-controlled.

One newly elected deputy was Imre Filaković, a survivor from the now shadowy Croat Peasant Party who took the acknowledged risk of suggesting that his group should preserve its national identity: "Some of my friends have told me, do not speak, you could foolishly lose your head and nothing will be gained." Yet despite having his speech interrupted by constant heckling he did suggest that, as all opposition newspapers were banned, the Assembly ought to have its own proceedings published. The rest of the group, who were enjoying some of the minor spoils of office, promptly and unanimously agreed to expel him.

But it is the rise and fall of the Serb Professor Dragoljub Jovanović which offers the classical cautionary tale for fellow-travellers. Jovanović had been leader of the left-wing section of the Serb Agrarian Party before the war. When all the democratic groups joined forces against the royal dictatorship he had been among the minority who wanted to bring the Communists into a united front. In 1941 he signed a deal with the Communists which Tito interpreted as an acceptance of Communist domination, and Jovanović as a partnership in which the Communists would represent the towns, and his own group the much more numerous peasantry.

Immediately after the war Jovanović publicly congratulated Marshal Tito for his wisdom in appreciating that the Yugoslav people, especially the Serbs, would never accept a single omnipotent party. In 1945 he merged his formation into the National Front and denounced Grol and the opposition as "internal émigrés". Indeed he had been so humble that when Tito decided that the time had come to get rid of him, Police Chief Ranković observed that it might be difficult to find a charge. "Well if there isn't a charge, you will have to invent one!" was Tito's reply.[14]

Jovanović's downfall began during the debate on the new constitution, when he objected to clauses which seemed to place the Communists above the law. Milos Minić, Public Prosecutor at Mihailović's trials and later Tito's Foreign Minister, reminded him that the purpose of the Judiciary was not to resolve disputes but to liquidate the class enemy. When Jovanović complained that the Communists seemed to be going back on their pledges to a plural society he was reprimanded for echoing the words of "international reaction". The political leaders then put in the boot: Kardelj alleged that Jovanović's speeches would delight the heart of the White Guard and the Ustashas, Minić commented on the similarity of the views now being expressed by Jovanović and those of the opposition politicians already in jail and, on 27 April 1946, Djilas finished him off: "The masses are moving forwards, creating a new life, subduing all obstacles; the masses are like a big river, like a flood throwing out mud on their banks, and so they will throw out Jovanović and his friends." Three weeks later, Jovanović and his friends were arrested and all given long prison sentences (in the Soviet Union, as Čavoški pointed out, they would have been shot).

In dismissing the non-Communists after the war, Western observers often claim that, following the inter-ethnic massacres, the Communists were the only group which stood for a united Yugoslavia (see Chapter 6). In this context it is worth going back to the experiences of Ljubo Sirc, a law student at the Ljubljana University when the war began, who had escaped from Yugoslavia to try and alert the West about Yugoslav internecine fighting. Having volunteered to return to his country to participate in its liberation, he was told by the British he could only be allowed to do so if he joined the Partisans. After his contacts with the Communists during the resistance he disbelieved that they would voluntarily share power with other groups. But from this he had drawn the wrong conclusion that the British would never have underwritten the coalition compromise unless they had intended to send in troops to enforce it. As one of the few educated soldiers in his unit, Sirc was befriended by the political commissar who showed him a document setting out the Party's war aims. They included a Communist dictatorship, the use of the National Liberation Front to promote Communist aims and the total destruction of all existing institutions. Back in Ljubljana he resumed contact with his older friend Dr Nagoda, a civil engineer who had been with him in the earlier phase of resistance and they decided to get into touch with political friends in Belgrade and Zagreb. Sirc had no difficulty in finding like-minded democrats, as eager as himself to form an all-Yugoslav political grouping to try and challenge the Communist monolith.

But OZNA caught up with them and in 1947 in a spectacular show-trial Sirc and his friends were condemned allegedly as foreign spies, in fact for having tried to implement Western views of democracy to which the Yalta agreement ostensibly entitled them. Nagoda was hanged, Sirc was also condemned to death but reprieved and spent seven years in prison refusing offers of release conditional on serving as a police informer. His father, who had nothing to do with his son's political activities, was also arrested as a hostage and when Sirc still refused to provide the required "confession" the old man was given a ten-year sentence and died in jail.

Among the Slovene Communists Kardelj, identified by Western intellectuals as a leading moderate, was the most Stalinist. Linking the Slovene political prisoners in an "unprincipled brotherhood", in which he included "White Guard, Blue Guard, Chetniks, Ustashas, atheists, capitalist scum and obscurantists from the top lawyers of the Catholic hierarchy", Kardelj ended his peroration on a challenging note: "Finally, all these were unmasked and turned out to be straightforward spies in the service of foreign imperialists. Down with them! . . . The conclusion which has to be drawn from all this is that we must sharpen and strengthen watchfulness, we must not believe the lies and stories spread by the enemies of our people, and we must hit hard at any action by which our enemies wish to put a brake on our progress."[15]

At the time when Nagoda was being hanged as a British spy, Fitzroy Maclean was also in Slovenia, enjoying a holiday with Tito whom he found "remarkably affable, considering the existing tensions between our two countries."[16]

In 1947, the year of the show trials, Maclean indeed made two official visits to Yugoslavia on behalf of the Commission for Refugees. On the first occasion he allowed himself to be hectored by Yugoslav ministers about the way in which the British were plotting with "nefarious Quislings" to kill Tito. He was happy to leave them and join his old friend for a hunting trip at Bled. His subsequent dispatch to the Foreign Office concedes that things are bad but characteristically exonerates Tito: "Living as he now does, in magnificent palaces and castles, he is no longer as closely in touch with the people of the country and their everyday affairs as when he shared their dangers and hardships as a Partisan. He has been obliged, too, to delegate authority to some who are unworthy of it. Thus he is not, I think, aware of a good deal that goes on in his own country and in the world at large and suffers also from the lack of someone who will tell him unpleasant truths."[17]

On his second visit after the British press had carried reports of the trials, Maclean told Tito that he was by now "deeply distrusted and disliked by almost all British opinion". But once again in his message to London he goes to Tito's defence: "It was quite obvious that Tito genuinely believed that we and the Americans were making use of the refugees for nefarious purposes" but Maclean was able to reassure him and the friendship survived: "Our talk which had opened rather stormily thus ended on a much more cordial note and the remainder of my visit to Zagreb was given up to merry-making with the Marshal and some of his intimates, all old friends of mine, in his suburban residence, an excruciating modern villa formerly inhabited by the notorious Pavelić."

Yet Tito made no concessions: pro-British prisoners stayed in jail, more were arrested, and Tito's judiciary and press continued to help his secret police in the task he had set them of "striking terror into the hearts of our enemies". And by 1947, trussed and bound, Yugoslavia must have seemed a dainty morsel for Tito to set before his Soviet master. Indeed in the period immediately after the war Tito's zeal, both in denouncing the West and in liquidating friends of the West in his own country, seemed to be promoting him to the rank of Stalin's favourite follower. In April 1945 he had been invited to Moscow to sign a treaty of friendship and Stalin, who rarely agreed to share the limelight with anyone, did him the signal honour of sending him on a triumphal tour of the USSR and allowing him to be welcomed as a war hero.

In May 1946 at the funeral of the President of the USSR, Kalinin, when Stalin, Beria, Zhdanov and Molotov were pall-bearers, Stalin again showed his special regard. As the cortège passed the diplomatic stand, he raised his arm and beckoned Tito to join him. Resplendent in his full Marshal's regalia, Tito stepped down and walked beside Stalin to the Kremlin burial place. "He stood there while the coffin was lowered in the grave and then walked with Stalin to the Lenin Mausoleum where the two of them stood to take the salute of the military parade which followed. Tito was, evidently, at that time *persona gratissima* in Moscow."[18]

The split two years later between Stalin and his most fervent disciple is incomprehensible except when seen within an international context. Having imposed his domination on Yugoslavia Tito was now extending his ambitions to the rest of the Balkans, a process for which he assumed he had Stalin's support. Indeed as early as October 1943 in relation to activities in Greece, he had felt able to write to one of his top commanders: "In our opinion and also in that of Grandpa's [wartime pseudonym for the Comintern] we should be in the centre of the Balkan countries, both in the military and political sense."[19]

Nor did his unconcealed intention of extending his power in the areas beyond Yugoslavia's pre-war frontiers in any way indicate a renunciation of his allegiance to Moscow. There is no reason at all to think that he would not have been satisfied to stay within the

Soviet bloc if Stalin had allowed him to expand his fiefdom to incorporate the rest of the Balkans—an ambition which by 1947 he was well on the way to realizing.

Having failed to take Trieste, Tito had turned his attention to Albania. If we are to believe Enver Hoxha, his treatment of his small neighbour was a carbon copy of what Stalin had done to Yugoslavia: exploitation through manipulating prices, joint companies, totally controlled by the senior partner and above all, infiltration into the military and political apparatus. The split with Stalin came just in time to save Hoxha: Tito had insisted on sending two Yugoslav divisions into Albania, ostensibly to protect it from Greece but, in reality, Hoxha was sure, to subjugate his country. Djilas was later to recall that he had asked Kardelj why on earth it was necessary to send two divisions into Albania and had been given a sufficient reason: "Well, you know how it is, the Old Man keeps on pressing for it. . . ."[20]

For Stalin, Tito's aggression was often a positive embarrassment. In 1946 Tito ordered his men to shoot down two American aircraft flying without his permission over Yugoslav territory. In the subsequent row, Stalin refused to take his side and Tito was forced to apologize and to pay compensation to the families of the dead American airmen.

In his designs on Bulgaria Tito also enjoyed only sporadic Soviet support. Whereas the Bulgarian Communists favoured unity with Yugoslavia on equal terms Tito wanted to break up Bulgaria, annex its Macedonian area to the Macedonian republic of Yugoslavia, and turn the rest of Bulgaria into a seventh Yugoslav Federated Republic. For the Bulgarians too the rupture came just in time.

In Greece in 1946 Stalin supported Tito when he helped launch and sustain the Communist revolt against the monarchy. In the subsequent hostilities it was the Macedonians from Yugoslavia who did most of the fighting—as contemporary Macedonian Communists like to recall. But after March 1947 when Truman enunciated his "doctrine", committing the US to defending the independence of Greece and Turkey, Stalin saw at once that both countries were now out of Communist reach. Tito was slower to get the message and the war went on.

All through 1947, Stalin still evidently hoped that he could satisfy his protégé's appetites within the Soviet orbit. That year he revived the old Comintern, dissolved in 1943, now under the less sinister name of Communist Information Bureau—Cominform, in which he encouraged the Yugoslavs to play a leading role. At the initial meeting in September 1947 Kardelj and Djilas were cast in star parts and Belgrade was selected as the seat of the projected Cominform Secretariat.

For Stalin 1948, the year of the Czech *coup* and of the Berlin blockade, was particularly dangerous. In the difficult task of avoiding the ultimate catastrophe (the US still had a nuclear monopoly) while consolidating Soviet power in Eastern Europe, Stalin understandably felt that he needed to exercise total and unquestioning control over his subordinates. As he had told Khrushchev, he was confident he could get rid of Tito by shaking his little finger—but in practice he preferred to operate through more substantial instruments: his armed forces and secret police. Soviet efforts to penetrate the Party and recruit spies were reported to Tito who responded by ordering that any information requested by the Russians should be channelled through his own office.

Stalin thereupon summoned Tito to Moscow but he excused himself and sent instead his closest associates, Kardelj and Djilas. Before they left Moscow Stalin had signified his displeasure and Molotov called in Kardelj and made him sign a treaty then and there, under which Belgrade would have to consult Moscow before taking any initiative in international affairs. Kardelj later claimed that he had been too frightened to refuse.

Even so, the Yugoslavs could not bring themselves to believe in the possibility of a breach. Reporting back to Belgrade Djilas was still reassuring: "There is no need to doubt for one moment the great love that Comrade Stalin has for our entire Party and particularly for Comrade Tito."

According to Alex Bebler, future Yugoslav representative at the United Nations, it was the Soviet military penetration which triggered off the final rupture:

> On Stalin's orders, Russian officers penetrated deeper and deeper into the organisation of our army and that is how the trouble started. There were amongst us hundreds of Russian officers who acted as instructors in our army. They were placed all over the country. Russian officers started behaving as if they were the masters and wanted to command our unit. Our officers did not like it and began to protest. Our officers were all Partisans who fought in the war, and naturally objected to being deprived of their commands.

"The Soviet attempt to penetrate the army and to infiltrate the officer corps and to turn its highest leaders from their allegiance to Tito," wrote Adam Ulam in his perceptive analysis of the collision, "were among the most important factors in convincing the Yugoslav régime that for its sheer survival it had to stand up to Soviet Russia."[21]

When Stalin heard of Tito's recalcitrance he retaliated by officially informing the Yugoslav government on 18 and 19 March, that the Soviet military and economic advisers would be called home. On 20 March Tito wrote pleadingly to ask Stalin to spell out his grievances. A week later he received a long and irate letter signed by Molotov as well as Stalin, in which the Yugoslav Communist leaders were linked, in an improbable combination, with both Trotsky and the Mensheviks. The Yugoslavs took three weeks to assess the state of the Party and on 23 April Tito and Kardelj sent another humbler letter assuring Stalin that he must have been misinformed: "Is it possible that the men who have served 6, 8, 10 years in jail amongst other things for their work popularising Russia could be as you suggest. . . . We shall always remain grateful to the Soviet Communist Party for its Marxist–Leninist teachings that have guided us until now and will guide us in the future as well. . . ."

It was to no avail: in May Stalin told them that their differences should be settled at a special meeting of the Cominform. Tito knowing that his case was hopeless refused to attend and on 28 June a brief message from the Cominform announced to a dumbfounded world that Yugoslavia had been expelled. The overwhelming majority of Tito's close associates supported him. Those who had fought at his side during the hardships of the war had developed a personal loyalty and this would be reinforced by the knowledge that if Tito hanged, they would all be strung up with him.

In the subsequent panic potential enemies of all colours were arrested. And as in Stalin's Russia, the worst treatment was reserved for the old revolutionaries who had failed to stay in the dictator's good graces. The most famous victim was the Croat Communist leader Andrija Hebrang, the man Stalin was known to have designated as Tito's successor.

He was arrested, placed in solitary confinement, given no access whatever to the outside world and accused of every conceivable crime, including having been an agent of the Ustashas. The public was informed that he had admitted everything and been so ashamed of himself that he had committed suicide. To this day members of his family and most politically conscious Croats remain convinced that he was never a Stalinist at all and that, having refused to succumb to torture, he had been murdered in prison.[22]

Goli Otok, a desolate island on the Adriatic, was selected as the location for the internment of over 50,000 men and women allegedly Cominformist who were tortured, humiliated and starved. It took a long time before those who survived dared to reveal even to their own children the inhuman punishments they had been made to inflict on each other, which included dipping the heads of prisoners into buckets of excrement. Inmates were forced to compete with one another in beating up new arrivals. Many years later, a Yugoslav refugee in Leningrad was still showing Russian friends the lacerations on his back which he said he received at Goli Otok.

Many of those rounded up were not Stalinist either in word or deed. The parents of a Montenegrin woman told her 30 years after these events how a letter from the Yugoslav leadership openly challenging Stalin's infallibility had suddenly been presented at a local Party meeting and those present asked to express their views. Having never heard anything but praise for the Soviet Union they looked astonished and their expression alone was enough to condemn them both to Goli Otok. Many of those sent to the camp had fallen into disfavour for reasons that had nothing to do with the Cominform. Rodoljub Čolaković was one inmate who rightly predicted he would never emerge alive. In 1938 he had been in Moscow at the same time as Tito and, being better educated, had drawn the attention of the Comintern to the inadequacies of Tito's translation of Stalin's *History of the Soviet Communist Party*. Though the errors did no more than pinpoint Tito's intellectual limitations, his enemies presented it as a case of sabotage and Tito was lucky to escape with his life. Tito later told his associates that his premature grey hair dated from his Moscow sojourn.

But though inside the Party the breach with Stalin caused consternation and disarray, among ordinary Yugoslavs it vastly enhanced Tito's popularity: he was now identified no longer as a Soviet agent but as a national hero. Only a few fellow-conspirators remembered how dutifully he had served Stalin during the time when Party policy included the demolition of the Yugoslav state. Now, with a genuine sense of patriotic pride, he could announce,

"No matter how much each of us loves the land of socialism, the USSR, he can in no case love his country less."

The response of Tito and his team to Stalin's excommunication developed in three distinct phases: the first until the early 1950s when they tried to demonstrate their fidelity to the Bolshevik camp; the second, until 1955, when they accused Stalin himself of having betrayed the revolution; and finally reconciliation on the basis that the two countries could proceed towards the same Communist goal though "along separate paths".

The first phase produced an apparent anomaly: whereas in other newly sovietized countries, repression was at its worst when Soviet control was tightest, in Yugoslavia terror reached its peak after the breach with Stalin.

The fulfilment of the overambitious Five Year Plan, which depended primarily on the forced labour of half-starved prisoners, became an essential part of the policy of Yugoslav Communist politicians designed to demonstrate that they were no less committed to national planning and the realization of national targets than the Russians. Further the Yugoslav Communists rose to the Cominform challenge that they pampered their kulaks, by becoming the first Party after the Russians to collectivize the land. By 1952 the newly collectivized farms had taken over much of the most fertile land and the peasants were responding by sporadic rioting and, more devastatingly, by starving out the cities. According to one US estimate in 1952 as much as 30 per cent of the arable land was left untilled.[23]

And by this time any opposition at all was formally prohibited: "If someone wants to implement a programme outside the programme of the National Front," Tito said, "then it is not a socialist programme but a programme hostile to socialism and naturally we will not allow such a programme at the elections. There cannot be two programmes in our country, comrades, but only one: the programme of the National Front, the programme of socialism."[24]

The programme of the National Liberation Front by this time however was in the process of turning Yugoslavia into a disaster area. And it was not before the country was on the brink of starvation that Tito renounced his efforts to be a Yugoslav Stalin and realized that he had no alternative but to turn to the West.

As Khrushchev later acknowledged it was Stalin's intransigence which almost pushed Tito over the edge. Having discovered that he could not destroy Tito by shaking his little finger, "he shook everything else he could shake". And in 1949 and 1950 troops from the Soviet Union and the satellites were redeployed for a prospective invasion. Skirmishes started on the Slovene and Croat Northern frontiers which in November 1952 Tito listed: in 1950: 936; in 1951, 1,517; and in the first ten months of 1952, 1,530. The Russians he alleged had killed 40 Yugoslav frontier-guards and civilians without themselves suffering a single casualty.[25]

Just how close Stalin came to ordering a full-scale invasion was revealed by the Hungarian defector General Bela Kiraly:

> I was designated commander of the army which was supposed to invade Yugoslavia. The Hungarian Army was supposed to break through between the Danube and the Tisa river, creating a bridge-head on the Danube, and stop there. The privilege of invading the heretical capital, Belgrade, was reserved for the Soviet Union. In other words, everything was prepared. What saved Tito against military invasion was the Korean War. America stood up. Consequently, the Russians assumed that if they invaded Yugoslavia, Americans would stand up again. I'm absolutely convinced of that because what we did was not military exercises: it was a systematic build-up and a systematic preparation for war, which was supposed to come sometime in 1951 or about then.[26]

While the invasion was being prepared, the satellites vied with each other in the virulence of their anti-Tito rhetoric and their campaigns culminated in a series of show-trials. Those hanged for Titoism included Rajk in Hungary, Kostov in Bulgaria, and Slansky in Czechoslovakia. The excesses of the indictments and the brutality of the judicial proceedings were as remote from Western concepts of justice as the postwar trials of liberal politicians had been in Tito's Yugoslavia.

At the same time the Yugoslav Communists were called upon to throw out their leaders, identified by Molotov as "a criminal bunch" and by the Cominform, at its meeting in November 1949, as "murderers and spies".

There was one issue however on which Tito felt vulnerable. As Stalin had said, since coming into power he had ruled Yugoslavia like an old-fashioned despot, surrounding himself with cronies and using *ad hoc* groups when he needed them regardless of their status in the Party. As Djilas later recalled, there was no effective politburo at the time and no operational Central Committee.[27] Now everything was institutionalized and Party organs reconstituted. Work began at once for the convening of the first Party congress which was held a month after the breach had been publicly announced.

In the Western capitals the Stalin–Tito rupture was welcomed with enthusiasm bordering on ecstasy. The US *chargé d'affaires* reported home: "No event could be more momentous for the attainment of our foreign policy objective than the permanent alienation from the Soviet Union of this key region." Soon afterwards, Secretary of State Marshall endorsed the views of his Policy Planning staff: "By this act the aura of mystical omnipotence and infallibility that surrounded the Kremlin has been broken. . . ."[28]

After a brief interlude, the Soviet economic boycott, which Stalin had intended as a punishment, began to yield rewards. The deals with the USSR, as the Yugoslavs themselves revealed, had been both exploitative and undependable, but once the tap of US aid was turned on supplies were lavish and unconditional. And it was with almost embarrassing haste that US policy shifted. Within two weeks after the rupture was announced the Americans released the 30 million dollars worth of gold, deposited in the US by the royal government and blocked since the war. And a few months later negotiations began for material and financial support which, in the course of the 1950s, amounted to over two billion dollars: more per head then received by any other country.

At the same time, while the Russians were deploying troops along the Yugoslav frontier Tito was receiving the first US military mission. In the subsequent decade this sufficed to re-equip eight of Yugoslavia's 27 infantry divisions and to replace much of the battered wartime equipment of the Yugoslav Navy and Air Force.[29] During the same period, the US also sponsored the first of a long series of loans from the World Bank and IMF on which Yugoslavia never ceased to depend.

Without this massive rescue operation Tito's régime would probably not have survived: on this point at least Stalin and the Western leaders were in agreement. A series of bad harvests had exacerbated a situation which was already appalling. Industry as well as agriculture was breaking down. Boycotted by the Communist countries, the factories lacked raw materials and thanks to Titoist policies they were lacking in technical proficiency. The few surviving Yugoslav managers had been replaced by new inexperienced men coming up through Party or Partisan ranks.

Further, the first Yugoslav Five Year Plan, modelled on Stalin's policy of crash industrialization, represented an extravagant dis-

tortion of national resources. This was the view not only of the
Russians, who might be accused of opposing Yugoslavia's mod-
ernization, but also of many Yugoslav economists and the critics
were known to include the former planning chief Hebrang, which
may have been one of the reasons why Stalin had picked on him to
be Tito's successor. The same note of disapproval was to be struck
later when representatives of the US government and of the World
Bank began visiting Yugoslavia. None the less, the American
Administration decided that, for political reasons, they would turn
a blind eye to the plan's excesses and Tito was given the material
support he said he needed to reach his targets.

With the anti-Communist mood now prevailing in the USA the
Truman administration had to extort aid for Yugoslavia from
Congress, as Secretary of State Dean Acheson later recalled "in
bits and pieces", but he happily recollected that by 1952 "it had
carried Tito through his troubles".[30] The rescue operation was all
the more difficult, both to work out and to justify before Congress,
as the Yugoslavs, like other Communist governments, conducted
their business in conspiratorial secrecy, leaving the Americans to
depend on the unverifiable say-so of the interested party.

The Yugoslavs themselves were astonished by American cre-
dulity. As Tito's friend and confidant, Svetozar Vukmanović
Tempo, later recalled: "We did not shrink from publishing ficti-
tious data in official documents so as to obtain more aid and thus
enable our own resources to be diverted for financing industrialization. In this operation we had considerable success."[31]

Vukmanović Tempo later gave Khrushchev a melodramatized
version of his dealings with Washington: "The Americans tried to
take advantage of our troubles, imposed the most one-sided,
shackling sorts of conditions, clearly of a political character,
designed to take Yugoslavia off its social course and force us
towards capitalism. I walked out and slammed the door. The
Americans gave in. . . ." In fact, as the US records reveal, the
Americans, at this stage[32] of the cold war, were so eager to secure
Yugoslavia, that aid was not only unconditional but it was deployed for purposes of which American economists expressly
disapproved.

Requesting emergency aid for Yugoslavia, Truman predictably
refrained from revealing that it was the régime itself which was
primarily responsible for the economic disaster. Instead he attributed the penury and near-famine exclusively to the combined
consequences of the Soviet blockade and the drought.

In his "save Tito" policy, Acheson had no trouble squaring the British. Though Foreign Secretary Ernest Bevin had no illusions about any kind of Communists, he quickly agreed: "Tito is a scoundrel, but he is our scoundrel."[33] And when Churchill returned to office in 1951 he was emotionally predisposed to re-embrace his wartime protégé. Those on the British side who had unstintingly lobbied for the Partisans during the Yugoslav civil war, led as before by Maclean, now a Conservative MP and Deakin, now Warden of a college at Oxford, came back into their own. And when in 1953 Tito paid his first official visit to London the welcome was euphoric.

Churchill volunteered to underwrite the security of Tito's régime: "Should our wartime ally in Yugoslavia be attacked, we would fight and die with you . . ." to which Tito replied "This is a sacred vow. It is enough for us. We need no written treaty."[34]

The meeting was recorded a triumph though there were still a few liberal-minded journalists like David Astor, then editor of *The Observer*, who hesitated about whether or not they wished to participate in the rejoicings. But these reservations were quickly overcome and from then on succeeding generations of British diplomats, academics and journalists (including those of *The Observer*) came to accept Tito as an asset to the Western world.

A discordant note was struck by Evelyn Waugh, in an article "Guest of Dishonour", published by *The Daily Express* when the visit was announced, in which he wrote about Tito's persecution of the church, which, as a British Liaison Officer with the Partisans, he had witnessed at first hand: "Mr Eden would not invite into the country, to feed and flatter, a notorious Jew baiter. Only when Christianity is at stake do our leaders show bland indifference."[35] It is significant that 31 years later in a highly appreciative review of an anthology of Waugh's articles, *The Economist* selected this particular piece as one of the exceptions when Waugh's views were preposterous.[36] Yet in the light of what we now know about what was going on in Yugoslavia at the time, Waugh was nearer to reality than Lord Fisher, the Archbishop of Canterbury, who allowed himself to be photographed beaming benevolently at a man who, in an overwhelmingly Christian country, had just abolished the Christmas holiday.

We cannot know what Tito himself was feeling as Moscow went on hurling abuse and the Western allies—except for the odd man out—lavished him with praise. But certainly by this time he was allowing his associates to challenge Soviet orthodoxy. It became fashionable to denounce the Soviet economy as "state capitalism" and to propagate, instead, the new ideas of self-management: factories to be run not by officials but by the workers themselves (see Chapter 7).

In the period of retreat from Stalinism, the Communists lower down the line no longer knew what to think. It now seemed safe to talk about competition and market-laws, and in the Ljubljana prison, a warder in charge of "cultural work" invited Sirc to lecture on the workings of "economic automatism". It did him no good: "For the political commissar who heard me, consulted other prisoners who knew something about economics, and reported to his superiors that I was propagating enemy doctrine."[37]

At every level previous certitudes were shrivelling and Djilas later recalled that during this time Tito positively encouraged his immediate entourage to think the unthinkable.[38] They talked between themselves of the possibility of associating the Yugoslav League of Communists with the Second (i.e. non-Communist) International. They discussed joining the Marshall Plan (under the European Recovery Programme, participants were required to cooperate in sharing out aid and to move towards free trade and currency convertibility: unfortunately for the Yugoslavs, the Americans attached no such conditions on the aid they lavished on Tito).

Further, recognizing that the Soviet Union was now the only military threat, Tito seriously contemplated joining the North Atlantic Alliance: indeed, indirectly and fleetingly, he nearly did.

Having been deprived of Stalin's military support, he had abandoned the Greek Communists and given up his designs on Albania, Trieste and Bulgaria. And under the Soviet menace he negotiated a Balkan Pact of Mutual Defence with Turkey and Greece signed in August 1954: as both his partners were members of NATO Yugoslavia had in effect become part of the Western defence complex.[39]

The choice which confronted Tito in the mid-1950s was historically unusual, perhaps unique. A politician's freedom on the international scene is generally narrowly circumscribed by the balance of external forces. At this juncture however Tito was free to go in two diametrically opposite directions. He had already defied Stalin who had "called the spirits from the vasty deep" only to find they would not come. And Washington was offering him anything he needed without imposing political pressures. Yugoslavia had reached a cross-roads and, for Tito, the choice between the two directions was more than a matter of foreign policy.

Linking up with the West, as he could have done and nearly did, would almost certainly have transformed Yugoslavia into a plural society. As the experience of the rest of Europe suggests, this would have made it more productive, but would have deprived Tito's party of their monopoly of power and its supporting pillar: the Marxist–Leninist monopoly of truth.

The other way was the preservation of one-party Communist rule, coercive, incompetent and (as future decades were to confirm) insolvent, but a society in which Tito could preserve his control over the tripod on which he always relied: the party cadres, the secret police and the army. Predictably, for a man of his background, the second alternative was preferred.

Though East was East and West was West, for a brief time the twain met in Belgrade—and the oddest feature of this encounter was that the man who came to incarnate Western values turned out to be the former Communist fanatic, Milovan Djilas. In his writings and interviews he was to show himself the ablest defender of the two fundamental concepts which distinguish Western from Marxist–Leninist thought: the notion of objective—or as the Communist would say "bourgeois"—truth and the rights of the individual against the Party and its secret police: acting, as the Communists see it, in their capacity as the vanguard of the proletariat.

During the war, Djilas had headed the Communist *agitprop* machine and, in their despatches, Western liaison officers frequently named him along with Tito, Kardelj and Ranković as the Partisans' Big Four. The story of his metamorphosis has been well told by Stephen Clissold, in *Djilas: the Progress of a Revolutionary*.[40] But fully to understand how a man of Djilas's integrity could ever have been swept into the Stalinist maelstrom (for which many of his compatriots have never forgiven him) it is useful to go back to the first volume of his autobiography, *Land without Justice*[41] depicting the primitive semi-feudal society in which he grew up. In his region of Montenegro, most peasants lived on the edge of starvation, from what their stony soil could produce, and many of Milovan's father's and grandfather's generations had been wiped out in the vendettas which were part of local life. Leaping straight from this inherently violent society into the cosmopolitan atmosphere of Belgrade university, Milovan saw Stalinism as the best hope for despoiling the rich and eliminating oppression.

The disenchantment came only after the war when he was able to see the contrast between the Utopia for which he had fought and the reality of the new society and its acquisitive ruling class. And as it happened, the disenchantment coincided with his first contacts with the West.

After the 1946 upheaval Tito had entrusted him with the job of striking up relations with the Western socialists as a possible line of escape from Yugoslavia's ideological isolation. As Clissold commented,

> Djilas's informal manner and the breadth of his intellectual interests made him, in the early 1950s, the ideal liaison officer with the British Labour Party and the Democratic Socialist Parties of the West. But it was in Aneurin Bevan that Djilas found a real friend, a natural rebel like himself and sufficiently open-minded and undogmatic to listen as well as to preach. Bevan certainly helped Djilas to recognise that there could be no personal freedom nor any protection from arbitrary rule without responsible government and a legalised opposition. In return, there is every reason to suppose that it was Djilas who helped Bevan to understand the nature of Soviet power.

Lady Falkender, then Marcia Williams, working at the headquarters of the Labour Party, still recalls today the interest which Djilas's case aroused in a party where foreigners normally play only a peripheral role. Eight years after his first meeting with Djilas Bevan repudiated his earlier belief in unilateralism: one-sided nuclear disarmament, founded on what Djilas regarded as the dangerous illusion that the Soviet Union would follow the Western lead rather than respect the Marxist precept and the dictates of Soviet self-interest, by taking advantage of the new correlation of forces.

Indirectly, in this way, Djilas may have played a crucial role in British politics. For the impact of what Bevan's biographer Michael Foot and other "Bevanites" still consider their leader's apostasy, was shattering. It postponed for a generation the conquest of the Labour Party by the pro-Soviet left and its consequence: the breakaway of the Social Democrats to form a new party.

Tito's disavowal of Djilas was gradual. At the Sixth Party Congress in 1952 they were still speaking the same language —though it had changed a great deal since the Fifth (1948), when

Djilas's *agitprop* was inspiring the slogan "Stalin! Tito! The Party!" Now for both of them the villain was Stalin and Tito opened proceedings with an eight-hour speech diatribe against his former master. But it was Djilas who formulated the new ideas and, as Clissold wrote, "did more than anyone to make the Congress a notable milestone in the Party's history and a high watermark of the trend towards liberalism". The occasion flustered his old mother: "It is not well with our Djido when they applaud him more than Tito." It was at this Congress which Tito later regretted, that the party renamed itself the League of Yugoslav Communists and abjured the right to executive office.

But though Tito felt free to trounce Stalin he was not ready to accept limitations on his personal power in Yugoslavia nor on the monopoly which the party continued to exercise over Yugoslavia's political life. And Tito was coming to recognize that his personal ascendancy was incompatible with the concepts of democracy which his former favourite, Djilas, now seemed to endorse.

In Djilas's view, his clash with his party was inevitable though he attributes his nine years of subsequent imprisonment to Tito's eagerness to placate Moscow.

Stalin died in 1953 and as soon as he was embalmed the new Soviet leaders started sending out conciliatory hints to which Tito responded fast and favourably. Meanwhile Djilas was increasingly withdrawing from public life to reassess his political creed: by the end of that year he had reached the radical conclusion that Yugoslavia was now governed by "a new class" of self-serving toadies and that it was his bounden duty to say so.

Most surprisingly of all in the doctrinal confusion of the time, he was able to develop his liberal thesis in the pages of the official Communist newspaper *Borba*, which remained his responsibility. The following extract from one of his articles exemplifies the tone: "The greatest crimes of horror in history, from the fires of the inquisition to Hitler's concentration camps and Stalin's labour camps, occurred ultimately through the absence of free thought, from the exclusive claim of reactionary fanatics who exercised a political monopoly. . . . We must learn to respect the opinion of others even if they seem to be stupid and conservative and we must get used to the idea that even when we are right, our views will remain those of a minority. . . ."[42]

Tito reacted first with astonishment and then with rage and Djilas found himself shunned by his former friends. The general state of political disarray spread from the top of the party down to its lowest ranks. Even in prison, Sirc recalled, which now contained many Communists who had fallen out of favour, by December 1953 Djilas's articles were the main topic of conversation. As Djilas had been so close to Tito it was assumed his writings must represent the new party line: "Dolenc [a Communist fellow-prisoner] stood between two beds and mused 'we shall have to learn everything anew when we come out of here when things go on like this . . .' Duško, another Communist, was equally amazed, 'Things do seem to change very quickly.' "[43]

Sirc's own suspicion that the articles were "just another Communist trick" were allayed when Tito decided that the matter would be settled once and for all at a meeting of the Central Committee which would be broadcast live. We cannot know whether he would have dared take the risk had it not been for a story written by Djilas in the literary weekly *Nova Misao* of January 1954 which, as Tito rightly guessed, would ensure him the Party's frenetic and unanimous support for Djilas's political execution.

In a fictional form, Djilas recounted the wedding of the Partisan General, Peko Dapčević, to a beautiful young actress, which he had attended as best man. As the girl was neither a party member nor a former Partisan, she was ostracized and humiliated by envious women of impeccable credentials but with the gaudy tastes of the *nouveaux riches*.

By exposing the new leadership to ridicule and contempt Djilas sealed his fate. His trial took place in a splendid marble and bronze office previously belonging to a Belgrade bank. The proceedings were heard in the prisons over the inescapable loudspeakers and Sirc recalled his own reactions: "It was appalling to see those former friends and comrades assault him [Djilas] one after another, for having taken seriously slogans about equality of citizens and socialist legality. Djilas had at first tried to resist and then gave in. Many people were shocked by his behaviour. They probably did not know what it was like to stand alone against former friends criticizing you in the name of a doctrine which you, not so long ago, yourself so ardently believed . . ."

Indeed, on the second day Djilas crumbled and Tito won another famous victory. The recantation started with a pledge: "I shall go on working to carry out the decisions of the League of Communists and the government authorities, as I have always done in the past." Djilas not only admitted his errors but repudiated Bevan and his other Western friends: "I can see that the abstract democratic theories would, if concretely applied, mean exactly what the comrades here have underlined: the mobilization of the *petite bourgeoisie* of the Social Democrats of the Western Camp."[44] On the thirtieth anniversary of these proceedings, the Student Centre at Belgrade produced a sketch, based on the authentic records, contrasting the official adulation of Djilas before the hearing with the venomous sneers afterwards. Djilas's wife Štefica—who was to display Fidelio-like solidarity with her husband during his ordeals—enjoyed it so much that she went to two performances.

Tito questioned the sincerity of Djilas's self-criticism, but declared himself satisfied: "The League of Communists had demonstrated its monolithic unity". The party ideology was by now in tatters but on the basic principle of "what we have we hold", the Communists, in Yugoslavia as elsewhere, remained united.

Djilas has described his own self-disgust as he watched himself behaving, for the last time, like an obedient party member: "If you belong to the Communist Party," he said later, "it cannot be long before you have to sacrifice your beliefs and castrate your conscience." Within a few weeks he recovered his self-respect and handed in his Party card. At the end of 1954 he and his friend Vladimir Dedijer submitted a formal request to be allowed to form a Social Democratic party. It was refused and Dedijer spent a long time abroad; after he returned to Yugoslavia he repudiated Djilas and climbed back into Tito's favour.

Djilas's disgrace opened the way for the reconciliation with Moscow. In the summer of 1954 Khrushchev pointed out that, now that the Russians had rid themselves of Beria and the Yugoslavs of Djilas, there were no further obstacles to renewed friendship. Arriving in Belgrade in May 1955 Khrushchev conceded that Moscow had been misinformed about Yugoslavia: an error ascribed to "the machinations of foreign imperialists".[45] In the West the visit was heralded as a Soviet Canossa. But its practical consequence was to quash the newly signed Balkan pact and extricate Yugoslavia from the Western defence system.

Even after his public disgrace Djilas would not be silenced. Having had the exceptional experience of having been hugged by Stalin and having participated in Communist rule from the top, he felt a personal obligation to testify publicly about the nature of the system he had repudiated. All domestic outlets were closed and when he addressed his writings to the outside world Tito was able to have him charged with anti-state activity and from then on to use his own prestige to vilify and dishonour his former favourite.

Since his release from prison in 1967 he has lived at home under police surveillance. Sporadically, the Yugoslav media renew hate-campaigns to which he is unable to reply. All his writings, even his non-political novels and short stories, are banned.

And, as Khrushchev had predicted, the downfall of Beria and Djilas did indeed lead to a new chapter in Soviet–Yugoslav relations. The reconciliation between the two states was followed in 1956 by renewed ties between the two Communist parties. Tito went back to the USSR to celebrate the occasion and felt able to say: "I feel at home in the Soviet Union because we are part of the same family: the family of socialism."[46] And it is in this familial context that we need to reassess the concept of non-alignment.

Chapter 5

NON-ALIGNED AGAINST THE WEST

NEARLY TWO YEARS after Tito's death, on 8 March 1982, the Yugoslav agency Tanjug was able to announce that the Russians had paid him the compliment of giving his name to a square on the border between the old and new parts of Moscow. A tribute was inscribed in gold letters on a plaque at the top of Krassyn Street: *Josip Broz Tito Square. In memory of an eminent combatant for the Communist and Workers' movement, Josip Broz Tito (1892–1980)*.

An eminent combatant for the world communism was not the way Tito was perceived in the West. On the contrary, the breach with Moscow and Tito's subsequent preoccupation with the countries of Africa and Asia and, later on, Latin America, produced the misleading impression that his Yugoslavia had ceased to be part of the Communist movement. The misconception was encouraged by the title "the non-aligned movement" adopted by the new association: an epithet suggesting neutrality between the Eastern and Western blocs.

In reality, in common with other political leaders who depend for their right to rule neither on tradition nor on free elections, Tito directed his foreign policy primarily towards propping up his political structure. And in his case this had to depend on being part of the Marxist–Leninist world and therefore distancing his country from the plural societies which deny the Communists any vanguard role and *ipse facto* the right to monopolize power.

This did not mean that Tito ever reapplied to join Comecon (in 1949 he had sought membership and been refused); nor that Yugoslavia officially became part of the Warsaw Pact (the Soviet military alliance, set up in 1955). It was along their own path that Tito and his successors reserved their right to advance towards the common Marxist–Leninist goal.

The Marxist–Leninist creed shaped the past as well as the future and this basic identity of attitudes explains why during the war, just as the Soviet Ambassador Maisky had added up Allied and Nazi losses in the same column,[1] so Tito and his team lumped the Western Allies with the Germans as their "class enemies". And it is this perception which explains why, to this day, Yugoslav historians have continued to sustain Edvard Kardelj's thesis that in 1942 Churchill and Hitler were struggling on the same side to destroy the Partisans.

Though Stalin was ready to settle in his own time for "Communism in one country" neither Soviet nor Yugoslav Communists ever abandoned their belief that they represented the future. According to Kardelj's own account, already in 1945, during the time when he represented Yugoslavia at the Paris peace negotiations, he was privately pressing Molotov to abandon the Soviet Union's exclusive preoccupation with Europe and instead to extend its anti-capitalist, i.e. anti-Western policy to the wider world:

> I once mentioned that it seemed to me that Socialist countries must give greater consideration to the many small and semi-colonial or independent countries which were practically American colonies and certainly members of the American voting machine in the United Nations but who nevertheless would prefer complete independence and speedier economic development. As I said, I did not think it necessary for the contemporary world to be divided into capitalist and socialist states but that it should be possible, with a suitable policy towards the small nations and semi-colonial countries, *to split the capitalist world* [my italics]. My theory failed to convince Molotov."[2]

What Kardelj called his theory stayed in the freezer for several years. Immediately after the war Stalin and Tito were both preoccupied with extending and consolidating their share of Europe and, after the political earthquake of 1948, the Yugoslavs were desperate to re-establish their doctrinal fidelity to the collectivist cause. It was only three years later, by which time Stalin had turned "Titoism" into a capital offence and in the satellite states had arranged for the hanging of alleged Titoists, that Tito finally hit back. It was then that Yugoslavia went through a now forgotten, fleeting interlude, during which Tito and his team, who had climbed to power on the Marxist–Leninist bandwagon, even opened their minds to the possibility of changing sides.

Curiously at the time when Tito delivered his devastating exposure of Soviet imperialism, a large part of the liberal intelligentsia in the West were still inclined to be pro-Soviet. The bias had been relaunched by the genuine injustices of Senator J. R. McCarthy's purges and though, compared to Stalin's atrocities, these were negligible they took place in an open society and therefore evoked a much stronger public reaction.

Few Europeans in the West were listening when on 27 July 1951, Tito, who knew the Kremlin from the inside, dared to ask:

> Where is the German Republic of Volga, where one of the most gifted of peoples used to live? It is in the forests of Siberia. Where is the Tartar Crimean Republic? It doesn't exist any more; it is in Siberia, vanished amidst forests and swamps. Where are the Chechens of the Caucasus? They no longer exist—they've been driven out of the hills where, as a free people, they have been fighting for centuries for their liberty; they have disappeared into Siberia, swallowed up in the gigantic forests where they must slowly die as they cannot stand the climate. Where are the thousands and tens of thousands of Estonians, Latvians and Lithuanians? They do not exist any more; every day they are being sent to Siberia, to labour there in the hardest conditions and perish from the face of the earth. This fate awaits every country and people which lets itself fall into their [Soviet] clutches. . . .[3]

At the Sixth Party Congress on 3 November 1952 he returned to the theme: "Has Soviet imperialism not made of the former independent European countries such as Czechoslovakia, Poland, Hungary, Romania, Bulgaria and so on, mere colonies in the heart of Europe? Not to speak of the enslavement of the Baltic states before the war. . . ."[4]

Tito's popularity peaked and though the Soviet danger loomed, the people, particularly in Belgrade, seemed possessed by a devil-may-care attitude, evoking memories of the short-lived euphoria after the March 1941 *coup* when, once before, a Yugoslav David, in the person of the little King, had taken on another Goliath.

In practice, as we saw, however, Tito was not ready to forfeit his monopoly of power. And, as he showed when he disavowed Milovan Djilas, he recognized that denunciations of the Soviet dictatorship could not have failed to raise questions about his own one-man rule, which derived its legitimacy from the same source. It was vital for his political survival that the economic and military aid which he needed from the West was not made conditional on a continuation of his quarrel with Moscow. In the post-Stalin era, he was thus able to return to the safer issues of "proletarian interna-tionalism" without antagonizing his Western backers. Indeed he ordered that open assaults on Soviet imperialism, of the kind he had himself delivered, were in future to be treated as a criminal offence—as they still are today.

As we know from the Khrushchev memoirs, the Soviet leaders, on their side, were by no means unanimous in wanting the return of the renegade. Khrushchev says that he himself regarded Tito as "a lively person and a simple man" and judged him "a good Communist and a man of principle", but that his colleagues still needed persuading. "After 1956, we set up a special commission to decide whether Yugoslavia had become a capitalist state and it reported back: banks and all means of production were socially owned. And the state relied on the dictatorship of the proletariat [Leninist euphemism for Communist dictatorship]. I never had any doubt, but it took an authoritative commission to prove it to the others."[5]

It has to be said that both a mastery of double-speak and an appropriate international climate were prerequisites for the survival of a régime, which, to this day, is underpinned ideologically by the East and economically by the West. But it was primarily Tito's own dominant personality, his wartime legend and his engagingly friendly manner which made this possible. His favourite home in the Adriatic island of Brioni became a place of international pilgrimage. Khrushchev and Bulganin were followed, later in the same year, by John Foster Dulles, a symbol of anti-Communism who was enchanted by his reception. A year later John's brother Alan, Director of the CIA, listed Yugoslavia among "the free nations of the world".[6]

The Western powers never tried to bring Yugoslavia into the North Atlantic Alliance nor even to put pressure on Tito to respect the Balkan Pact which he had just signed with Greece and Turkey. All that was hoped was that this strategically important stretch of territory, which had extracted itself from the Soviet bloc and now depended on Western aid, would be set towards neutrality.

A policy of genuine neutralism would indeed have commended itself to the many educated Yugoslavs, who shared Western cultural traditions. But Tito and his men, engaged then as now, in the struggle to defend their monopoly of power, could rightly have feared that there would have been something dangerous and subversive in getting too close to Europe's established neutrals: Finland, Sweden, Switzerland and Austria. All of them had opted for a multiparty political system and for competitive rather than a collectivized economy, and were not the kind of people with whom the Yugoslav Communists could comfortably re-align.

Before being readmitted into good Communist company, Tito therefore began to seek friendships outside Western Europe, and it was in the colonial world that he found other charismatic, anti-capitalist leaders like himself. The most important of them and the co-founder of the non-aligned movement were Indian leader Pandit Nehru and Egyptian dictator Gamal Abdel Nasser. From then on Tito's declared policy of non-alignment did not merely mean not belonging to either of the big power blocs. It acquired a positive stance: an association with what later came to be called "the Third World", which had anti-colonial antecedents and was and remains dominantly anti-Western.

The establishment of a Yugoslav mission in New Delhi in 1949 was a first step in the new direction. It was followed soon afterwards by the despatch to Burma of Yugoslav military aid. Later, Tito sent his associates to help set up an Asian Socialist International and in the summer of 1953 arms were also being delivered and links established with the newly radicalized Egypt.

The first head of state to visit Tito's Yugoslavia was the Emperor Haile Selassie of Ethiopia, welcomed as an early pioneer in the anti-Fascist struggle. In 1955, Tito returned the Emperor's call and then went on to India and came home by way of Egypt. Here he held the first of many meetings with Colonel Nasser, who came to regard Tito as his spiritual father and whose signed photograph was always on his desk.[7]

Between themselves, the ex-colonial countries had little in common apart from burning resentment against their former masters. Nevertheless in 1955, even before Yugoslavia's links with them were institutionalized into the "non-aligned movement", they had already held their first summit in Bandung, Indonesia and had resolved to unite against any form of Western dominance and to blame the West for all the forms of slavery, poverty and exploitation suffered in the Southern hemisphere.

In Yugoslav history books however the new movement started not at Bandung (where the Chinese were the moving force) but one year later at Brioni, on the occasion of a joint visit by Nasser and Nehru, the Indian leader being the first to coin the term non-aligned. "In the harsh winter of the world, the Brioni meeting was more than a symbolic event," wrote the editor of an authorized and glossily illustrated book on non-alignment, published in Sarajevo in 1982. "It was a genuine call to the conscience of mankind, a vernal announcement of new forces that would offer the peoples of the world the way to extract themselves from the labyrinth of suffering and from all forms of subordination and colonial gloom." In the event, no new forces emerged and in the subsequent decades most of the newly emancipated peoples suffered from hunger, war, chaos and internecine slaughter: often all four at once. But, in terms of rhetorical flourish, the movement never looked back.

The Russians took some time before recognizing that the non-aligned movement could profitably be turned, as Kardelj had once suggested, into an adjunct of anti-American policy. Indeed, its anti-colonial principles commended themselves to the Americans, who traced their own political system to a rebellion against an imperial power and, at first, they greeted the movement with more eagerness than the Russians. The benevolent attitude is reflected in an academic study, *Yugoslavia and the Non-Aligned World* by A. Rubinstein, published by Princeton University and financed by the Simon Guggenheim Foundation. "The heroic period of non-alignment", which Rubinstein dates between 1955 and 1964, is attributed to "Tito's forthright advocacy of the independence of all colonial peoples". Sharing Tito's post-1953 oblivion of the peoples colonized by the Russians (a *volte face* from Tito's 1951 pronouncements), Rubinstein felt able to commend Tito for having maintained "a constantly principled position". Reflecting the general pessimism of American intellectuals, Rubinstein affirmed that "socialism" (used here in its Marxist sense) "is the most potent word in the twentieth century." The author accepted as inevitable that the ex-colonies should be "more suspicious of the West than of the USSR", and so justified Tito's dual role: advocate of a Marxist–Leninist world and also spokesman of the non-aligned.[8]

Tito found no difficulty in accommodating his reconciliation with the Russians to the new linkages he was forming with the ex-colonies. He was more than ready to swallow his words about Stalin's colonialism (which Stalin's successors never reversed) and to fall in line with his new overseas associates identifying imperialism exclusively with the West. (Later when a term to describe Soviet global expansion was needed the non-aligned preferred the less loaded word "hegemonism".)

As for Khrushchev, having won his battle against Tito's opponents, he was free to blame the earlier rupture on Stalin's "shameless rule" and to announce that the "abnormal relations" between the two countries had been liquidated. Normal relations, in

Khrushchev's sense of the word, were no more than the readmission of Yugoslavia into a now more loosely articulated Soviet bloc.

With aid now pouring from the West, Tito was careful not to lose his inter-bloc bargaining position. When Khrushchev tried to use the fortieth anniversary of the Bolshevik revolution as an occasion to negotiate tighter links between all the Communist ruling parties, Yugoslavia kept its distance. The former Yugoslav ambassador to Moscow, Veljko Mićunović, recalled that Tito's delegation led by Kardelj avoided embarrassing confrontations by staying in the villa allotted to them on the Lenin Hills (where they discovered that their Russian hosts had installed nineteen microphones) and whiled away the time playing cards.[9]

By then Stalin's planned invasion was part of a forgotten world and indeed Mićunović points out that it was in the military field that the association between Yugoslavia and the USSR was closest: "It is our armies, which in the main carry on our joint struggle, which symbolizes the comradeship-in-arms and the close links which were formed in the past. The Russians are very strong in the manufacture of weapons and military equipment and it is in this, more than anything else, that they can put us in a position of dependence in view of our need for arms."

While the Western leaders went on supplying weapons which they supposed the Yugoslavs needed against the Russians, the military ties linking Moscow and Belgrade, though loose and stretched, were never broken. For, as Mićunović reflected: "The imposition of limitations on Yugoslavia's independence in domestic and foreign policies has been the central issue of all quarrels that have so far taken place between the USSR and Yugoslavia. It will probably be the same in the future." Tito contested the degree but not the existence of these limitations.

In the last resort, as events in Hungary and later in Czechoslovakia were to show, Tito could be relied on to rally to Moscow. The popularization of the idea of National Communism, first postulated by the Yugoslavs, is sometimes held (in the West as well as the East) to have inspired the East European demands for more independence. But after Khrushchev's speech at the Twentieth Congress in February 1956 the East Europeans did not need Tito's help to appreciate that Moscow's grip was weakening, and this was what triggered the subsequent eruptions. Indeed when in 1956 enraged Hungarians began hanging local Party officials and security policemen from the lamp-posts of Budapest, their comrades in nearby Belgrade had even greater reason to tremble than those in Moscow.

Before deciding to send in the tanks, Khrushchev took the trouble to fly to Brioni to clear the invasion with Tito. And once order had been restored, Tito told the Yugoslav Communists that, in their decision to repress the Hungarian insurrection, the Russians had been right. He deplored the circumstances which led to the trouble and the Stalinist era of repression and he conceded that not everything could be resolved by force. But he added the important proviso: "Of course, if it means saving socialism in Hungary [which in Tito's meaning of the word socialism, it certainly did], then, comrades, we can say, although we are against interference, Soviet intervention was necessary."[10]

Tito's endorsement of the Soviet invasion of Hungary must have been useful to the Russians as a counterweight to the damaging publicity which the action had elicited in Western Europe. Ostensibly it might seem surprising that after such a helpful gesture the Russians and Yugoslavs were again at odds before the end of the decade. But Khrushchev's foreign policy in the later part of the 1950s, as Professor Zagoria has shown,[11] was dominated by efforts to avoid a final breach with China and it is only in this light that his attitudes towards Yugoslavia can be understood.

At issue was the party programme which the Titoists had prepared for their Sixth Congress in 1958 and which Tito had circulated to the leaders of the other Communist countries before submitting it for the ritual rubber-stamping by his own party.

Having never been replaced or amended, this programme remains the last word on the Party line and there is in fact nothing in it which could have changed the verdict of the Kremlin Special Commission clearing Yugoslavia of charges of capitalism. Domestically, it reversed the liberalizing trends of the previous congress and reaffirmed the Party's totalitarian claim to control every aspect of human life (a claim which no Communist party, in Yugoslavia or anywhere else, has ever effectively been able to enforce). On international matters, it committed the Party unambiguously to "the great idea of proletarian socialist internationalism" and declared the conflict between capitalism and socialism to be "the decisive antagonism in modern life".[12]

The clauses on personal freedom are a posthumous tribute to George Orwell. They proclaimed the rule of law and the rights of citizens against the state but reserve the benefits exclusively for the régime's supporters: "In certain situations, the only way of establishing freedom for all is by abolishing the freedom for oppressors and for those who try to restore the oppressors [categories which only the Party can identify] . . . The great socialist, democratic, humanitarian and revolutionary goals that Yugoslav Socialism has set itself can be achieved more quickly and less painfully if the enemies of socialism are allowed no opportunity to introduce obstacles and disturbances into our internal social life. . . ."[13]

In a manifest effort to conciliate Moscow the programme justified the creation of the Warsaw Pact, declaring it "a natural defensive reaction" to the Atlantic Alliance and to German rearmament—Tito preferring to forget that the Western military coalition and the reaffirmation of US concern for Europe had probably saved Yugoslavia from Stalin's projected invasion.

Yet Khrushchev was still reluctant to concede that a Communist country could stay outside the Soviet bloc and, in Marxist terms, the programme was heretical insofar as it attributed the danger of war not to the innate war-mongering of imperialism but to the existence of two hostile military blocs.

Initially, however, Khrushchev was anxious to keep the campaign against Yugoslavia within sober limits. As Zagoria pointed out, "he still considered Tito was useful for a number of Soviet diplomatic purposes"—and Tito evidently thought so too. It was only after the Chinese broke off relations with Yugoslavia in May 1958 and launched into vituperation on the Stalinist 1948 level that the Soviet leader, in a final effort to placate Peking, sharpened his differences with Belgrade from mild reproval (unlike the Chinese he had gone on referring to Tito and his men as "Comrades") and followed the Chinese towards overt hostility. An opportunity was provided at a Bulgarian Party Congress when Khrushchev set a new line, naming Yugoslavia "a Trojan horse within the Communist movement".

As Sino-Soviet reconciliation proved impossible, the Yugoslav issue became irrelevant. Khrushchev no longer needed to sustain his anti-Yugoslav stance and could allow himself to be publicly reconciled to Tito, a man whom he evidently found personally congenial. Temperamentally they were very different. Khrushchev impulsive and hot-headed, Tito cold and self-disciplined —qualities no doubt reinforced during his experiences as a Comintern agent. Yet socially the two men had much in common: both were anti-intellectual from peasant stock and both had cocked snooks at other leading Party members drawn from the better educated élite. By 1962 the Trojan horse was forgotten and during

Tito's visit to Moscow that year he received the outstanding honour of being invited to address the Supreme Soviet. He took the occasion to deplore "the artificial barriers" which separated the two countries. Then early in 1964, after a meeting in Leningrad, he and Khrushchev issued a joint communiqué calling for a "monolithic structure for the Communist and Workers' movements, based on Marxist–Leninist principles".

Khrushchev's downfall in October of that year surprised Tito as well as himself. Nothing more was ever heard of "the monolithic structure" though Tito was quick to reassure the new leadership of his goodwill: "We will continue constructively to promote close co-operation with the Soviet Union and with other socialist countries."

Tito's promotion of his new, non-aligned movement may have contributed to his usefulness to the Russians. In Belgrade in 1961 he presided over the First Summit meeting of non-aligned leaders, and a former British Ambassador suggested that by lining up such a number of political leaders, "some of them of particular interest to the USSR", he had made himself a more valuable partner. And Tito on his side by sharpening the anti-Western tone of the proceedings may have been working his passage back into Moscow's favour.

The crucial international issue at the time was how the world would react to the Soviet nuclear explosions, which happened to coincide with the non-aligned conference and were on a bigger scale and far more powerful than any atomic tests carried out before or since. The tests were not only a breach of the moratorium agreed three years previously with the USA and United Kingdom in Geneva, they were also a defiant rejection of an anti-nuclear appeal from the Bandung conference which had been attended by almost all of Tito's guests. Yet, after a private meeting with the Soviet Ambassador to Belgrade, Tito successfully managed to scotch all initiatives for associating the non-aligned summit with the world-wide protests.

It was during the 1960s that the Soviet Union came round to accepting the Kardelj viewpoint that non-alignment could be a useful weapon in the East–West ideological confrontation. The movement was given hyperbolic treatment in books and pamphlets published in the Soviet Union (30 were shown at the New Delhi 1983 Summit Conference) and the Soviet leadership adopted what is still today the Party line: the invincibility of the combined forces of the peoples of the non-aligned countries and of the Communist bloc, predestined to join in a common struggle against the imperialists of the West. The official benediction was pronounced in Berlin in 1967, where a conference of Communist parties declared: "The movement of non-aligned countries, which includes the majority of the developing countries, is one of the most important forces in world politics. It renders an active contribution to the fight for peace, security, détente and equal co-operation, for the establishment of a just system of international and economic relations and to the struggle against imperialism, colonialism and neo-colonialism and all forms of domination and exploitation." In 1973 Brezhnev sent a personal message to the Algerian Summit, declaring that the Soviet bloc were the movement's "natural allies".

In the West some doubts were raised over Tito's readmission to Moscow's good graces but the State Department never wavered in its belief that the only alternative to Titoism was a totally Sovietized Yugoslavia. Though by this time direct aid, except in the military sphere, was tapering off, Yugoslavia still received surplus food from America and enjoyed easy access to low interest loans. Further, the World Bank and IMF, incited by the US, were making additional funds available while then—as now—discreetly waiving the conditions normally imposed on recipients of credit: notably a single exchange-rate, fair-trading practices and progress towards convertibility.

Tito's great stroke of luck at the time was President Kennedy's choice of George Kennan as US Ambassador to Belgrade. He arrived in 1961, the year of the first non-aligned Summit, with extensive experience of Eastern Europe and delighted to find Yugoslavia far less oppressive and suspicious than the countries of the Soviet bloc. Yugoslavia, as he recalled in his eloquent memoirs, appealed both to his aesthetic and to his historic sensibilities.[14] Yet, though he admired and liked the Yugoslav people, he expressed one important reservation: "Under all this charm and hospitality there lay a relatively low threshold of violence." The relief that this threshold was never crossed was perhaps a main reason why Kennan turned into an apologist and later into an active supporter of Titoism. A man of Kennan's integrity, intelligence and implacable non-conformity might have been expected to feel repelled by the totalitarian aspects of the creed. The prevention of violence was the extenuating circumstance which recommended the system not only to him but also to a great majority of Western diplomats who, then and later, were

happily accredited to Tito and his successors. Peace reigned in
Belgrade. By the time Kennan arrived the American ecstasy over
Tito's breach with Stalin was beginning to subside. In Washington DC, for the first time since 1948, the lobby of Yugoslav
emigrants (over half a million) were finding it possible to pressure
their congressional representatives against aid to a Communist
régime, even one which was anti-Soviet.

It was this lobby which sabotaged Kennan's efforts to smooth
relations with Belgrade. They are portrayed in his book as relics of
pro-Axis forces, defying America's wartime allies. The community
did include war-criminals (and indeed the CIA had helped some
of these to escape), though for the most part they were no more
anti-Communist than other Americans. Their reputation was
tarnished by a handful of Croats of Ustasha provenance, who
mounted terrorist actions against Tito's representatives abroad.
(The Yugoslav secret police retaliated in kind—so that when in
1979, the White House denounced Colonel Qadhafi for exporting
terrorism, he was able to retort: "Why this country? When Tito
does it nobody complains!") But the general run of anti-Titoist
Yugoslavs in the USA, like other émigrés from Eastern Europe,
did no more than take every occasion to protest against what they
perceived as the seizure of power in their own countries by a
Communist minority, which had never submitted itself to free
elections. And, in the person of the Senator from Wisconsin,
William Proxmire, the Yugoslav émigrés found a powerful champion. For a brief time the Senator and the anti-Titoists prevailed
against Kennan, despite the latter's special links with Kennedy,
who accorded him the unusual privilege of communicating directly with the White House. Proxmire persuaded the US legislature
to exclude Yugoslavia from the list of countries receiving US food
surpluses and from the benefits proffered in the Most Favoured
Nation accord (which, as Kennan bitterly recalled, the Serbs had
enjoyed ever since 1881, when the Kingdom signed its first
agreement with the United States). Kennan was particularly
outraged when Congress forced the President to include Yugoslavia in the list of captive nations: implying the expectations that
they would one day be liberated. "By this," wrote Kennan, "we
were morally committed to the overthrow of the Yugoslav government." It seems not to have occurred to him that the reverse was
also true, as Tito frequently supported anti-capitalist resolutions.

Proxmire made the dispute public in an article accusing Tito of
helping the Russians "by proselytizing the newly emerging coun-

tries of Asia and Africa in what he [Tito] calls international proletarianism."[15] This was indeed what Tito was telling the Russians but it was not what his representatives were saying in Washington nor indeed what American officials wanted to think. Kennan himself knew enough about Communism to accept Tito's ideological leanings: "The Soviet dominated Communist movement remains for Tito, through all vicissitudes, his European family and it was its opinion of him not ours that really counted." In Kennan's view, however, as long as Yugoslavia remained outside the Warsaw Pact, ideology did not matter. He observed that after 1948, the Soviet Union had lost its easy access to the Adriatic naval bases and claimed that, since then, the Yugoslav Army provided "a highly successful barrier" between the Warsaw Pact and NATO's southern flank: "Needless to say, this constituted a vast improvement on the situation which had prevailed in the period before Yugoslavia's break with Moscow. The Western powers, therefore, had an important stake in its preservation."

After Kennan had been overruled he resigned and while he was waiting to go home, he was invited for a private visit to Brioni. This gave him the chance, on an informal basis, to set out what he felt should be "sensible mutual expectations" between Yugoslavia and the United States. The Americans would agree that Yugoslavia would remain "a socialist state" and, on world issues, continue "to manifest a high degree of solidarity with other socialist countries". On the other hand, it would not join the Warsaw Pact or "make any special arrangements for military collaboration with the USSR". In return, the US would offer good credit terms for the sale of surplus food, revive the Most Favoured Nation Treaty and provide spare parts for military equipment already delivered. The Americans would also do their best to encourage favourable relations between Yugoslavia and Western Europe. Over drinks at Brioni, Tito cheerfully endorsed Kennan's plan. Soon after the ex-Ambassador came home the US boycott was lifted and in effect the Americans carried out their side of the Kennan proposals. And, as time went on, State Department officials, less well-informed than Kennan, brought themselves to believe that Tito was indeed doctrinally non-aligned.

In the Kennan–Proxmire dispute, it is received wisdom that Kennan was right. But Khrushchev's memoirs describing Nasser's relations with the Communist bloc fully confirm Proxmire's indictment of Tito for his proselytizing role:

At first we were unimpressed by Nasser, unsure whether he would create a progressive régime. He still hadn't touched the banks and the bourgeoisie. Tito replied that Nasser lacked political experience and if we gave him the benefit of the doubt we might later be able to exert our influence on him, both in the interests of the communist movement and of the Egyptian people. . . . When Tito and I met, he always defended Nasser vigorously and praised him to the skies. He always said that we might help Egypt, and he was absolutely right. . . .[16]

And in the subsequent years, contrary to Kennan's expectations, Tito did indeed make a whole number of "special arrangements for military collaboration with the USSR". They were particularly important in the Middle East, where it was Tito rather than the Russians who set the pace. For it was as an eager protagonist of the Palestinian Liberation Organization, seen to be analogous with Yugoslavia's Partisans, that Tito identified himself with radical movements in the Middle East, sharing the mantle of gallant guerrilla with the PLO leader, Yasser Arafat, who liked attending non-aligned conferences in battledress, carrying a gun. And therefore it was with Tito's active support that, in the post-Khrushchev era, the Russians actively involved themselves in Middle Eastern affairs and built up a large naval force in the Mediterranean. This was all the more welcome after the 1967 *coup* in Greece, where the Colonels who had seized power, unlike those in Egypt (though equally illiberal), were of right-wing rather than left-wing extraction and could therefore be seen in Belgrade as a potential challenge.

Having extended their attention beyond Europe, the Russians fell in with the Yugoslavs and started sending large consignments of weapons and munitions to Egypt. In the period before the Six Day War in 1967 Tito and Nasser met no less than seventeen times and it seems impossible that Tito was not consulted when, on 16 May, Nasser expelled the United Nations peace-keeping force and announced on Radio Cairo: "This is our chance, Arabs, to deal Israel a mortal blow of annihilation."[17]

The collapse of the Egyptian and Syrian armies, despite their numerical superiority and up-to-date equipment, evidently took both Tito and the Russians by surprise. The Soviet defector and former tank commander Boris Suvorov later recalled that, in the Officers' Mess at Kharkov, during the hostilities, everyone was expecting a radio announcement that the Soviet tanks (of which their own units were deprived) would by now be rumbling through the streets of Tel Aviv.[18]

In coming to Nasser's rescue Tito made himself an *ad hoc* member of the Warsaw Pact. He personally attended two ministerial meetings of the Pact countries, the first during, and the second immediately after, hostilities. No minutes of the meetings were ever published but Tito was reported to have pleaded for direct military intervention. After the meetings, he and his Warsaw Pact colleagues issued a joint communiqué blaming the war on "a conspiracy of certain imperialist powers, the United States in the first place, against the Arab countries".

The 1967 war was the first of many occasions in which Yugoslavia allowed the Soviet Air Force overflying and refuelling facilities. When Nasser's ambassador in Belgrade called on Tito to make sure there would be no delays, he was told "as far as Egypt is concerned, I am not non-aligned".[19]

The provisional incorporation of Yugoslavia into the Warsaw Pact needed explaining and Tito summoned an extraordinary meeting of the Central Committee to endorse his new line. The resolution, presumably drafted in Tito's office, linked Israel's pre-emptive attack with the war in Vietnam: "Both parts of the planned and long-range offensive strength of the imperialist forces in the world, particularly the United States."

Between the Middle Eastern wars of 1967 and 1973, in both of which Belgrade and Moscow worked together, their military collaboration was interrupted by the Czech crisis. The vast majority of the Yugoslav people, including a large part of the Communist Party, were highly sympathetic to the "Prague Spring" and Tito hoped Soviet intervention would not be necessary. In July 1968 the Yugoslav Central Committee allowed itself a highly independent attitude:

> The LCY takes the position that the working class and its Communist Party and other socialist and progressive forces in Czechoslovakia are the only ones called upon to assess the situation in their country and to solve the problems that have been piling up over a number of years. . . . The CC of the LCY feels that any outside action representing interference or an effort to limit the independence of the CP of Czechoslovakia or, in any way whatsoever, to jeopardize the sovereignty of Czechoslovakia would have given consequences for development of socialism in Czechoslovakia and in the world.

The news of military intervention aroused paroxysms of rage in Belgrade and a few days afterwards 300,000 people attended a protest meeting in the Marx-Engels Square. It was addressed by a well-known Communist veteran, Mijalko Todorović, who declared that in Czechoslovakia at that moment "they are breaking the spines of true patriots". In denouncing "Soviet National-Fascism" Todorović was cheered to the echo; within a few months however he had disappeared from public life and Tito had gone back to the notion of Communist solidarity.

Contrary to a view widely held in the West, the Yugoslavs have never specifically repudiated what came to be known as "the Brezhnev doctrine": the proposition that the Soviet Union has the right to intervene militarily to preserve a Communist régime. A few days before the invasion, in August 1968, Tito had been to Prague and had spoken of the dangers of Western imperialism and German *revanchisme*, implicitly warning the Czechs not to go too far. Later he claimed that his talks with Dubček convinced him that the Czech leadership was determined to prevent "any attempt by anti-socialist elements to hinder the normal development of democracy and the normal socialist development". After the Soviet invasion, he protested, "the entry of military units into Czechoslovakia, without invitation or consent by the legal government, has given us the cause for deep concern. By this step the sovereignty of a *socialist* [my italic] country has been violated and trampled upon and a serious blow inflicted on socialist and progressive forces all over the world."

At his Party's Ninth Congress Tito went further: "In some East European countries there appeared an acceptable doctrine about 'collective', 'integrated' and, in essence, restricted, sovereignty. This doctrine negates, in the name of an alleged higher degree of relationship among socialist countries, the sovereignty of these countries and strives to make it legal for one country to impose its will upon other *socialist* [my italic] countries, according to their own judgement, even by means of military intervention."

It was plain from these speeches that the issue which divided Tito and Brezhnev was whether or not in Dubček's Czechoslovakia "socialism" (in the Communist sense of the word) was at risk. For what Tito was implying, as he had done over Hungary, was that if Communism had been at risk, the Soviet Union would have been right to send in the tanks. Dubček's commitment to the Communist cause, as Tito told his Congress, had been confirmed in their joint communiqué after the Prague meeting. Yet, those

who witnessed the intellectual turmoil in Prague generally agree
that, whatever the communiqués said, by the time the Russians
arrived, the whole one-party edifice was crumbling. Indeed, that
view was confirmed many years later by Tito's deputy, Kardelj:
"During the so-called Czech crisis, a search for a really democratic
and simultaneously socialist way out of the troubles was made
impossible by the inundation of empiricist, liberal phrases. This,
of course, subsequently meant calling in a third power on to the
scene."[20] For Tito, as for Kardelj, there had to be a limit on what
the Russians could be expected to allow.

Tito used the excitement that followed the Czech crisis, to
reorganize his armed forces. It has been generally assumed, not
only abroad but also at home, that the new system was designed to
resist the application of the Brezhnev Doctrine to Yugoslavia. In
fact, reorganization by that time was anyway essential. The
former reliance on the regular army operating under a single
command had not only become too expensive, it also collided with
the growing demand among Communist cadres for the decentralization of power from Belgrade to the provinces (see next chapter).

The Jacobin concept of "a nation at arms" (wrongly attributed
by Yugoslav leaders to Karl Marx) had first been tried out by the
Serb ruler, Prince Michael Obrenović, almost a hundred years
before. In the 1968 conditions, the new territorial units, serving
under local command and drawing on the Partisan tradition were
manifestly a cheaper and more acceptable method of mobilization.

There is no doubt that after the Czech crisis, relations between
Tito and Brezhnev went through a frosty patch. The Russians
accused the Yugoslavs of extending asylum to Czech rebels and in
Belgrade and Zagreb wildly anti-Russian feelings were openly
expressed. None the less, the quarrel between the two leaderships
blew over remarkably fast. Too fast, in fact, to sustain the generally accepted belief that a threatened Soviet invasion was the real
reason why the whole Yugoslav defence system was reorganized.
Before the end of the year Tito was publicly warning the press "not
to over-dramatize" the differences: "The Soviet Union and
ourselves have an inherent interest in good relations, since we are
both socialist countries." Though in 1969 the Yugoslavs did not
attend the International Conference of Communist Parties, the
participants, including Dubček's Soviet-appointed successor,
issued a public statement declaring themselves "completely in
favour" of a further rapprochement between the USSR and
Yugoslavia.

In 1971 and 1972 the liberals inside Yugoslavia were treating Tito to his own series of "Prague springs" (see next chapter) and on these occasions, though he did not need Brezhnev's proffered military help, he did turn to the Russians for funds. By now, he had come to see that the increasingly intimate links with the Western democracies were exercising a destabilizing impact on his own régime and he guessed rightly that, after the Czech upheaval, the Russians would be ready to pay a considerable price to rescue Communism—even of the heterodox Yugoslav variety—from collapse.

Indeed in 1972 the Soviet government provided a credit reportedly of 1.3 billion dollars (the figure was never officially confirmed), a sum far greater than the Yugoslavs were then receiving from the World Bank, and which in political terms was to prove itself a sound investment. Tito was now free to turn his attention to suppressing internal opposition and to tightening Party orthodoxy (see Chapter 7). And, as an additional bonus for the Russians, *Komunist* (the Yugoslav party organ) was able to list among the liberals who had been dismissed from leading positions, three markedly pro-Western federal ministers "who had failed to sustain a class position in our foreign policy".[21]

In the Yom Kippur War of 1973, Tito's collaboration with the Russians was as close as it had been in 1967. Already at the beginning of 1970, overflying and refuelling rights had again been extended by the Yugoslavs for another massive Soviet airlift, this time designed to strengthen Egyptian defences on the Suez Canal. After hostilities broke out, between 10 and 23 October, the number of flights of Soviet aircraft over Yugoslavia was reported to have exceeded one thousand.[22]

By the mid-1970s, the Czech events were so far forgotten that on 1 May Tito felt able to tell a group of visiting Czech officers: "We are not formally members of the Warsaw Pact. But if the cause of socialism, communism of the working class, should be endangered [as the Russians could well argue it had been in Prague] we shall know where we stand. We hold our aims in common with the Soviet Union."[23]

When Sadat turned towards the United States and visited Jerusalem, Tito terminated his special relations with Egypt and lined up beside the Russians and his colleagues of the non-aligned movement, in unconditional support for the "rejectionist states". The chief beneficiaries of Yugoslavia's favours were henceforward Libya and Algeria and Iraq, pledged to continue fighting till Israel

was destroyed. Libya and Iraq were particularly valued by the
Yugoslav leadership both as suppliers of much needed oil and
willing purchasers of Yugoslav arms and equipment. Political
leaders frequently exchanged visits and Iraqi and Libyan Air
Force cadets came to Yugoslavia for their training. When Qadhafi
decided to close the access to the Gulf of Sirte, it was the Yugoslavs
who provided the contact mines.[24]

Tito's willingness to accommodate Soviet aircraft extended to
Africa as well as the Middle East. In his analysis *Yugoslavia and the
Soviet Policy of Force in the Mediterranean*, written for the Centre of
Naval Analyses, Milan Vego gives two lists of cases of Soviet use of
Yugoslav air space between 1967 and 1978. The first relates to
crisis-related airlifts: in 1967 for Syria and Egypt and then for
South Yemen, in 1970 for Egypt, 1973 for Egypt and Syria, 1975
and 1976 for Angola (Castro had visited Tito and obtained his
approval before sending in troops) and November 1976, 1977 and
1978 for Ethiopia. The rescue operation to support Ethiopia
against Somalia was the biggest Soviet airlift ever assembled and
reportedly involved fifteen per cent of all Soviet air transport. And
Yugoslav assistance on this occasion had no ideological motivation. For Somalia had set up what it called a Marxist–Leninist
dictatorship several years ahead of Ethiopia (though, as in the rest
of Africa, the definition Marxist–Leninist in the absence of trained
Communist cadres was hardly more than an epithet for a régime
using revolutionary rhetoric and accepting Soviet arms and in-
structors).

But although Somalia was also a fully accredited and indeed
senior member of the non-aligned movement, it was Ethiopia
which dominated the Horn of Africa and for the Soviet Union and
their Yugoslav associates, was therefore the side to back. Deprived
of Soviet supplies, Somalia turned—as Tito had once done—to
the United States for military and economic rescue. Following
Tito's footsteps, however, did not earn them his sympathy or
approval and he continued to help the Russians in their intervention on Ethiopia's behalf.

In his list of non-crisis operations, Vego notes overflights in aid
of Egypt, India, Syria, Tanzania, Guinea, Libya, Mali, Somalia
(before the change of sides), Chad, Algeria and Nigeria. Almost all
these countries were also receiving arms and political support
directly from Yugoslavia.

On the naval side, he noted that, though there were no official
Soviet bases on the Adriatic, their warships in the Mediterranean,

and the large fleet of commercial ships which kept these warships supplied, made constant use of Yugoslav docking and repair facilities. At Kotor Bay in Montenegro, special docking facilities were available for large ships which could only have been required to meet Soviet needs. When Soviet ships, including submarines, were anchored in Yugoslav ports, the public was—and still is—excluded from the surrounding areas.

All in all, however, Khrushchev's judgement of Tito as "a good Communist" was ultimately vindicated even more in political than military terms. With his left-wing and guerrilla credentials, Tito offered the leaders of the new countries the model of the charismatic leader, who had seized power, eliminated opposition, confiscated property, richly rewarded his followers (giving them a vested interest in preserving the régime) and made himself leader for life. Though only a minority declared themselves Marxist–Leninists—in some cases officially placing themselves under Soviet protection—the overwhelming majority of the leaders, whether soldiers or civilians, whether right or left, were at one with Tito in rejecting Western concepts of the rule of law and in abolishing any traditional or constitutional restraints on their exercise of power.

Not that in promoting non-alignment Tito's motives were exclusively ideological. Straddling the world as leader of a vast international movement suited his personality. It confirmed his stature as international statesman (the non-aligned summit conference came to attract some 1,000 journalists and broadcasters) and it offered him ample opportunity, over three decades, to indulge his lifelong propensity for foreign travel. In his eighties, he was still visiting a dozen capitals and two or three continents a year. And, at least in the early phases, many of his compatriots took a proxy satisfaction in seeing such a fuss being made of the leader of their small and previously neglected country.

Tito's biggest single contribution to the Soviet cause was to help redirect the hostility of the non-aligned movement from the disappearing issue of "colonialism", i.e. direct rule, towards neocolonial, i.e. indirect rule, through economic control. For, as the European empires disintegrated, it was only by shifting the focus of attack from political to economic issues that there could be any way of sustaining anti-Western passions and implicitly pro-Soviet policies. No one knew better than Tito how to combine tear-jerking demands for Western aid with implacably anti-Western rhetoric.

The world climate was propitious. The leaders of the newly formed states had encouraged their peoples to expect that once they were rid of their colonial masters, they would live as well as their former colonizers. A capitalist conspiracy, mounted by Western governments and multinational corporations, provided the indispensable scapegoat to attenuate the subsequent disillusion.

Under the grandiose title, the New International Economic Order, this policy was launched by the non-aligned countries in 1973, after the imposition of the Arab oil boycott. This itself gave weak and primitive countries the illusion that they now had the industrialized West at their mercy. The new programme, which became a permanent plank in Yugoslav foreign policy, required a massive transfer of resources and technology from the industrialized countries to the developing world: the Russians to be excluded on the grounds that, as they were anti-imperialist, world poverty was not their fault. Inspired by the tenets of Marxism–Leninism the New Order would operate on an exclusively government-to-government basis. Private enterprises, and more specifically the multinational corporations, considered inherently malevolent, were to be severely curbed.

The New Order which Tito preached, and, when ever circumstances permit, his successors go on preaching, was based on the premise that the whole developing world shared a common interest. An analysis of the composition of what the United Nations calls the less developed countries (LDCs) by Professor Alan E. Goodman, Dean of the Foreign Service Programme of Georgetown University, forcefully demonstrated the reverse.[25] Of the one-and-three-quarter billion people who lived in these countries, Goodman calculated that roughly one-third, inhabiting 24 countries, had either physical or human resources which enabled them to enjoy incomes above world averages. All these aimed at maximizing their earnings and gaining access to markets, capital and technology. Some 72 other countries contained some but not all the necessary ingredients of growth. These needed trade preferences, economic assistance and government-sponsored "soft" loans. The rest lived in extreme poverty and needed external help to feed their people.

Since President Truman's time, the voluntary transfer of capital by Western governments to the undeveloped regions had become a regular feature of Western policies. Indeed, American donations to Asia, Africa and Latin America far exceeded the sums which the

Marshall Plan provided for European reconstruction. Predictably however free enterprise countries, better run and more productive, not only remained much richer than the rest of the world but the gap between them was constantly growing larger. To many in the West this seemed inherently unfair and they felt a justifiable sense of guilt when they heard of the destruction of domestic food surpluses at times when millions of human beings were dying of hunger. A number of alternative programmes for helping the developing countries were for that reason put forward in the West both by institutions and by individual experts. They were designed to be more acceptable than Tito's New Order to the non-Marxist world which would have to pick up the bill. These included the Utopian *Programme for Survival*,[26] sponsored by the former German Chancellor Willie Brandt, envisaging something close to a global welfare state alongside more modest plans, favouring trade rather than aid, and which would leave the human problems of famine and disease to privately funded charitable foundations.

But Tito, by then in his ninth decade, went on promoting a programme which could never conceivably commend itself to those countries which had anything to give. "The developing countries have no need for so-called aid, through which they are generally provided with an insignificant part of what is being taken away from them under the present system of international relations. That is why this superannuated system must, once and for all, be changed in favour of the New International Economic Order, including a thorough reform of international credit and monetary institutions. . . ."[27]

The first, and still the only, US Ambassador to Belgrade who challenged America's benevolent view of Titoism, was Lawrence Silbermann. In *Foreign Affairs*, Spring 1977, he argued that, despite their expressions of goodwill, in practice the Yugoslavs did their utmost to stir up anti-American feelings. He cited cases in which Yugoslav officials in Belgrade had circulated information about Washington which he knew to be false, including allegations of US assistance to Croat terrorists. Though he conceded that, in the non-aligned movement, the Yugoslavs sometimes moderated extremely pro-Soviet resolutions, he suggested that they did so only because otherwise the movement would have fallen apart. Even the re-worded resolutions, he said, changed no more than to become "grossly offensive rather than outrageous".

Opposing the Silbermann view, Western diplomats pointed to

the 1979 Non-Aligned Conference in Havana, in which Tito made his last appearance and managed to defeat two plainly pro-Soviet resolutions. The first would have accredited the representative of the Vietnam-appointed government of Kampuchea; the second would have expelled the Egyptians for participating in President Carter's peace initiative. Though the Yugoslavs were, at the time, actively denouncing the Camp David agreements and were supporting the "rejectionist" states, they knew that for a movement which depended for its effectiveness almost exclusively on its numbers, the precedent of an expulsion could have been fatal.

And while the West was applauding the Yugoslavs for resisting Soviet-sponsored resolutions and for standing up to Castro, few people noticed that they were, at the same time, distributing among the African and Asian delegations in Havana a number of English-language tracts, which had been published in Belgrade but, both in style and content, could have been compiled in Moscow. One of these included a damning indictment of the capitalist conspiracy which had allegedly inspired the Brandt report.[28]

In these circumstances the Soviet authorities could plan the invasion of Afghanistan without worrying about "Third World" reactions. Brezhnev knew he could act on the justifiable assumption that the non-aligned movement (of which Afghanistan was a senior member) would be more impressed by the balance of force than by the balance of rhetoric. Immediately after the event, a Yugoslav delegation told the UN General Assembly: "No one likes to be dominated by someone else. One likes independence. And that is what the Soviet Union has violated: a people's independence." Yet when it came to the crunch, the Yugoslavs refused a British request that they should co-sponsor a censure motion against the Soviet invasion. Further no subsequent resolutions adopted by the UN on Afghanistan until 1984 named the Soviet Union as the aggressor. The grip of the Communist propaganda machine was demonstrated too by Soviet success in conducting its colonial expedition without arousing any excitement among the students at Western universities. This was in marked contrast to the riots and disturbances provoked by the US involvement in the Vietnam war which spread all the way from Berkeley to Berlin: the presence of Soviet troops in Afghanistan was accepted as a matter of Afghan internal affairs. The Soviet nominee from the puppet Afghan government attended the non-aligned conference in New Delhi in 1982 and was accredited by the 103 delegates without dispute. At the end of that summer, the final communiqué, considerably amended from the first Indian draft, included 23 separate denunciations of the United States and none of the USSR. Doctrinally non-alignment is now elevated to being part of the Tito cult, and no Yugoslav official would dare make a foreign policy speech without including the ritual tribute. Tito's palace at Brioni has been donated to the movement as "a place for fostering its ideas and aims".

In the post-Tito era, however, Yugoslavia and the non-aligned movement are less important to each other than they were and the present leaders spend far less time on non-aligned affairs than they do on more important transactions with members of the two power blocs. In economic terms the non-aligned movement has yielded very little. Even at its peak, the proportion of Yugoslavia's trade with the developing countries never reached more than fifteen per cent and several Western firms which have invested capital in joint enterprises in Yugoslavia have been surprised and disappointed to find that products made in Yugoslavia enjoy no special access to non-aligned markets. Indeed Tito's friend and frequent visitor, Colonel Qadhafi, told Dow Chemicals, when they were setting up business in Yugoslavia, that he made it a practice to import his petro-chemicals only from the West.

By far the most important of Yugoslavia's trading partners is the Soviet Union, though the balance cannot be calculated, as exchanges are based not on money but barter. When Yugoslavs announced that they received 5.5 million tons of Soviet oil in 1983, they did not indicate how much of it was on credit nor whether the Russians extended to Yugoslavia the favourable prices ceded to the regular members of Comecon.

Increasingly as Yugoslavia's living standards decline (see Chapter 7) and the supplies of hard currency dry up, it is turning towards the Comecon bloc. Trade with the group has increased twentyfold since 1964, when the first cooperation agreement between Yugoslavia and Comecon was signed and, during that period, trade with the bloc was going up annually almost by three per cent faster than trade with the rest of the world. Yugoslavia now participates in 23 out of its 33 specialized commissions and by 1983 the Comecon countries were taking almost half of Yugoslavia's exports.[29]

Further, unlike the other Communist states, which have signed a co-operation agreement with Comecon, the Yugoslavs now send a senior member of the Federal government to attend Comecon ministerial meetings. Both in 1983 in Berlin and in 1984 in Havana the Yugoslav representative was Vice-Premier Borislav Srebrić, whose speeches were given the same prominence as those of the full Comecon participants.

The EEC, on the other hand, with which the first trade agreement was not signed until 1970, was in 1983 taking only around 23 per cent of Yugoslav exports and supplying 36 per cent of imports. It was only in the general worry about what might happen after Tito's death that the EEC Commission was hustled by member governments into signing a new cooperation pact which eliminated customs and quotas from most industrial, and from some agricultural, products. Under the arrangements made when Greece joined the EEC, the Yugoslavs complained they had lost markets for their meat worth several hundred million dollars a year. Yet when in 1982 the quotas were raised, there was not enough of the right quality meat to fill them.

Besides trade, however, Yugoslavia also depends on the EEC countries for the regular remittances from its emigrant workers and for hard currency tourism. Further, the EEC countries provide 70 per cent of the foreign loans to Yugoslavia, plus an additional 200 million dollars from the EEC investment bank (the Yugoslavs are now asking for more) to help finance the Yugoslav electricity grid and its railways and roads.

It is one of the ironies of contemporary history that the West has underwritten the present Yugoslav régime primarily because of its non-aligned status while, at the same time, from the point of view of Tito and his successors, their relationship with the developing countries has been principally useful in sustaining a continued onslaught against the Western collective conscience. In terms of physical strength, the vast conglomerate calling itself non-aligned represents nothing; most members buy their military equipment on world markets primarily for conflicts against each other. On the other hand, as the Yugoslavs learnt from experience, numbers count a great deal in the propaganda battles at the UN, Unesco and other international agencies.

The existence of an automatic anti-Western majority in the UN goes back to 1960, when the number of UN members rose from 83 to 100; it is now 160. Almost all the new recruits were from newly decolonized territories and automatically members of the non-aligned group which, between the summit conferences in Belgrade in 1961 and New Delhi in 1983, quadrupled its membership. Those non-aligned governments which have private reservations about the credibility of the New Order have not wanted to diminish the movement's effectiveness by parading its divisions.

The anti-Western pattern set in Tito's lifetime has hardened since he died. In the years between 1981 and 1982 more than 84 per cent of the non-aligned countries voted with the Soviet Union. On the 100 issues which the State Department judged to be of particular political or economic interest to the United States, the figure was 88 per cent. There were slight variations between the records of the various non-aligned countries supporting the Americans on the 100 selected issues. With a total of four pro-American votes Yugoslavia came bottom of the list. The non-aligned group, according to one Yugoslav delegate to the UN, provides "the basic influential component for democratizing the United Nations".[30] He did not show how "democratization" could be advanced by an organization working on the principle of one country, one vote, and so giving the same representation to one billion Chinese or 225 million Americans as to the peoples of Antigua and Dominica, where the totals do not reach six figures.

The significance of the votes depends only of course on the importance which Western observers attach to them. And as the Yugoslavs have been able to see, many Western politicians, diplomats and opinion-formers, take them very seriously indeed. "The present anti-American guise of the non-aligned movement can only represent a serious failure of American diplomacy since the early 1960s", wrote Richard Jackson in his book *The Non-Aligned: The UN and the Super Powers* published by the New York Council of Foreign Relations in 1984. If Jackson had read Edvard Kardelj's book *Historical Role of Non-Alignment*,[31] he might have recognized that what the Americans needed was not better diplomacy but more effective weapons of psychological warfare. Kardelj identified Marxism–Leninism as "one of the essential sources of non-aligned policy" and demanded that the existing political structures in the backward countries be replaced "by the ideology and practice of contemporary socialism".

Jackson, like Kennan and so many US diplomats before him, refused to admit any ideological components in international affairs and went so far as to claim that, after the 1948 breach with Stalin, it was the disagreement with Italy over Trieste which kept the Yugoslavs from joining the Western bloc. (The real reasons are examined in Chapter 4.) He concluded with a hopeful prediction that, in dealing with non-alignment, Tito's successors are likely "to redouble their efforts to preserve a more centralist leadership".

But is "centralist", indicating a central position between the Eastern and Western blocs, really the adjective appropriate to Yugoslavia's postwar foreign policy? It is true that since 1948 Yugoslavia has never been an obedient satellite. The evidence is heavily weighted against the thesis of the KGB defector, Golytsin, who suggests that, after Tito's initial clash with Stalin, all the subsequent squabbles were no more than part of a giant disinformation campaign.[32]

Genuine Soviet–Yugoslav differences have shown themselves on many issues, and on many occasions. At least four times the Russians have withheld promised credits as an indication of political displeasure. They also have frequently unleashed and then re-leashed the irridentist claims of their Bulgarian satellite on the Yugoslav republic of Macedonia. Further, there seem to have been a number of incidents in which the Russians encouraged subversive activities by the pro-Soviet elements inside the Yugoslav Communist Party. (Though in view of Yugoslavia's judicial record, it is possible that these charges were fabricated.)

On several occasions the Yugoslavs have preserved a well-rewarded appearance of impartiality by siding publicly against Moscow. Like the Romanians, they refused to participate in the Soviet boycott of the Olympic games in Los Angeles and, going further than the Romanians, have supported the Euro-Communists in Western Europe. A speaker on Zagreb Radio in March 1984 took the Russians to task for backing a splinter Communist group against the official party in Spain, predicting this would lead "to a dangerous growth of anti-Communist and anti-Soviet sentiments".

After Mao Tse-Tung's death, both during and after Tito's time, the Yugoslavs also tried to keep a balance between the Chinese and the Russians. On 9 November 1984, the Yugoslav news agency Tanjug carried a Yugoslav criticism of an anti-Chinese article in *Pravda* in which the Russians complained that the Chinese were trying to create friction between them and three other Communist states: North Korea, Romania and Yugoslavia.

Whether the Yugoslavs ever caused the Russians any serious inconvenience is an open question. For obvious reasons, Yugoslav diplomats and journalists in their dealings with the West tend to exaggerate the differences. Anti-Soviet feeling certainly exists: the ordinary Yugoslavs including, no doubt, the vast majority of the two million Communists, know that the only threat to their country is from the Soviet Union, perhaps via Bulgaria, and it is on the northern or eastern frontiers that the Yugoslavs generally conduct their military exercises.

But, as Yugoslav recruits are repeatedly reminded, their prime job is "to defend the achievements of the revolution": a mission to which the Russians can hardly take exception. Tito and his successors seem to have regarded both their regular forces and the territorial army primarily as an instrument for sustaining internal security. Indeed, any study of the composition, equipment, ammunition, means of transport, food supplies—not to mention the wider issue of morale—rules out any possibility that the Yugoslav army, on its own, could offer any effective resistance to a full-scale Soviet invasion. Educated young Yugoslavs returning from their military service say that they are trained and indoctrinated primarily to prepare them for handling internal riots, as the Yugoslav army has already been called to do in the Kosovo region (see Chapter 6). The only resistance which the Russians could expect would be sporadic: there are individual peasants on the Northern frontier near Kikinda who keep a gun hidden and have let their neighbours know that if the Russians arrive they will shoot it out before being killed. In the wildly improbable event of the Russians attempting to occupy Yugoslavia for any length of time, they would, of course, like the Nazis, be up against guerrilla resistance in the hinterland; but most probably this would have nothing to do with any of the existing institutions.

From the NATO point of view, a pro-Tito policy is generally defended in negative terms: at least the régime has kept Yugoslavia outside the Warsaw Pact. But the recent history of Romania suggests that this is a doubtful advantage. Romania is a full member of the Pact, yet, like Yugoslavia, it refuses to allow Soviet troops on to its territory and, by 1984, was giving less support than Yugoslavia to the Soviet Union's global ventures.

For, as during Tito's day, Yugoslavia systematically supports "Movements of National Liberation": an epithet reserved exclusively for groups fighting against pro-Western régimes. Thus on a visit to Castro in 1983 the former Party Chairman, Mitja Ribičič, claimed that the basis of the friendly relations between Yugoslavia and Cuba rests on "the authentic revolution of our two countries" and lauded the contribution both were making "in the fight for socialism".[33]

The same year Grenada Radio reported "an extremely cordial

and fruitful encounter" between the Yugoslav leaders and Bernard Coard, the Grenadian Communist who later led the *coup* against another Cuban-installed left-winger, Maurice Bishop, who had himself fallen out of favour for visiting Washington.[34] During the subsequent US invasion of Grenada, the Yugoslavs joined with other non-aligned countries in protesting but could do nothing to prevent the arrest of their recent guest, and his trial on the charge of mass murder. The shadow of these events was not however allowed to darken the previously arranged visit of Mika Špiljak to President Reagan, which took place during crucial negotiations for new US credits for Yugoslavia. Nor did it prevent both leaders from affirming that Yugoslav–American relations have never been better.

A conference on Movements of National Liberation was organized by the Yugoslav Communist Youth Federation in March 1984 and according to the Tanjug news agency sent goodwill messages to "the struggling youth" of South Africa, Namibia, the PLO, the West Sahara and El Salvador. It offered no consolation to those resisting Russian rule in any of the states that Tito had once listed as Soviet colonies. Nor were any messages sent to the muhadjeen fighting against the occupiers in Afghanistan, much as the Partisans had fought in Yugoslavia 40 years before, though now in even harsher conditions and with less external aid and sympathy.

The Communists of Nicaragua have been particularly faithful to the Tito model. The Sandinista National Liberation Front initially included a whole array of other left-wing parties and responded to the same liberal and patriotic slogans which had inspired the Partisans. But in 1979, when the Party seized power, the Communists proceeded, as they had done in Yugoslavia in 1945, to eliminate their partners, to close down the non-Communist press, to take over education and the media and to set up the standard Communist-controlled mass organizations for veterans, women, youth, children, and trade unionists. On 9 November, the Yugoslav leaders sent congratulations to the Sandinistas after the electoral victory. Though, with the Americans watching, the Nicaraguan Communists had not dared to be as ruthless as Tito and his team, they were evidently headed in the right direction.

Yugoslavia's flourishing trade in light weapons (now one of its principal exports) is motivated, of course, by commercial as well as ideological considerations. No Western government has pointed out the discrepancy between the sales of guns to non-aligned associates (to be used either to fight each other or to repress internal resistance), and Yugoslavia's support for an endless flow of anti-Western "peace-loving" resolutions, regularly adopted at non-aligned summits.

Yugoslavia's Western benefactors have even agreed among themselves that, during the crisis years, Yugoslavia, though insolvent, must be provided with extra funds to enable it to continue extending unrepayable credits to the developing countries. In 1983 the governments which put together the 5 billion dollar rescue operation, which saved Yugoslavia from default, agreed to pay an additional 200 million dollars, to enable the Yugoslavs to continue to extend credits to their non-aligned partners. Yet, even where the money is used for civilian purposes, there are no indications that the Yugoslavs invest money in a socially more justifiable or constructive way than the profit-seeking commercial banks of the West. According to *Le Monde*, 16 February, 1984, Guinea, after being ruined "by years of incompetence and repression", was still spending huge sums on "prestige parade"; a superluxury hotel intended only for rare international conferences, was cited as a particularly extravagant example: it had been jointly financed by East Germany and Yugoslavia.

As Tito's successors have recognized, it is still thanks to his legend and to his authority that they go on being able to combine, on the one side, playing an active role in the world Communist movement with, on the other, continuing to receive Western financial and diplomatic support. It was Tito who played a leading role in rallying the ex-colonies under the "peace and progress" banner and it was his prestige which gave international credibility to the vociferously anti-Western non-aligned movement.

In his *History of the Modern World* Paul Johnson justifiably ridicules the reverence displayed by Western leaders for a movement which has included in its membership acknowledged cannibals like the Emperor Bokassa and General Amin, homicidal fanatics like Colonel Qadhafi and Ayatollah Khomeini, and such aligned politicians as Castro and Pham Van Dong, who survive on Soviet subsidies.[35] In failing to mention Tito however, Johnson does less than justice to the Yugoslav contribution in preserving the movement's "progressive" image and respectability among Western opinion formers.

It is easy to see why during his visit to Belgrade in 1982 the

Soviet Premier Nikolai Tikhonov felt able to say: "The USSR and all socialist countries have a high assessment of the contributions being made by the non-aligned movement to the struggle of peace, against the arms race, for preventing nuclear war and for international independence of oppressed peoples against neo-colonialism and Fascism."[36] It is less easy to see why the British Prime Minister, Margaret Thatcher, receiving her Yugoslav opposite number, Milka Planinc, in London a year later felt able to congratulate her guest on the "record of keeping the non-aligned movement truly non-aligned" or why President Reagan had to speak along the same lines during a visit from the Yugoslav Head of State, Mika Špiljak, meeting soon afterwards.

Yugoslavia's present leaders, following in Tito's footsteps, have continued to demand and to receive Western material and political support, while still penalizing any of their own citizens who publicly advocate political pluralism or private enterprise. Yet they know that it is only countries with Western forms of government which have shown themselves able to generate enough wealth to roll back Yugoslavia's debt and keep them in business. Also for the purposes of self-preservation, the collective leadership has continued to denounce and discredit Western forms of democracy and to oppose the penetration of Western capital among their associates in the non-aligned movement: Marxist–Leninist régimes have to be supported wherever they operate because, as the Yugoslavs as well as the Russians know, the fall of Communism—even as far away as Nicaragua—could set off dangerous ripples.

None of this would have been possible without Tito's leadership and legend. The Soviet politburo may sometimes have been exasperated by his demonstrations of independence and self-satisfaction; but, all in all, he had earned his little niche in Moscow.

Chapter 6

NEITHER BROTHERHOOD NOR UNITY

THE WESTERN RESOLVE to help implant and sustain a Marxist–
Leninist régime in Yugoslavia has rested principally on the belief
that only one-party rule, sanctified by the Tito legend, would be
capable of preventing the country's disparate communities from
tearing one another apart. Yet, contrary to Yugoslavia's reputation, until the massacres of the Second World War, there had been
very little internecine strife between her component nationalities;
although conquering armies had made ample use of native manpower, from the time of the Turkish Jannissaries until the 1914–18
war, when the Habsburg Emperor marched Corporal Tito against
the Serbs. But the inter-communal atrocities of the 1940s had
given Yugoslavia a bad name and when the Partisans adopted the
slogan "brotherhood and unity", while the members of the royalist government were locked in inter-communal disputes, it was the
Communists who emerged as the indispensable unifiers.

The "brotherhood and unity" platform, adopted at the AVNOJ
conference of 1943, had indicated a final Communist break with its
on-and-off support for various separatist movements which at
different times conspired to detach Croatia, Slovenia, Macedonia
and Kosovo from Serbia. During the hostilities Tito had left the
nationalities issue to his local Party chiefs and these had exploited
the patriotism of the separate communities in accordance with
tactical convenience or personal preference. Tito himself, half-
Croat and half-Slovene, showed no greater attachment to his
ethnic roots than Stalin.

The 1943 resolution committed the Communists to a single
Yugoslavia, but within a federal framework which would recognize the separate identity of the various peoples. Conclaves of
Communist leaders got to work at once delineating the new federal
boundaries. Though it was decided to retain Belgrade as the
capital it had to be made clear to the non-Serb Communists that
rule from Belgrade would in no way imply a revival of "Serb
hegemony"—the Communist charge against the defunct kingdom. As we have seen, the Serbs of Serbia had played a minor role
in Partisan fighting and, at the rank-and-file of the Partisan army,
at least until the Italian surrender, were Serb refugees from the

THE PROVINCES OF YUGOSLAVIA AND OUTLYING COUNTRIES

Ustashas, residents of Croatia and Bosnia and Montenegrins.

The Communists decided that Montenegro would form a separate republic though it contained only two per cent of the Yugoslav
population and it is highly debatable whether Montenegrins are
anything other than Serbs by another name. Montenegro had
indeed maintained a separate existence for centuries, but this was
because the Serb-speaking Orthodox Christians up in the Montenegrin mountains were able to hold out against the Turks,
whereas their compatriots in the valleys were conquered or expelled. The sense of separateness was subsequently consolidated
by the vested interests of the local political and administrative
apparatus, which was soon to become—and has remained—
Montenegro's only growth industry.

The Serbs of Western Yugoslavia, driven to desperation by the
genocidal Ustasha attacks, had fought like lions and it was Tito's

old mentor, Moša Pijade, who suggested forming them into a separate federal entity, within the prospective federation. Tito's other close associates shared his reluctance to make any concession which would boost Serb morale.[1]

Eagerness to humble an over-mighty Serbia seems also to have been behind the design to give its northern province of Vojvodina a separate status. This region north of the Danube had been annexed by Serbia from the ruins of the Habsburg Empire and though it was predominantly Serb (particularly after the expulsion or flight of its half-million German minority) the survival of Hungarians, Romanians, and other small minorities was used as an excuse for giving it the title of Autonomous Province, still nominally part of Serbia but with separate federal status.

The province of Kosovo is treasured by the Serbs as the cradle of their great medieval empire though 80 per cent of its population is by now Albanian. If Tito had had his way Kosovo would have been detached from Serbia altogether and been transferred to Albania which he had intended to incorporate into the Yugoslav federation. According to Enver Hoxha (not necessarily a reliable source), during his 1946 visit to Belgrade, Tito told him that he personally believed that Kosovo belonged to Albania but that in view of strong Serb opposition the transfer at that time would be "inopportune".[2] Kosovo thus became, like Vojvodina, an Autonomous Province within the Serb Republic.

Under the new dispensation, Macedonia, for which Serbia had gone to war 30 years before, was to be a separate republic. So was Bosnia-Herzegovina, also an area of mixed nationalities. The Communists had considered linking the region with either Croatia or Serbia but decided that after the wartime killings neither option was feasible. Further, as Djilas recalled: "The Bosnian leadership too, like every authority which grew out of the uprising, insisted on their own state and later, even on their own outlet to the sea."[3] Herzegovina was extended to include a 25-mile strip along the Adriatic coast, carved out of Dalmatia. The rest of the Dalmatian coast was assigned to the Republic of Croatia, which preserved the shape of a *croissant*, almost encircling Bosnia-Herzegovina. As a consequence, the Croats, like the Serbs, came to regard themselves as territorially deprived.

During the war, Slovenia, in the north-west corner of Yugoslavia, had been treated by the Germans as conquered territory and Tito had left it in the charge of local Communists who chose to base their resistance on an appeal to Slovene rather than to

Yugoslav patriotism. When in 1945 Tito paid his first visit to "liberated" Ljubljana he found himself surrounded by Slovene national flags: "What is this supposed to mean?" he asked, "What is this separatism?"[4] The leading Slovene Communists, including Kardelj and Kidrič, were quick to fall in line; in the drafting of the first centralist constitution and the equally centralist first Five-year Plan it was they who played the leading role.

By the end of the war the eight-member federation was already established within its existing frontiers: six Republics: Serbia, Macedonia, Montenegro, Bosnia-Herzegovina, Croatia and Slovenia and two Autonomous Provinces, Vojvodina and Kosovo. The concept of federation satisfied not only the desire of the various communities to assert their national identity but it also commended itself to the Western allies, on whose support, during this phase of the war, Tito very much depended. To the West, the word federation had a reassuringly democratic and liberal connotation. Though it was known to cover a wide variety of institutional practices it was generally held to imply that executive power would be shared between the centre and the component parts, with an independent judiciary to ensure that the constitutional prerogatives were respected. Federalism, for Tito and Kardelj, both of them trained in Moscow, had a quite different and specifically Bolshevik meaning. Lenin had shown how to harness the national and separatist aspirations of the Czar's subject peoples to the wagon of the Red Revolution and Tito intended to do the same for those of the Karadjordjević dynasty. Once the Communists were in charge, it was assumed that the phenomenon of nationalism—being no more than a relic of bourgeois ideology —would disappear. Meanwhile as in the USSR the nationalities could be fobbed off with "cultural autonomy": the right to use their own language and alphabet, but only to express one-and-the-same party line.

The first Yugoslav constitution was a close replica of its Soviet model though in one important respect, in the choice of words, it was less liberal. The Russians have always discreetly camouflaged the coercive aspect of the Soviet dictatorship acknowledging the right of the separate Soviet Republics to secede. In practice the concession is meaningless as any challenge to the integrity of the USSR constitutes high treason, punishable by death. Yet even this nominal freedom was more than the Yugoslav leadership dared to concede. For, as Tito told his associates: "Our situation is different from that of the Russians, we cannot do this. Say something changes in Macedonia and they demand secession, what then?"[5]

For this reason, in Yugoslav double-speak, successive constitutions while also acknowledging the principle of the right of secession, declared that, during the Partisan struggle, all the peoples of Yugoslavia took an irreversible decision to stay united: in the words of Yugoslavia's leading constitutional lawyer, Professor Djordjević, commenting on the present 1974 constitution: "As regards to the right to secession, there is no change from the earlier constitutions. Such a right legally does not exist . . . for the constitution confirms the historical process which led to the creation of the Yugoslav community." In reality, as Professor Ivo Lapenna of the London School of Economics has pointed out, the peoples of Yugoslavia were never consulted, at any time, about whether or not they wished to be incorporated into a single state.[6]

There were, however, two fundamental reasons why it would have been impossible to repeat the Soviet experiment on the Yugoslav body-politic. First, whereas in the USSR the Russians were unchallengeably the dominant people and Russian nationalism could be evoked in times of danger, without provoking countervailing passions on a considerable scale, in Yugoslavia the Serbs, though the largest single group, represented only 40 per cent and were not strong enough by themselves to dominate the country. Further, whereas in the USSR national minorities tended to live in compact territories, in Yugoslavia, as a consequence of centuries of invasion and emigration, the national communities are inextricably intermingled. Apart from the relatively homogeneous little Slovenia, all the regions of Yugoslavia contain mixed populations and almost half the Serbs live outside their federal boundary.

The monolithic Stalinist dictatorship was indeed so unsuited to a country of Yugoslavia's diversity that it was only the combination of war weariness and police terror that made it even temporarily tolerable. By the end of the war Tito had told his colleagues, when they were squabbling over internal frontiers, that, under Communism, the nationalities issue would disappear: "With us, these demarcation lines will anyway be no more than administrative divisions, instead of fixed frontiers, as with the bourgeoisie. . . ."[7] For a while he seems indeed to have believed that a unitary Yugoslavia was feasible. There is no doubt that Yugoslav patriotic fervour had been kindled by the expulsion of the Axis occupiers and when the public learnt of Tito's breach with Stalin had received an additional boost. The Russians were being defied in the name of Yugoslavia and well into the 1960s "Yugoslavism" remained official party doctrine.

Inevitably, however, the centrifugal forces began to make themselves felt. The Communists at first suppressed any signs of nationalism, identifying it in Serbia with the Chetniks, in Croatia with the Ustashas and in Slovenia with the White Guard, so doing their best to preserve the atmosphere of civil war. But two of Tito's top advisers, Vladimir Bakarić from Croatia and Edvard Kardelj from Slovenia, began to complain that they were losing contact with their own compatriots and Tito himself could not remain unaware that the Communists were in danger of finding themselves isolated from the rest of the country. It was against this background that the leadership introduced a new constitution in 1963 which began Yugoslavia's gradual metamorphosis: from a Soviet-style monolith into a veto-ridden confederation of eight mini-states, run by their respective Communist parties: which is how Yugoslavia is governed today.

Central to the new system was the use of quotas in which the eight federal entities shared out power and patronage. A "key" was imposed for all federal institutions which gave the six republics two representatives each and the Autonomous Provinces one. The Communists were encouraged to play a bigger role locally and Tito agreed that the eight Party congresses would in future meet before rather than after the federal congress: so acquiring authority to do more than merely rubber-stamp Belgrade's decisions. And the Central Investment Fund, which had allocated capital from Belgrade, was abolished and its funds transferred to the banks though three of the largest of these happened to be in Belgrade (infuriating the Croats, who claimed that this deprived Zagreb, previously Yugoslavia's financial centre, of its traditional place).

The turning-point away from the centralist and repressive Stalinist era is generally dated 1966, the year of the dismissal and disgrace of Aleksandar Ranković, the former head of the secret police and one of Tito's closest wartime associates. Though a former tailor with very little education, Ranković had been Tito's right-hand during the time when Tito was openly saying that he wanted to strike terror into the hearts of his opponents and Ranković's name was linked with arbitrary arrests, torture and forced labour. Further, he made no secret of his opposition to the concessions being made at that time both to nationalist feelings and to economic liberalism (see next chapter). His police kept a close watch over all the top party members and after his demotion Tito let it be known that he had even placed a bugging device under Tito's conjugal bed. This titillating frill on the story is rarely believed by those close to the centre, who recall Ranković's dog-like devotion to his master, which he was further to demonstrate by never saying anything in his own defence after he fell from favour. It seems more probable that Ranković was a scapegoat whom Tito thought useful to eliminate when he needed to display, both to his own countrymen and to the outside world, that his liberalization was authentic.

After Ranković's fall the Eight acquired control over their own police apparatus, a system which enabled some republics to become a great deal more oppressive than others: in this respect Bosnia generally headed the league and Slovenia always remained the freest. But all over Yugoslavia, as before, the judiciary were still required to administer what the Communists call "class justice": i.e. to deprive anti-Communists of the protection of the law.

In 1968 the eight Communist parties acquired the all-important right to select their own candidates for the top jobs, and in the following year Tito set up a collective Presidency, representing all the federal entities, with the chairmanship rotating annually among them—though he stayed President until he died.

By 1970 the word "sovereignty" was coming to be used to define the status of the eight federal entities and almost all the prerogatives of government were yielded up by the federal government. The impression that power was being handed down to the local communities was however misleading. In reality, the party blanketed the entire country and no federal unit had the right either to tamper with the constantly changing rules and decrees regulating the Titoist version of self-management (see next chapter) or to give any encouragement to private enterprise or to Western forms of economic and political freedom.

The reassertion of nationalist feeling convinced Tito that the party cadres could only exercise effective authority if they came to be identified with the local interests within their regions. In the federal capitals the party leadership had to be seen, like the local football team, fighting for their own victory and for the defeat of everyone else. They were given the patronage and funds to make and break individual careers, but in return were expected to remain faithful to the Party creed and, in times of crisis, to the Party leadership.

The 1974 constitution confirmed the "sovereignty" of the Eight and gave them full control over the administration and the economy, including foreign trade and the allocation of foreign currency. Besides running their own party and controlling the police and judiciary, each of the Eight was given the right to set up its own French-style Academy of the Arts, entitling it to nominate its own "immortals".

As we shall see in the next chapter, after 1972 the liberalization of the 1960s went sharply into reverse, but Belgrade never reimposed central control over prices, pay, investment, distribution and foreign currency. On the contrary, the decentralization went remorselessly forward, creating a new system which economists dubbed *polycentric étatisme*: state control which operated not from Belgrade but from all the eight federal capitals.

The carving up of the national dichotomy made nonsense of Yugoslavia's One-Year and Five-Year Plans, even though, for ideological reasons, these remained obligatory. The anomaly was stressed by Yugoslavia's leading Marxist economist, Branko Horvat: "The Soviet system is inefficient but it is logical. Our system is both inefficient and illogical. If in the eight centres (six republics and two provinces) everybody does things in their own way, we no longer have one economy but eight separate economies, administratively shattered. There are no state boundaries between the Eight yet statistics show that economic exchanges (the circulation of goods and money) between the republics have, to a large extent, dried up."[8] Indeed, according to the Public Auditing Office, the capital investment crossing internal frontiers in Yugoslavia in 1983 was only 0.18 per cent, even less than the previous year.

"While I lived in Belgrade," Horvat recalled, "I had a savings account with Yugobanka in Belgrade. When I moved to Zagreb I went with my Belgrade savings-book to the Zagreb branch of Jugobanka to withdraw my money. They told me: we cannot pay you. Why not? I asked. Because the capital in the branch in Zagreb belongs to Croatia and cannot be transferred to another republic. They told me to go to Belgrade to get my money. You must agree that behaviour of this kind goes beyond economics into psychiatry."[9]

The local cadres, in return for Party loyalty and the elimination of effective opposition, were given power and patronage over every aspect of public life. And to the immense detriment of the Yugoslav economy and the well-being of the Yugoslav people, all the essential services, including the railways, electric power, transport and the post office, were carved into eight and managed by the eight separate authorities. Everyone recognized that the system was absurd but nobody knew how to change it. On 2 October 1983 Belgrade TV showed that whereas it took only 55 seconds for a car to cross the bridge which separates Zvornik from Mali Zvornik, a letter might take several days as the two towns are in different republics, Bosnia and Serbia, and the post has to go via Tuzla and Belgrade.

The dismantling of the Yugoslav economy deprived the country of any regular supply of energy. As *Politika* reported on 16 November 1983 "local authorities have regarded it as far easier to reach a deal with a foreign power than with an energy producer just a few hundred kilometres away." Electricity failures became a regular part of everyday life and in the winters of the early 1980s Yugoslav citizens endured long and regular periods of blackout, often lasting sixteen hours a day, which reminded elderly British visitors of their wartime experiences.

There need have been no energy crisis, according to the Yugoslav experts, if inter-republican rivals had not effectively obstructed two major hydro-electric projects.[10] The first, to be partially financed by the World Bank, was located at the mouth of the Rivers Pliva and Tara near Foča, and was held up by disagreements on the share-out of benefits between Montenegro and Bosnia; the second on the Drina River by a similar dispute between Bosnia and Serbia.

During his last years Tito recognized that he was presiding over the disintegration of Yugoslavia: "If we go on like this, there will be no Yugoslavia. There will be eight dwarf-like economically autarchic states, and it will have no standing whatever in the outside world." But they *did* go on like this and Westerners doing business with the dwarfs came back asking: "Is Yugoslavia really a country?"

To most Yugoslavs by this time the answer would have to be a qualified no. As *Borba* wrote on 7 November 1982: "Every branch of Yugoslav industry, including ferrous and non-ferrous metallurgy, machine construction, electronics, petro-chemicals and automobiles, have been built up in accordance with the formula Six plus Two" (referring to the six Republics and two Autonomous Provinces). Even how much you were legally allowed to eat began depending on where you lived. For as shortages spread the local authorities began introducing separate and different rations. Though after prolonged consultation, the constitutional court decided that local rationing was illegal, the practice continued. According to *Politika*, 18 June 1984, the defiance of rules and orders of the federation by its constituent parts amounted to "a negation of the state".

The system would have collapsed under the weight of its own extravagance had the Yugoslav leadership not suddenly been showered with manna from heaven, in the form of apparently limitless supplies of petro-dollars. After the quadrupling of the price of oil in 1973 and subsequent leaps, Western banks were awash with money and desperate to find borrowers. And in 1977 a law, giving the Eight full right to raise their own funds and to look after their own international accounts, removed any restraint on Yugoslav borrowing. The weak federal government allowed itself to be pressured into holding down the price of domestic oil, while the eight Party leaderships went on independent buying sprees. Each of them, even the poorest, was eager to outbid the rest in equipping itself for an automated and industrialized world. In the West, where the old heavy industries were in deep depression, governments and traders were euphoric at finding insatiable customers: "Who, except the Yugoslavs, in these difficult times, would be building a new steel mill?" asked a merchant-banker in the City of London in 1980, explaining why he was syndicating a loan for yet another mill in the unprofitable heavy-industry complex of Smederevo in Serbia. Several Western governments (though never Germany) put pressure on their banks to undercut competitors by offering easy credits.

The federal regions not only failed to cooperate, but, in order to snatch trade from one another, subsidized and gave other forms of aid to their own producers. For this reason, foreigners who had engaged in joint enterprises (permitted in Yugoslavia after 1968) and had installed themselves on the assumption that they would have access to the whole Yugoslav market, discovered on the contrary that a neighbouring republic, to spite its rival, would bring in a competing Western firm to set up a similar plant.

Even so, some of them made quick profits from the eight little booms, particularly easy to come by as their own governments generally guaranteed them against risks. Loans were syndicated without any serious study of the borrowers' profitability or even solvency. Some Western banks later admitted that money had been raised for Yugoslav enterprises which were unable even to produce a meaningful balance sheet.

As international funds began to dry up, the fight between the Eight for diminishing resources became increasingly ferocious. In a market economy the contest would have been between firms; in Yugoslavia it was between competing national groups and the victory went not to the commercially profitable but to the politically strong. In 1981 the Yugoslavs were unable to meet their international obligations and the swarm of visiting officials and bankers from the West were shaken to discover the quantity, unaccountability and elusiveness of their Yugoslav creditors. Demands began being voiced for more central direction and in the summer of 1983 as a condition for desperately needed credits, the Yugoslavs were obliged to give supervisory powers back to their Federal Bank. But the Eight retained their veto and local feeling made it impossible to exchange *polycentric étatisme* for the centrally directed *étatisme* of the Stalinist era.

As an excuse for the internal chaos, Yugoslav officials like to compare Yugoslavia to the European community: decisions being obstructed in both cases by diversities of national interests. The comparison is however misleading. In Western Europe, despite government interference, goods and investment cross national boundaries for commercial reasons. In Yugoslavia every aspect of the economy is publicly owned and the criteria are never commercial but always political.

The system as it operates in contemporary Yugoslavia has been compared by Milovan Djilas and others to the *millet* administrative system of the Ottoman Empire. This differed from the European feudal system, in which the barons rested their authority on their ownership of the land, which gave them an autonomous power-base. In the Turkish as in the Communist systems, the criterion for leadership was ideological. In the Ottoman Empire, the Sultan delegated his absolute authority in each *millet* to the religious leader belonging to the prevailing faith. In present-day Yugoslavia the diversity of faiths is assumed not to exist and the party's unchallengeable authority is handed down to the local Party's head-man.

The purpose of the Titoists in handling the nationalities would seem to have been not so much to reconcile the different groups as to make sure that the feuds between them would serve—as they have done in the past—to consolidate the régime. The local party cadres, built up on a solid territorial base, are primarily engaged in fighting each other: this had meant that, until now at least, there has never been any coordinated opposition. However much the Serbs, Croats and Slovenes, who form three-quarters of the Yugoslav population, differ between themselves, Marxism–Leninism is in conflict with the religious and cultural traditions of all three. Their identification of their nationality with their own churches inclines them to reject the party's atheist claim to monopolize the truth and the peasant tradition, which still survives, makes them the natural opponents of a bureaucratized state. Nonetheless, in spite of all this, the authorities have been remarkably successful in diverting the anger and frustration away from themselves and focusing it instead on inter-communal and inter-ethnic strife. Two encounters, within 48 hours, with two eminent, well-educated and widely read intellectuals, one in Zagreb, the other in Belgrade, gave me an unnerving Tweedledum-Tweedledee impression. In almost identical terms each of the two blamed all his people's distress, both past and present, on the misdeeds of the national group to which the other one belonged. Srdja Popović, a leading Belgrade lawyer who travels around Yugoslavia and defends civil rights cases in different capitals, blames this pathological condition primarily on the prohibition which the régime imposes against open dialogue about Yugoslav history and politics. This repression of normal outlets, he believes, drives the ethnic groups back into themselves and sustains their paranoid attitudes towards each other.

Any possible understanding between the Serb, Croat and Slovene educated élite fills the Communist authorities with alarm. When in 1966 the writer Mihajlo Mihajlov was prosecuted (and later jailed) for trying to publish an intellectual magazine which could appeal simultaneously to Slovene Catholics, Croat nationalists and Serb liberals, he was declared guilty of "inciting nationalism". Logic suggested that, as his magazine was specifically designed to bring the traditionally rival groups together, he was doing precisely the opposite: but that made him all the more dangerous.

On the federal structure itself, both Serbs and Croats are equally discontented. The Serbs believe that non-Serb Tito based his régime on the principle, "Yugoslavia can be strong only if Serbia is weak." Whether this really was his view is not clear, though he was obviously eager to prevent Serb domination and it was not until a year after his death that a Macedonian member of the collective presidency publicly repudiated the doctrine as unworthy of modern Yugoslavia. The Croats, for their part, have always felt that the reimposition of Belgrade as capital city relegated them permanently to a junior role. Slovenia never had a state of its own but they too remain eager to re-emphasize their identity. Back in London after a chance meeting with a Slovene businessman in Ljubljana I received a yard-long parcel containing an unsolicited gift: the replica of an ethnic map of Slovenia dated 1853, which included within its frontiers the whole of Istria Peninsula and all of the now Austrian province of Carinthia.

Both the Orthodox Serbs and the Roman Catholic Croats and Slovenes incline to identify their patriotism with their religion.[11] Yet, although both faiths (unlike Moslem) have been harassed and repressed and both have suffered restriction on the number of their priests and on any activities outside church premises, they seem incapable of combining against their common atheist oppressor. Asked why this was so, an Orthodox Serb replied that, whereas Communism was no more than a transitional phenomenon, the struggle between the churches was for souls: it had started long before Communist supremacy and would continue long after.

In recent years, there have been moves, principally from Slovenia, towards more oecumenical attitudes but the nationalist barriers still seem insurmountable. Asked whether as a man of God he did not feel he had more in common with a Catholic priest than with a local Party secretary, the editor of a widely-read Orthodox weekly newspaper *Pravoslavlje* answered: "Of course, I do, but not with the enemies of my people." Inevitably conversation turned towards the notorious wartime concentration camp of Jasenovac, where the editor claimed "the Croats" had killed over 800,000 Serbs. Historians agree that though slaughter was horrific, the Ustashas had neither the Nazi technique nor equipment for massacres on the German scale and a nought should probably be subtracted from the propaganda figure. But few Serbs would dare say so: for many of them, the higher your figure the greater your patriotism. Further, the Jasenovac victims were not only Serbs but also the Ustasha Croat enemies, including many Croat Communists, as well as large communities of Jews and gypsies. Justifiably the Croats refuse to accept collective guilt. A Serb demand that the Pope should prostrate himself as a penitent at Jasenovac, as Willie Brandt had done at Auschwitz, was the reason why by 1984 this very Catholic community had still not received a papal visit.

The Serbo-Croat disputes centre round language almost as much as religion. This is particularly difficult for outsiders to comprehend as the two languages are so nearly identical that in the nineteenth century a common tongue was the base on which the Croats launched the idea of a united Yugoslavia. An early pioneer, Ljudevit Gaj, went so far as to suggest that the Croats should adopt the Cyrillic script used in Serbia. Instead they clung to Latin lettering and the two communities still fight furiously over the finer shades of linguistic difference.

A language truce was patched up in 1954, at a writers' meeting at Novi Sad, but later, during the postwar nationalist revival, the Croats disavowed it.[12] When further work on a Croat encyclo-paedia which had been started under the German occupation was prohibited, the Croats protested against "cultural genocide". From Zagreb's point of view, the Serbs are often provocative. One Croat lawyer negotiated an international treaty, sent the text on to Belgrade where it was "translated" into Serb and then retrans-lated back again into Croat (he claimed incorrectly). The retrans-lation then became an official text. Even the Slovenes who have a perceptibly different though also Slav language are currently engaged in a campaign against Serbo-Croat verbal infiltration.

Since the end of the Ranković repression, it has been the Croats who have come nearest to open insurrection. The Catholics rally to the memory of Cardinal Stepinac, whose grave in Zagreb cathedral is always covered in fresh flowers. The non-believers now have their own hero in the rehabilitated person of Andrija Hebrang, who is seen in Belgrade as a Stalinist but whom the Croats believe was a liberal-minded Communist, murdered for his loyalty to Croatia.[13] National sentiment focused on Matica Hrvatska, a patriotic organization set up in the middle of the nineteenth century and revived in 1967. The success of its publica-tions and meetings eclipsed those of the Communists and although it was nominally only a cultural institution, it represented a formidable political challenge. The Communist leaders fell out about whether it should be suppressed or conciliated within the Party. Hebrang's associates had been liquidated with him. But in the 1960s a new generation true to his tradition was emerging of which the two most prominent figures were Party Secretary Savka Dapčević-Kućar and Prime Minister Mika Tripalo. But Tito's old-time supporter Bakarić was still Croatia's leading Communist and it was he who persuaded Tito that the demonstrations and rallies were getting out of control. Assembling the leaders at Brioni

in April 1971 Tito let them know that Brezhnev—three years after
the Czech invasion—had been on the telephone offering Soviet
help. In the same month the students of Zagreb University
signified their defiance by electing as President of the Students'
Union a nationalist rather than the approved Communist candidate.

In July of that year Tito came to Zagreb and spoke of reports
that Serb villages in Croatia were arming and drilling in dread of a
repeat of the Ustasha massacres (though there was no violence)
and he referred again to his talk with Brezhnev: "I'd sooner restore
order with our own army than let others do it"—a remark which
implied that in any case "order" was to be restored. In September
Brezhnev paid an official visit to Belgrade, demonstrating that the
fraternal assistance was available if needed.

Before the end of the year it was all over. On 5 November 1971,
at the biggest public rally in Zagreb since the war, Savka
Dapčević-Kućar, a university professor and skilled orator, declared: "We would be wrong to act as though we in the Communist
Party are a closed sect which thinks that society and the working
people exist for us and not we for them." In an effort to ward
off the now inevitable repression, the Zagreb students went on
strike and tried to rally working-class support. They selected a
very unrevolutionary issue (later partly conceded) that the
Croats be allowed to retain the foreign currency that they
earned. (They were then being compelled to transfer it at unprofitable exchange rates to the Belgrade Central Bank. As Croat
industry depended on imports, access to hard currency was
vital.)

Meanwhile the Matica Hrvatska press carried the campaign
one stage further, publicly demanding that the Croats be allowed
the right, should they wish it, to secede. By this time Tito had had
enough. After a private meeting with the Croat leaders, he went on
TV and denounced them, not only for pandering to nationalism
but also for tolerating "anti-Marxist and in a large part pro-
Western ideas in schools and universities". Ten days later the
army organized a pre-emptive display of force, the police arrested
the student leaders and resistance petered out. Four hundred
leaders were tried and though no evidence was produced to
show any link with terrorism or foreign conspiracy, most of them
were given long prison sentences. Though Tito had accused the
students of spreading Western views, they received very little
sympathy from the West, which accepted his claim that they

represented a threat to Yugoslav unity.[14]

Looking back ten years later, Mika Tripalo said he still believed that the young Croats could have been calmed down if they had been allowed to sing their songs and wave their flags (it is still illegal to raise the flag of any of the Yugoslav nationalities, with the exception of the Albanian, unless it carries the Communist emblem. The special concession to the Albanians was conceded personally by Tito after the 1968 troubles and much resented by the other seven). Yugoslavia must be one of the few countries in which singing the wrong song can be a crime. One elderly Zagreb citizen recalls that when he was young, and while the Croat Communists were still separatists, there was a well-known nationalist song for which the singer could be arrested as a Communist; today the singer of the same song could be picked up as a counter-revolutionary.

Though quieter, the resentment simmered on. Besides the initial trials, the opponents of the system claim that some 32,000 people were either arrested, dismissed from their jobs, interrogated or harassed in other ways. Two of them, both still in prison at the time of writing, are revered as martyrs: university professor, Marko Veselica, whose father died fighting with the Partisans, had first asserted his sense of Croat solidarity when he challenged and defeated the Titoist candidate in the 1969 election: the only postwar occasion when any freedom of choice was allowed. During the troubles, Veselica had helped the students to articulate their claims and afterwards he was expelled from the Party, lost his job, and was given a seven-year prison sentence. After Tito's death he was sent back to prison after a West German magazine had published an interview with him in which he declared himself "a former Communist, who is now a Christian, a democratic socialist and a believer in political pluralism."[15] A description of the subhuman conditions of his imprisonment and the reassertion of Croatia's case against the régime, was declared enough to convict him of anti-State activities.

The other was Dobroslav Paraga, who was nineteen years old when he was arrested for collecting signatures pleading, immediately after Tito's death, for an amnesty for non-violent political prisoners. While in jail Paraga organized a hunger-strike, partly against the way political prisoners were being treated but also against the exclusion of priests from the prison, even when called in to administer the last rites.

Contemporary Croat nationalists including Veselica and Para-

ga tend to combine a belief in asserting their own national identity
with Westernized concepts of a plural society and the rule of law.
Most of them accept that freedom of religion and language has to
be extended not only to Croats but also to the half a million Serbs
who live within Croat frontiers.[14]

In recent years, while the whole of Yugoslavia has been in
economic trouble, the Croats coped least well with the recession.
The Party tried exhortations and activists carved into the paving-
stones the slogan: "We must, we can, we shall!"—"But we aren't
allowed to", was surreptitiously added.

It is hard to prove any connexion between political mood and
economic performance and Croats were inclined to exaggerate
their misery. Zagreb is crammed with cars and taxis and when
leading citizens complain—as they often do—that unlike Belgrade they have no new hospital or sports stadium they never
suggest providing such amenities for themselves. Indeed the sense
of desolation is outwardly visible. The centre of Zagreb looks
shabby and neglected, the façades of buildings are being allowed
to crumble and streets are in disrepair. In Zagreb after 1971, as in
Prague after 1968, at least temporarily, people seem to have
stopped caring.

It was not until one year later, in 1972, that Tito intervened to
domesticate the Serb Communists, though from the time of the
Chetniks, Serbia has consistently been the régime's principal
problem. The Serb people are traditionally averse to authority, a
characteristic deplored in the mid-nineteenth century by the
monarch of the time, Prince Michael Obrenović: "Until now with
us the chief entertainment of everyone, regardless of social class,
has been political argument. This goes on behind the plough and
the counter, behind the office desks and tavern bars, while few give
much thought to matters on which the existence of the state and of
us all depends."[16]

By the turn of the century the Serbs had done better than many
much richer communities in establishing the right of the citizen
against the state. Peter I of the Karadjordjević dynasty came to the
throne in 1903, after a military *coup* in which his predecessor Prince
Alexander Obrenović and his wife had been hacked to death and
defenestrated. Peter was already 60 years old and had spent his life
in the West and translated John Stuart Mill's essay on liberty into
Serbo-Croat. During his reign Serbia was a constitutional monarchy and one of the few countries in Europe to enjoy a free press, a
multiparty system and autonomous universities.

In material terms, the creation of Yugoslavia benefited the Slovenes more than the Serbs. Though the court, the bureaucracy and the officer corps were mainly Serb, succeeding royalist governments made no effort to channel wealth into the Kingdom's Serb regions and in the years between the war the *per capita* investment in Serbia is reported to have been only one-quarter as high as in Slovenia.

The Serbs were given some concessions within the Communist state. With the help of Western capital and engineering skills, they at last obtained their long-held ambition of a railway across the mountains, linking Belgrade with the Montenegrin port of Bar —which most economists would agree was a serious misallocation of scarce capital. But on the whole, they did not do well out of the federal arrangements. Though most of Serbia is far poorer than Croatia and Slovenia, the Republic of Serbia was designated part of modern Yugoslavia and consequently obliged to transfer large sums annually to the regions qualifying for underdeveloped status; a condition certainly prevailing in much of Serbia itself. Further the Serbs were specially harmed by the postwar Party policy, only recently changed, of encouraging industry by holding food prices far below market levels. The Serbs more than other Yugoslavs had stayed on the land.

In Serbia, as in the rest of Yugoslavia, the lifting of political repression after 1966 provided new outlets for rumbling discontent, and there were strongly hostile reactions when, after the Croat troubles, Tito decided to put the liberalization policy into reverse (see chapter seven). In 1972, after publicly repudiating the 1952 Party congress, which under Djilas's inspiration had set Yugoslavia on its moderate course, he issued a new directive which regressed back to Marxist fundamentalism. The banks, commercial conglomerates and insurance companies (which in the 1965 economic reforms—described in the next chapter—had been partially released from state control) were declared to be "alienated centres of financial power" and were identified not just with a revival of capitalism but also with "increasingly articulate nationalism".

Repressing the Serbs was harder than Tito had expected. On 9 October 1972 he held a conference assembling not just the leaders of the Serb party but also a number of lower-rating cadres, whom he assumed would be more pliant. Yet after four days' argument he conceded that things "were taking a completely different direction from the one I wanted", and hinted that power of persuasion might be insufficient: "We must settle accounts with those who stand with the class enemy on the other side of the barricades." Yet even after Tito had publicly berated the Serb leaders the Serb Central Committee still refused to accept their resignation and it gave in finally only after ten days of manoeuvring, warnings of impeding civil war, and threats to bring in the army. A new Central Committee had to be installed and 1,000 members of the Serb Communist party were expelled—which meant the end of their careers.[17]

In Slovenia, the principal victim of Tito's return to dogmatism was Stane Kavčič, who had distinguished himself by his management of Slovene affairs and consequently in 1970 been invited by Tito to become Federal Prime Minister. Kavčič not only dared to decline the offer but as Slovene leader proceeded with his policies for improving relations with the EEC countries and trying to provide greater outlets for private business.

Materially as leader of Slovenia, Kavčič had had a relatively easy time, as the Slovenes have done less badly out of the system than any other Yugoslav republic, and, unlike the rest, they still today enjoy virtually full employment. As before the war their consumer industry was relatively advanced and with the absence of foreign currency which excludes imports, Slovene commodities have often been able to monopolize the Yugoslav market. As a Belgrade economist ironically commented: "Slovenia is the last of the empires. The British, French, Dutch, have lost theirs, but Slovenia still has its captive markets and its undeveloped colonies. . . ."

Opportunities for Slovene efficiency and expertise were plentiful in the federal bureaucracy, and what the Western chancelleries refer to as "the Slovene mafia" plays a leading role in the nation's financial affairs. Yet the Slovenes tend to compare themselves not with other Yugoslavs but with the Slovene minorities who live more comfortably than themselves across their borders in Italy and Austria. They have little in common with the Bosnians and Albanians, of whom many have emigrated into Slovenia to do the menial tasks which the Slovenes shun.

In general, the Slovenes, whose language others find difficult to understand, are freer than other Yugoslavs to speak and write as they please. Nonetheless the Yugoslav civil war left them, too, like the Serbs and Croats, with wounds that have not been allowed to heal. There is still a taboo on any public discussion of the fate of thousands of Slovenes who disappeared without a trace in the post-war terror. Until he died in 1981, the poet-Partisan veteran Edvard Kocbek did more than anyone to investigate and expose the facts.[18]

Kocbek's Partisan record and literary reputation protected him from prosecution but, 21 years after the slaughter, the Communists decided to discourage further embarrassing revelations by making an example of a well-known magistrate, France Miklavčič, whose offence was to have allowed himself to be interviewed by a Trieste newspaper, on the postwar casualties. These were still a forbidden topic in the Slovene press, even though Miklavčič said nothing which in privately circulated documents Kocbek had not already revealed.

When Miklavčič's house was searched the police discovered a diary revealing that he and a group of friends, meeting in their own homes, had discussed the possibility of a more humane and open society. The judge, who had five young children, was jailed for two years and made jobless for life.

Kocbek's cause has subsequently been taken up by the literary magazine *Nova Revija* which has gathered around itself the best writers and leading non-conformists and seen to it that the Partisan crimes are not forgotten by those (including most of the staff) born after the civil war. They have been taken to task for "spoiling the younger generation" by a prominent survivor, Josef Vidmar, himself a major beneficiary of the Communist régime. The magazine has retorted by accusing Vidmar of being anti-intellectual, jealous of Kocbek's literary eminence.

Yugoslavia is the only Communist country which has tried to operate a significant decentralization of powers, and the local leaders to whom authority has been devolved are engaged in a delicate balancing act. On the one side, they need to make concessions to avert excessive and potentially explosive local discontents. But, if they go too far, they risk unleashing the unmistakably Westernizing and pluralist aspirations of the Yugoslav heart-land: Serbia, Croatia and Slovenia. And one of the ways in which the party has retained its grip on the central regions is to play off the peripheral parts of the country against the core. And it is with this exigency in mind that the party's record in Kosovo, Macedonia and Bosnia-Herzegovina can be understood.

Whatever the régime, the region of Kosovo, historically Serb but now ethnically Albanian, would present problems. But these have been almost certainly exacerbated by Communists' efforts to solve them, first by policies of Stalinist repression then by financial largesse, and now by a little of both. During the Yugoslav monarchy many Albanian Moslems were driven out (figures vary according to source) and their land distributed to some 40,000 Serb and Montenegrin peasants. Nonetheless the majority remained Albanian and at their conferences of 1928 and 1940 in Zagreb the Yugoslav Communists agreed that, when the Balkans were Sovietized, Kosovo would be allocated to Albania.

In 1941 Kosovo was indeed annexed by Albania, then a Mussolini protectorate and in 1945 it took several Partisan divisions to reimpose Yugoslav rule. As long as Tito was planning to annex Hoxha's Albania, Kosovo's fate was uncertain but after his rupture with Stalin when annexation became impossible, there were no further restraints on the police repression masterminded by Ranković against Yugoslavia's own Albanians. Predictably, it did not take long after Ranković's departure for the Albanians to reassert their rights. "Why do 370,000 Montenegrins have their own republic while 1.2 million Albanians do not even have local autonomy?" asked a former Partisan leader Mehmet Hoxha (no relation to the Albanian dictator). The case was reinforced by a series of riots and demonstrations, which induced Tito to turn his previous policy upside down.[19] The Albanian Communists were given the same economic and political powers as those exercised by the leaders of the six republics and Tito developed closer personal relations with the Kosovo Party secretary Mahmud Bakali. Previously the Albanians communicated with the federal authorities through the channels of the Serbian republic; now Tito allowed Bakali direct access to his own office.

During the Ranković era, Kosovo received hardly any external help and had virtually no industry and was greatly impoverished by Belgrade's practice of holding down the price of all raw materials. After 1968, Kosovo obtained the lion's share of the federal development funds which became its principal source of investment. The Kosovo experience might serve as a warning to the defenders of the New International Economic Order, who favour giving unconditional aid to the irresponsible leaders in developing countries. Federal funds went mainly to a few highly capitalized industrial complexes and to the construction of conspicuously grand office buildings, and hardly anything was done to alleviate the acute poverty of the average Albanian peasant.

In Kosovo's capital, Priština, contemporary and pre-industrial society exist side by side. The local bank built a glass and concrete skyscraper, topped by a magnificently panelled board-room which would dwarf anything in the City of London. Meanwhile the peasants took their products to market in carts dragged along by little donkeys with red ribbons plaited between their ears to ward off the evil eye. Though part of Kosovo is very fertile, the essential jobs of irrigation and of improving farming methods were left to the experts of the World Bank, and it is they who have created a few successful oases in the otherwise bleak landscape.

The average income of individual residents of Kosovo compared with that throughout Yugoslavia slumped, between 1947 and 1962, from 52.4 per cent to only 34 per cent. In 1980, after more than a decade of federal cherishing, it had still risen to only 40 per cent—a lower figure than when the Communists took over. In the postwar years, the Kosovo average living standard was about one-quarter of the Slovene level: by 1980 it was less than one-seventh.

Before foreign currency dried up and while the local bosses still had money galore, a group of Albanian leaders were invited to Texas. Having decided they needed to learn English they addressed themselves to an expensive English language school on the Sussex coast, specializing in intensive tuition, and asked for an immediate despatch of qualified teachers. Told that the money was no barrier, the director waived doubts about whether he could spare the staff, and, as a consequence, during my first visit to Kosovo in 1979, I ran into a group of bemused and amused language specialists, who suddenly found themselves plumped into this primitive community, applying the world's most modern teaching methods on a small group of half-educated and very friendly Albanians.

The Priština college, which had previously been a branch of the University of Belgrade, acquired its own independent status after the 1968 disturbances and, before books were available, it proceeded to build itself a grandiose gold-domed library. At its peak in 1980, it enrolled 45,000 students, so becoming one of the largest in Europe. As most of these were unwilling to go back to their own villages they did nothing to grapple with Albanian illiteracy, now at 31.5 per cent, more than double the national average. Indeed it is difficult to see how the vastly increased number of university graduates, most of them likely to remain unemployed, can fail to exacerbate tensions. After 1968 the Albanian language replaced Serb as the first in teaching, and a large number of professors and text-books were brought in from Tirana, storing up troubles for the future.[20]

The suddenly demoted Serb minority was seriously threatened by Tito's transfer to Bakali of the police and the administration. Though a rigorous censorship was enforced to keep the facts from the rest of Yugoslavia, within a decade over 100,000 Serbs were induced or harassed into leaving and the police stood idly by while Serb homes were destroyed and cemeteries desecrated. Visiting Kosovo, Tito warned against nationalists and irredentists: "All these foes have the same aim: to try and provoke dissatisfaction among the Albanians in Kosovo and to sow discord among the multiracial population."

And indeed, soon after he died, violence erupted again and on a much larger scale. What started as a university demonstration against canteen food developed quickly into a politically inspired insurrection. Army units recruited from all parts of the Federation were rushed in, and after a show of force and several weeks of curfew, order was at least superficially restored. Belgrade reported nine fatal casualties and Tirana reported 1,000. As outside observers were excluded and as neither capitals respects "bourgeois" objectivity, the true number remains unknown.

The situation was still explosive when I visited Priština for the second time in the summer of 1983. Bakali had been ousted from his job but remained free to roam around the city and was warmly applauded wherever he appeared. On the other hand, savage sentences were passed against obscure activists. Thousands of students were given long prison terms and some school children were inculpated for offences such as throwing dirty water at Tito's statues. In the hall of the newly constructed Grand Hotel, where the black marble produced the atmosphere of a mausoleum, officials of the World Bank said they watched each morning for the arrival of the old Albanian bootblack. Normally, he plied his trade at the hotel entrance and his absence indicated that it would be sensible to stay indoors. My Serb companions drove back into Serbia for the night feeling it would be unwise to leave a smart car with a Belgrade number-plate in Pristina overnight.

The censorship was lifted after the 1981 riots and reports began being published about Albanian efforts to eliminate the Serbs in order to create "a pure Albania". In one almost "pure" Albanian village, the head of the last remaining Serb family had been murdered and his widow and children threatened. A delegation of Serbs called on the President of Serbia, General Ljubišić (formerly Tito's Defence Minister, later the Serb member of the collective presidency) to seek protection and compensation for the bereaved family. They were told he could not intervene as this was an internal Kosovo affair.

Part of Peć Monastery, the seat of the Serb Patriarch, was burnt down by Albanian terrorists. A local priest told me of the Church's gratitude to the Communist authorities for financing the reconstruction, but at the same time nuns were informing my Serb driver that village boys threw stones at them and poisoned their cattle. The arsonists were never caught. Yugoslav officials often draw an analogy between Kosovo and Northern Ireland, in both of which violence is endemic and the communities are split by nationality and religion. But in Northern Ireland, those demanding change represent one-third of the population, whereas in Kosovo four-fifths are Albanians. Indeed it is doubtful whether in the post-colonial world, any European democracy would try to refuse the right of secession to an alien territory of more than a million people.

But on Kosovo's demand for its own republic Tito was adamant, and after hearing of continued troubles despite the economic largesses, he paid a visit to Priština in 1979, to denounce nationalist irredentists. The continued Communist refusal to allow Kosovo to have a republic of its own (for fear it might proclaim secession) will be more and more difficult to sustain as the ratio of Albanians to the Yugoslav population continues to increase.[21]

In June 1984, in what was almost a replica of the Tito saga, ten Albanian rebels were tried in Priština for setting up a National Liberation Front and taking a loyalty oath to the national flag which was hoisted in front of pictures of Marx, Engels, Lenin, Stalin and Enver Hoxha. Though there is no evidence that the Kosovo Albanians want to join the independent state of Albania, the Yugoslavs are unwilling to take the risk that one day they might. From 1953 to 1981, as a consequence of their high birth rate and the slump in the natality of the Slav groups, the ratio rose from 4.4 to 7.7 and it will not be long before the Albanians become the Federation's third largest nationality.

The impact of the loss of Kosovo on the Serbs is difficult to predict. Its surviving monuments bequeathed by the Serbian medieval monarchy are treasures of Byzantine art and are cherished not just as tourist attractions but also as vital links with a splendid past. Since 1981 there has certainly been a marked increase in the stridency and bitterness of Serb nationalism and in 1982 a group of Orthodox priests declared: "Kosovo has been our

tomb and our resurrection"—meaning that Kosovo had been
lost but had relit the dying embers of national and religious
fervour. When Peć's rebuilt church was consecrated Serbs poured
in from all over the country taking part in a ceremony which, as
a caustic journalist reported, had little to do with religious
devotion.

Braving the passion of his compatriots, the writer Dobrica Ćosić
has dared to suggest partition. The Serbs who have been evicted
would have the right to return and make their part of the province
into part of Serbia, while in the rest, the Albanians would form
their own republic and be free to decide where they belonged.[22]
The Kosovo irredentists are claiming not only republic status for
their province but also the annexation of many neighbouring
localities where the Albanians are now in a majority and which
include Tetovo, Macedonia's second biggest city.

A surgical operation on this scale would seriously strain Macedonia's own loyalty to Yugoslavia. It is a disputed question
whether the Macedonians are indeed a separate ethnic group or a
branch of the Bulgarian nation. Indeed by an historical quirk it
was the Bulgarians who were the first to recognize Macedonia as a
political entity. Before the First World War they sponsored a
unified Macedonia (within their own orbit) while the Serbs
favoured partition.[23] But the frenetic attachment of the Serbs to
their share of Macedonia has been vividly evoked in Ćosić's novel:
Times of Death.[24] In it he reprints the texts of authentic diplomatic
dispatches of 1915, in which the Allies entreat the Serbs to cede
Macedonia to the Bulgarians. But even though this is the only
hope of preventing the latter from joining the invading armies, the
Serbs refuse to give in. Instead the Serb High Command drags the
freezing remnants of a starved and defeated army across the
mountains of Albania to the Adriatic coast. They lost thousands of
men along the way, but as a result Serbia participated as an ally in
the postwar peace negotiations and its share of Macedonia was
re-annexed.

By the Second World War the rules were reversed: on linguistic
and ethnic grounds the Bulgarians claimed Macedonia as an
integral part of their own country (during the war Macedonian
Communists themselves rallied first to the Bulgarian not to the
Yugoslav Party). Since the war however the Titoists, with apparent success, have invested vast political capital in establishing
Macedonia's national authenticity. Its local dialect has been
turned into a literary language and the Communists have even set

up and financed an autocephalous church. Its present Primate is a former Partisan, archbishop Angelarije, whose office is not recognized by the Patriach of Serbia, head of a Church which has traditionally included Macedonia.[25]

Another area where the Communists have tried playing the periphery against the centre has been Bosnia-Herzegovina, a mixed community of approximately 40 per cent Moslem, 40 per cent Serb and 20 per cent Croat. The Moslems had done their best to stay out of the war in which they felt uninvolved. Sarajevo in 1942 had welcomed Hitler's friend, the Mufti of Jerusalem, before he went on to Zagreb to preach death to the Serbs as well as the Jews. The Ustashas never attacked the Moslems, treating them as honorary Croats, but many were the victims of indiscriminate Chetnik retaliation, and enough subsequently joined the Partisans to form several military units and to share the spoils of victory. Bosnia was rewarded with its own Republic but although the Yugoslavs followed the Soviet custom of including the nationality of each citizen in their census, nothing would induce the Serbs or Croats of Bosnia to declare themselves anything but Serb or Croat. The Communists therefore gave the word Moslem (with a capital M) a new meaning denoting not a religion but a national category. Anomalously, as a Party member may not practise religion, the Moslem members of the Central Committee in Bosnia had to call themselves Moslem atheists: a contradiction in terms.

Conscious of the religious realities, however, the Titoists did their best to appease practising Moslems. Their seminaries were generously endowed, their theologians treated as respected members of the academic community, and their publications received generous allocations of paper, enabling them to publish 100,000 copies of their religious books.

Further, whereas for the building of churches, permits were generally refused (in Belgrade the vast half-finished Cathedral of St Sava, intended by the monarchy to be the centre of Serb Orthodoxy, remains a physical reminder of atheist supremacy), there were no obstacles to the construction in Bosnia of about 800 new mosques, mainly paid for by Middle Eastern benefactors. Also, in foreign policy solidarity with the Moslems was demonstrated by the consistent support given by Tito and his successors to the PLO and all anti-Israel Arab states.

But with the Ayatollah Khomeini's accession to power (just in time to avert a scheduled visit of the Shah to Belgrade) Bosnia was penetrated by Islamic fundamentalism and it looked as if the

Communists, in promoting Islam, had created for themselves something of a Frankenstein monster. Pictures of the Ayatollah were pinned up in the windows of private houses (sometimes alongside those of Tito) and the young Moslems, particularly in the Medresa at Sarajevo, were swept away by anti-materialist, and implicitly anti-Marxist, religious fervour. The Ayatollah not only was the first "Third World" leader to withhold the ritual homage to Tito, but he publicly denounced him for persecuting religion "by corruption and by the gun".

The Communists did their best to cream off the Moslem élite: to ensure that this previously under-privileged community received its fare share of jobs, the quota system was introduced into all the Bosnian institutions, including even newspapers. But, even so, the success of the religious revival disturbed Tito's successors and, in the summer of 1983, they decided to make an example of thirteen Moslem intellectuals, allegedly associated with the *Moslem Declaration*. Claiming to be a programme for the Islamization of the Moslems, this document did not mention Yugoslavia but its implications were dynamite. It denounced Marxist materialism and the cult of personality (no need to specify Tito) and it enjoined the faithful to remember that there can be no separation between religion and public life. They must therefore prepare themselves to seize political power as soon as circumstances were propitious: action too soon would be as wrong as action too late.

After an extraordinary trial, in which some witnesses told the court they had been forced to give false testimony and were arrested on the spot, the prisoners were sentenced to a combined total of 90 years by a self-declared Moslem atheist, Judge Rozah Hajić.[26] On appeal, the sentences were reduced but the verdict upheld. "A mere farce" was the way in which the trial was described by a well-known Bosnian, Adil Zulfikarpašić, a former Partisan Commissar and member of the first postwar Bosnian government, who had emigrated to become leader of the Bosnian Moslem Association of exiles. Zulfikarpašić claimed that the people charged with conspiring did not even known each other and some of them were not fundamentalists at all, but modernizers like himself. He explained, however, that, whereas in the old days, he and his fellow-intellectuals had expressed their resistance to Serb rule by declaring themselves to be Croat, since the Islamic revival, they felt they had to go back to their roots and identify with the Moslem masses. He predicted that in a self-governing Bosnia, free to organize its own political life, the three communities would peacefully coexist, though he anticipated that the Serbs would hold fewer of the top jobs.[27]

The refusal of the Bosnian Moslems to go on thinking of themselves as Croats has further increased the Croats' sense of numerical—and therefore political—weakness in relation to the Serbs. As long as both communities go on believing that Bosnia belongs to them, there seems no end to the spiral of malevolence which divides them. Those Yugoslavs who favour government by consent rather than the present one-party rule, argue that if the matter could be openly discussed and the people given autonomy within their own religious groups, they could coexist peacefully as they did in the past.

Tito and his team were not the first to discover the old imperial principle of "divide and rule": but ruling is impossible if divisions go too far. In present-day Yugoslavia, there are constant references to the "disintegration" of the state, the word being used not only in unofficial comments but in the speeches of leading Communists. The view that relations between the Eight are worse than they were immediately after the war was suggested by several speakers at a meeting of the Central Committee of the Yugoslav Communist Party in March 1983. It has, of course, to be conceded that, under any form of government, the urge of the peoples of Yugoslavia to unite will be countered by the centrifugal forces of conflicting national loyalties. What has to be admitted however is that in 40 years of undivided power, the Communists, by their own admission, have deepened the cleavages.

Chapter 7

THE HOLY GRAIL OF SELF-MANAGEMENT

THE GREATEST CLAIM the Titoists have made for world recognition is that they have found a third way, between communism and capitalism. What they call "self-management" purports to free the worker, on one side, from the hardships and insecurity of the free enterprise system and, on the other, from dominance by the Soviet-style state bureaucracy. If the experiment had worked, the Western world would have been forced to re-examine the economic laws governing the market economy. Instead, it turned into a cautionary tale: efforts to manage the market diverted the pressures of demand and supply into such anti-social practices as high inflation, black markets in currency and commodities, smuggling, speculation, almost ubiquitous corruption and massive moonlighting in working hours. "The world owed Yugoslavia a debt", said a thoughtful young Yugoslav, representing his country abroad, "for those who believe in worker-control, we have shown how *not* to do it."

It is sometimes assumed that the 1948 rupture between Stalin and Tito exposed differences about how Communism should operate. This, as we saw in Chapter 4, reverses the order of events. The self-managing doctrine was initiated to fill the frightening ideological vacuum after Yugoslavia's expulsion from the Soviet bloc. Milovan Djilas, the brightest and, in those days, the most zealous of party theoreticians, plunged himself back into the Marxist–Leninist texts, the only political literature he knew. In it he found the syndicalist concept of a free association of workers in Marx's earlier works and in a pamphlet by Lenin written just before the Bolshevik revolution.[1]

It was after the imposition of the Soviet blockade and before the arrival of Western aid—and so at a time when the Yugoslav people were near starvation—that Djilas considered applying such a principle in Yugoslavia though he was unsure whether it would be wise to shift the responsibility for the catastrophe on to the workers' shoulders. His anxieties however were not shared by his two close associates, Kardelj and Kidrič, to whom he outlined his idea at a private meeting, in the unbugged privacy of his own car, parked outside his (later confiscated) villa. They seemed to approve in principle but favoured a few years' delay, and two days afterwards he was surprised to learn that work on the scheme would start at once.

According to Kardelj's reminiscences, the concept of self-management sprung spontaneously from the Partisan wartime practices,[2] but this, however, is unsubstantiated by any of the contemporary memoirs or despatches. On the contrary, at a time when the military aid was exclusively coming from the West, British and American liaison officers were surprised at the rigidly Stalinist line propagated by the political commissars attached to each Partisan unit.

Work on the new system lasted from four to five months and it was Kardelj who decided that the projected self-managerial powers should be attributed to workers' councils, of the kind already set up in the bigger factories. A new bill was already in draft when the three associates nervously broke the news to their master. At first Tito hesitated and it was Kardelj who won him over by convincing him that the idea of self-management could be a propaganda *coup*, particularly effective in rehabilitating Yugoslavia internationally within the workers' movement. "Tito paced up and down as though completely wrapped up in his own thoughts. Suddenly he exclaimed: 'The factories belonging to the workers: something that has never been achieved!' And with these words the theories worked out by Kardelj and myself seemed to shed their complexity and to acquire a better prospect of being carried into effect." And indeed it was Tito himself who, a few weeks later, introduced the new self-management proposal to the National Assembly, taking the opportunity to announce that, as the Yugoslav workers would henceforward manage their own factories, the category of wage-earner was here and now abolished.

Kardelj's belief in the propaganda value of self-management was to be amply justified. The Belgrade newspaper *Politika* was exaggerating when, immediately after Tito's death, it affirmed: "At one time it was written abroad that mankind would in future reckon its dates from the day Tito proclaimed the handing over of the factories to the workers: because he then went through the cosmos to absolute freedom for all men." But nonetheless the event did arouse international excitement, inspire countless books and monographs, and bring bevies of Western sociologists to Yugoslavia.

On the other hand, Tito's exclamation, "the factories belonging to the workers!'", though it did have a world-wide resonance, was in fact misleading. Under the self-management system Yugoslav factories, which were under public ownership, were never, then or later, handed over to their workers. Instead they were subject to a new legal framework which allowed the employees a share in some aspects of management. The means of production remained, as before, "socially owned", in other words, belonged to everybody and nobody, and were consequently at the disposal of whoever had the biggest political clout.

Though the general concept of self-management seems to have come from Djilas, there can be no doubt whatever that it was Edvard Kardelj who was its implementer. From 1950 until his death in 1979, Kardelj kept the self-management system, through all its permutations, under his personal direction. Indeed it is only by taking a closer look at the limitations of the man that we can understand the unbridgeable gulf which developed between, on the one hand, the legal texts embodying the principles of self-management and, on the other, the way management operated under one-party rule.

Unlike his leader, Kardelj seems to have been singularly devoid of personal charm which may have been an advantage: it meant that, despite his seniority in the Party, Tito knew he would never be a rival and he could totally trust him. After the other members of Tito's advisory triumvirate were disgraced—Djilas in 1954 and Ranković in 1966—Kardelj survived unchallenged as the second most important man in Yugoslavia. The contrast between the two men, whose partnership lasted for 40 years, was striking: Tito was a large, princely figure with strong exhibitionist inclinations; Kardelj was small, neat and inconspicuous, with a trim moustache, who, like his father before him, was trained to be a schoolmaster and all his life looked the part. Despite the eighteen-year age-gap between them, Kardelj's career in the Party went as far back as Tito's. In the mid-1920s, while Tito began his climb within the Communist-controlled trade-unions, Kardelj, still a schoolboy, was making his debut in the Communist youth movement. In the lax conditions of the time, he combined membership of an illegal and subversive party with a year's course in a teachers' training-school, which he completed in 1929. Nor did the authorities prevent the Ljubljana primary schools of the time from making wide use of a Marxist text-book he wrote for reading lessons. The police caught up with him after he had finished his training and he spent two years in prison for anti-régime agitation, and another two in Moscow, where he attended the Leninist school before becoming a full-time Comintern agent. He arrived in the Soviet Union with hardly any higher education and his mind was *tabula rasa* for the Marxist–Leninist imprint. Back in Ljubljana in 1933 he wrote an anti-bourgeois article "Trade and Merchants" for the schoolchildren's monthly *Naš Rod* (Our Generation).

As soon as Stalin allowed the Yugoslav party to reconstitute itself on home ground, Kardelj was appointed by Tito both to the Central Committee and Politburo. By 1941 he was Tito's right-hand man, and it was he who submitted the Politburo report to the first conference held in Yugoslavia by a purged and reconstituted party. When Moscow mobilized the Yugoslav Partisans, following the German attack on the USSR, Kardelj managed to combine the leadership of the Slovene Liberation Front (which at that time was promoting a separate Slovenia) with Vice-Presidency of the Yugoslav Central Committee.

At the end of 1943, Deakin met Kardelj at the Partisan Headquarters in Bosnia and, he later remembered, Kardelj "appeared, deceptively, to be a typical bookish Marxist intellectual". Deakin, already fully committed to the Partisan cause, claimed that it was Kardelj's "skill and moral stature" as the leader of the Slovene resistance movement which had turned Slovenia into "the only genuine regional all-party united front".[3] The image of unity was sustained only by eliminating any Slovene resisters unwilling to submit to Communist orders (see Chapter 3).

By the end of the war, when Tito was beginning to identify himself with Yugoslavia, Kardelj remained an unconditional Stalinist. And when, after the eruption over Trieste, Stalin had taken exception to Tito's protests that the Russians had let him down, it was Kardelj whom the Yugoslav Politburo chose to disassociate them from their leader's presumption. A dispatch to Moscow on 5 June 1945 from the Soviet Ambassador in Belgrade reveals the abjectness of his apology, which went so far as to suggest that the Soviet Union should annex Yugoslavia. It was published after the 1948 rupture and no Yugoslav has ever challenged the authenticity of the Ambassador's extraordinary report:

Today I spoke to Kardelj, as you suggested (Tito is not here). The communication made a serious impression on him. After some thought, he said he regarded our opinion of Tito's speech as correct. He also agreed that the Soviet Union could no longer tolerate similar statements. Naturally, in such difficult times for Yugoslavia, Kardelj said, open criticism of Tito's statement would have serious consequences for them and, for this reason, they would try to avoid similar statements. However, the Soviet Union would have the right to make open criticism should similar statements be repeated. Such criticism would benefit them. Kardelj asked me to convey to you fully his gratitude for this well-timed criticism. He said it would help them to improve their work.

In an attempt to analyse (very carefully) the causes of the mistakes, Kardelj said that Tito had done great work in liquidating factionalism in the Yugoslav Communist Party and in organising the people's liberation struggle. But Tito was inclined to regard Yugoslavia as a self-sufficient unit, outside the general development of the proletarian revolution and socialism. Secondly, such a situation had arisen in the Yugoslav party, because, as an organisation, the Central Committee did not exist. We meet by chance and we make decisions by chance. In practice every one of us is left to himself. The style of work is bad and there is not enough co-ordination in our work, Kardelj said. We would like the Soviet Union to regard them as representatives of another country, capable of solving questions independently, but as representatives of one of the future Soviet Republics, and the Communist Party of Yugoslavia as part of the Communist Party of the Soviet Union: that is that our relations should be based on the prospect of Yugoslavia becoming, in the future, a constituent part of the USSR. For this reason, they would like us to criticise them frankly and openly and to give them advice which would direct the internal and foreign policies of Yugoslavia along the right path.

The Soviet ambassador said he had warned the Yugoslavs they must recognize the fact that, under existing treaties and international obligations, Yugoslavia was at present an independent state with an independent party. But he reassured Kardelj: "We would never refuse advice, should you ask for it."[4]

Whether or not Kardelj took advantage of the offer is something we shall never know. But certainly in the postwar period his conduct was in accordance with the Stalinist model. Having, during the war, been principal advocate of a National Liberation

Front, in which all the participating political parties were supposed to be equal, he then took the lead in liquidating the partners in the coalition government, in whipping up hatred for those who tried to organize opposition (see Chapter 4) and in providing the theoretical justification for one-party rule.

Yet despite his actions and his writings, Kardelj has never forfeited the kindly image of himself in the West as a liberalizer and a moderating influence. In fact, in both word and deed, he showed that he believed not only that Marxism has revealed the absolute truth ("We Marxists know about the socio-historical roots of religion"), but also that all non-Marxists should be suppressed: during the civil war, by mass murder; afterwards, by selective incarceration. A natural gift for double-talk favoured this misconception. In defending the merits of Communism against Western-style democracy, he denounced the evils of the multiparty system as "monopolistic" and lauded "the pluralism" of one-party rule. In expounding the Marxist theory of the predetermined inevitability of the victory of Communism over capitalism, Khrushchev said it all in four words: "We will bury you!" Kardelj's approach was more oblique: "If we understand socialism, not as a perfect social ideal but as the process of the gradual transformation of social relations in conformity with the development of social ownership of the means of production, then the characteristic contestation in the world today is not between abstract socialism which is absolutely good and abstract capitalism which is absolutely bad, but between the concrete socialist system that is emerging and the concrete capitalist system which is breaking up."[5] In 1975, when Kardelj expressed this opinion, Yugoslavia was already living off Western loans.

Sceptics might suppose that Kardelj used abstruse language to conceal his meaning. But Slovenes who knew him believe, on the contrary, that the style was the man. The turgid, jargon-ridden prose of his political pronouncements faithfully reflects a stunted mind. In ordinary life he spoke like everyone else.

For Tito it was easy to see why Kardelj was the ideal choice as the man to develop and propagate the concept of self-management which was to make Yugoslavia and Titoism unique. A systematic account of all the laws and decrees, interpreting the doctrine, would fill hundreds of volumes and reveal very little about the Yugoslav economy. But in broad lines, the system developed in three main phases, covering three decades. The first, in the 1950s, allowed the workers' councils to share in the management of their factories, though the state held on to the main levers of economic power. The second, in the 1960s, represented a tentative move towards a market economy. The third, in the 1970s, marked a regress back to state-control, though, as we saw in the last chapter, the controls were now dispersed between the Federation's eight units.

In the first phase, selected groups of workers, acting under Party guidance and control, were given the right to be informed and consulted by the management. The managers themselves were selected—as they have been ever since—by the Party network, on which they have always relied for their appointment and promotion. But the most important of the first set of reforms was not the trumpeted introduction of self-management, but the dismantling of the Central Plan, and the transfer of the authority previously exercised by the planners, not to the workers, but to the party-controlled "people's committees". It was these which supervised the workers' councils, raised taxes, organized welfare, allocated investment and prevented political deviations.

These committees functioned within a territorial unit which Kardelj designated as communes inspired, he claimed, by the example of the 1871 Paris commune. (Not that there was any evident connexion between the gang of revolutionaries who temporarily ran Paris after the French defeat in the Franco–Prussian war and the newly installed Yugoslav committees, which Kardelj set up in the hope they would bolster the state's authority.)

In installing his new system, Kardelj relied not only on the party but also on the organizations it controlled. Of these the most important were the all-embracing Front known during the war as the Movement for National Liberation and renamed in 1952 the "Socialist Alliance of the Working People of Yugoslavia" (referred to in the West as SAWPY), the trade unions, the Youth League, and the Veterans' Association. These selected candidates for office and fixed the elections.

The fundamental weakness of the first phase of the system was that, having done away with coercive planning while still rejecting the guidance of the market's invisible hand, Kardelj had failed to provide any way of matching supply and demand. The communes competed against each other to build more and bigger plants and the rate of economic growth became the sole measurement of success. This produced a false dawn: most developing countries enjoy a spurt of industrial output during their initial take-off period of industrialization. (Dr John Moore of the Hoover Institution has noted a remarkable similarity between the Yugoslav and Soviet rates of growth during comparable periods of their development: in this respect, self-management seems to have made no difference.)[6]

And so the Yugoslav economy—like Topsy—just grew. The authorities, lacking any criteria for allocating capital, tried to satisfy everyone by the only available means of printing more money. And the first phase of self-management (like the other two) ended in a period of runaway inflation. The way was then open for a double act, with which the Yugoslavs were to become painfully familiar: on the domestic side, an indiscriminate monetary squeeze which, on the international side, opened the way for new credits from the IMF and Western governments.

After this inauspicious start, Kardelj's system entered its second phase: this time in a series of liberalizing measures, he did make concessions to market forces: some prices were decontrolled, some subsidies phased out, and the exchange rate of the *dinar* brought closer (though never too close) to its real value on the international monetary market. Socialized firms were encouraged, within limits, to compete against each other and some of the country's light industry was opened up to foreign competition.

The first to feel the pinch were city workers, who had previously benefited from highly subsidized food, energy, transport, housing and all basic necessities. And it was partly as compensation, that Kardelj conceded what has remained, from the point of view of the individual worker (though certainly not for the national economy), the system's most positive concession: the right they still retain to control the hiring and firing at their place of work. The most constructive innovation of the second phase of reforms was the recognition of the right of Yugoslav workers to seek jobs abroad. Unlike Kardelj's other initiatives this was a great creator of real wealth and also encouraged the independence and initiative of ordinary people. The concession was wrung out of the Communist leadership which was finding itself incapable of providing employment for the peasants coming in from the countryside. This process, common to all developing countries, had turned into a stampede as a consequence of their ill-judged policy of holding down food prices. The right to travel came while free-enterprise Europe was still short of labour; within a few years one in six of the whole Yugoslav workforce went West. The annual remittances of the emigrants' earnings was to make a vital contribution not only to the happiness of their own families but also to Yugoslavia's balance of payments. The newly granted freedom had however one grim side-effect: the mere threat of withholding passports, reportedly exercised against only a few thousand chosen victims (there are no official figures), was enough to tame most intellectuals. World travel was particularly necessary for the Yugoslav scientific community, deprived of the hard currency to buy equipment or journals. From then on, they rarely raised their voices against their political masters.

Freedom of travel was not accompanied by freedom to invest and the few years of stunted liberalism were insufficient to turn Yugoslavia into a market economy. Executives were ordered to improve the competitiveness by responding to market signals but, as Samuel Brittan wrote (in relation, not to Yugoslavia, but to British nationalized industries): "To publish a set of rules asking the managers of a state enterprise to behave as if they were profit-maximizing entrepreneurs in competitive private industry ignores the actual personal motivation faced by these men. . . . You do not make a donkey into a zebra merely by painting stripes on its back."[7]

Though, during the 1960s, Kardelj was a great painter of stripes, neither he nor Tito really liked to have businessmen making money independently of Party patronage. Soon they were associating themselves with an anti-managerial campaign launched by the Party hard-liners against "the red bourgeoisie". When in 1968 Belgrade students, following Western examples, started demonstrating, Tito turned the tables and took the side of the demonstrators. The "techno-bureaucrats" (a category which included managers, bankers and almost everyone with technical skills) became enemy number one. Not that Kardelj himself ever favoured equality. Workers, he believed, should be paid according to performance, at least until the coming of Communism, when, as Lenin predicted, everybody would have everything they wanted. It was Praxis, the far-left movement, which espoused the egalitarian and implicitly anti-Titoist cause. In 1967 it founded its own periodical (later suppressed) and its members gradually came round to favouring more Western concepts of intellectual freedom.[8]

The slackening of Party control during the period of reforms produced two unsettling results which, between them, led to the third and final phase of the Kardelj system. By releasing the energies of local nationalism, it obstructed progress towards a competitive and open economy (see previous chapter) while, at the same time, it stimulated what came to be known as "consumerism": demands of Yugoslavs for standards of living appropriate in the much more productive West. Everybody wanted cars, colour TVs, high-fi radios, and holidays abroad. Shaken by the first challenge the leaders tried to buy off the second by distributing more money.[9] By January 1971, the economy was again sliding out of control and this time Tito publicly promised: "Stabilization will not be at the expense of the working class." In the long run, it could not be at anyone else's, but the time of reckoning was delayed by foreign borrowing until Tito and Kardelj were dead.

Introduced in the 1970s, the third phase was primarily directed towards the control of the Party—or rather of its cadres. For since 1948 the Yugoslav League of Communists had quadrupled in numbers and the two million members of what was supposed to be the vanguard of the proletariat had little in common with its rear. Workers were a small minority and the overwhelming majority of the two million belonged to professions for which membership was a precondition for employment or promotion: notably the administration, the judiciary, the media, the army, the police, and higher education.

The final phase was introduced by Tito's directive to the Party cadres in 1972 (see previous chapter) which not only reaffirmed Party discipline but also reversed the liberalizing trends of the 1960s. The subsequent purge (by dismissal not death) affected businessmen as well as politicians: in Belgrade alone 50 managers of large enterprises lost their jobs.

The Tito letter was a prelude to two voluminous, legally binding documents: first, the 1974 constitution (the fourth since the Communists took over) contained ten basic principles of several paragraphs each plus 406 articles and, as Kardelj boasted, was one of the longest in the world. The second, the Law of Associated Labour, had 671 articles and was so complex and obscure that no labourers could hope to understand it.

The two texts, compiled by committees of Kardelj's disciples, are still in force—or would be if they were enforceable. They guaranteed the rights of people in general, and of workers in particular, but negated this proposition by leaving the party above and beyond the law. They also specifically guaranteed the right to work, although by that time Yugoslavia was already becoming one of the countries with the highest rates of unemployment in Europe.

It was in this final phase that Kardelj introduced the new delegate system: voters would elect not representatives to speak on their behalf but delegates to do their bidding (in practice, the bidding of the party). Such a change of name might seem meaningless as long as the candidates were, anyway, all selected by the Communist Party. But Kardelj informed the Party cadres that in future Party policy should be implemented "first and foremost at the delegate level". The main instruments Party control were the newly created "socio-political" organizations set up at each level of government. The committee system was generalized, so that, after Tito, leadership could be eliminated. Instead Kardelj introduced a system of permanent rotation, in which everybody changed jobs, in most cases every year, in others every two or four years, giving the whole political system the appearance of an Alice-in-Wonderland tea-party.

In practice this meant that a small ruling élite, selected by Tito and later by his successors, was constantly changing jobs, making it impossible to establish personal responsibility for any decision. The relative importance of the different institutions depended on the place occupied at the time by the most influential politicians. "All essential functions in the Federation and the states are performed by at most a hundred-odd people" said Štipe Šuvar, a Croat Communist, in 1972.[10] Most recent references to the continuation of "horizontal rotation", as it is called, suggests that nothing has changed; although by now Štipe Šuvar is a leading figure in Croat policies and one of the happy hundred.

One of the leading beneficiaries of "horizontal rotation" was Mika Špiljak. He was to become President of the Presidency and be received at the White House at the beginning of 1984. When I met him in 1981 he was top man in the Yugoslav trade-union movement. It was soon after the Solidarity explosion in Poland and as I was particularly interested in the relation between the Party and the trade unions, I had asked the authorities whether I could interview representatives of each.

A member of the Secretariat of Information told me cheerfully that I could kill two birds with one stone: Špiljak was a senior member of both institutions. We met at offices far more luxurious than those of any British trade union and he assured me that, though the Yugoslav workers were disciplined enough to have accepted the nine per cent cut in real wages as a consequence of the present economic crisis, if this should happen again they would take industrial action. Adopting a bluff, plebeian manner, he sounded as if he were speaking for the work-force rather than as part of the ruling body. The year 1984 when he was President was the third in succession in which real wages had fallen behind prices by between nine and ten per cent; as in other Communist countries, the Yugoslav trade unions had served their role as transmission belts for party purposes.

Just as on the labour front the Communists would not permit independent trade unions, so on the managerial front they were unwilling to lose their grip over production and distribution. In his third and last package of reforms, Kardelj set out to replace what he called "the blind forces of the market" by "social compacts": a nationwide network of deals in which compromise reached under Party auspices would replace competition.

In the industrial sector Kardelj institutionalized cartels: delegates from a whole branch of industry were brought together and made to agree on deals covering wages, prices, investment plans, foreign trade and the distribution of the always scarce hard currency.[11] The compulsorily applied agreements tore to shreds the idea of workers being free to dispose of the fruits of their labour—which had initially inspired the whole self-management dogma.

In the finance system, too, entrepreneurial initiatives were eliminated. During the semi-liberal era bankers had been encouraged to use their commercial expertise and had consequently enriched both themselves and their institutions. Kardelj hit back by abolishing the banks. He had them replaced by what he called 'Financial Associations of Associated Labour' (the Yugoslavs still call them banks), which belonged to the enterprises which were also their chief borrowers. The banks, by another name, continued to be responsible for distributing credits and, operating under no commercial constraints, stayed the principal agents of inflation until the 1980s, when the IMF blew the whistle.

Yet in this constitutional jungle Kardelj still went on advocating "scientific planning": the compacts were supposed to be coordinated into a collective national plan, elaborated from the bottom upward. Negotiations, at district, commune, republic and federal levels, now took up many millions of working hours. (A much-travelled Belgrade economics professor said that conferences are now as much part of the life of Yugoslav workers as tea-breaks are for the British: a fair analogy, except that tea-breaks are shorter.) Even so, agreements on prospective One-Year and Five-Year Plans are rarely reached until several months after they are scheduled to start. No one minds, for, as *Borba* wrote on 16 July 1984, "the common characteristic of development of many if not all One-Year and Five-Year Plans of development is that during the past decades they are never realized."

On the social side, in the various branches of welfare— education, health, social security, cultural facilities (including sport), public transport etc.—social compacts were negotiated under tripartite "Communities of Interest", representing the people who used them, those who paid for them and those who operated them. In line with Kardelj's other institutions, the massive participation of the workers in committees and consulta- tive bodies was largely a parade. Everyone knew that the real decisions were taken by a handful of political bosses in advance of the meetings so that on the days set for selecting delegates from the factories, the workers often contrived to arrive late, hoping their names would be left off the lists.

In many cases, to avoid unpleasant confrontations, extravagant social compacts were signed which satisfied everybody but for which there were no resources. In 1983 it was calculated that the compacts signed in the previous year could have been honoured only by doubling the national income and by tripling the foreign debt.

Far from reconciling conflicting interests the system exacer- bated class divisions. The local workers objected to having money deducted from their pay-sheets while the providers of services —teachers, doctors, nurses—resented never being paid enough to keep up with inflation. Today, even in relatively prosperous and traditionally incorruptible Slovenia it is common for doctors to expect a tip. As in the capitalist world, when the economic situation deteriorated the first squeeze was on social services. And though, theoretically and according to the texts, the Yugoslavs still enjoy welfare on a Scandinavian level, in reality, as reported in a Zagreb newspaper, by 1983 these services had declined "to a beggar's level".

Another central feature of the 1970s package was to break up Yugoslav industry into what Kardelj labelled "Basic Organiza- tion of Associated Labour": groups consisting of between 50 and 500 men, representing the smallest unit qualified to run separate accounts.[12] After the "big is beautiful" period of the 1960s, when the party dreamed of creating companies on the scale of General Motors and ordered the amalgamation of companies regardless of commercial criteria, the new industrial giants had begun to identify themselves with their own republics. Kardelj had then come round to believing that the smaller groups would be more closely linked with their own companies and so would manifest class, rather than national, solidarity. In practice, the decline of intra-federal trade continued (see previous chapter) and the integrity of the Yugoslav market, though constitutionally guaranteed, slid further away than ever. For the party, however, the dismantling of big business did have the advantage of providing large numbers of new managerial and clerical jobs and so creating another stratum of dependable cadres. Between 1977 and 1984 the figure of basic units rose from 10,000 to 29,661. The railway system alone was split up into 350 separate businesses.

The way the system operated varied according to region. Bosnia went on treating its big firms as single entities and in 1983 a leading member of the Bosnian Chamber of Commerce told me that three-quarters of his Republic's investments were concentrated into ten big companies. In Croatia, on the other hand, where the local people tended to be more educated, each unit stood out for what it knew were its rights, introducing an element of blackmail against the management. Thus the petrochemical company INA, which had been compelled to take over a whole lot of questionable ventures, now found itself deprived both of its assets (legally allocated to the basic units) and of its authority.

The consequences of managerial impotence were graphically described by INA's former marketing director, Djureković. Every subsidiary demanded additional jobs and investment capital, which the headquarters could neither afford nor refuse. Productivity was pitiful: as a result of local pressure, three oil refineries were built where one would have sufficed. In the refineries, which Djureković visited, Shell International employed an administrative staff of twelve or fifteen; for the same tasks in 1983 his own company was forced to take on several hundred. Djureković had given up and defected and, in the summer of 1983, a few weeks after visiting me in London and telling me INA's inside story, his corpse was found near his new home in Munich.[13] By this time, according to a British specialist on the Yugoslav economy, INA was losing one million dollars a day.

By splitting up firms or, as his critics would say, "atomizing" Yugoslav industry, Kardelj assumed that he would bring the workers closer to the management. In practice, as the sociologist, Professor Neca Jovanov, was able to show, the allegedly self-managed firms, whatever their size, were effectively controlled by a tight little group he identified as the *aktiv*: "Five, six leading officials of enterprises gather: the director and his aides, the chairman of the workers' council, the secretary of the League of Communists organization, who is usually a supernumerary. There, mainly under the pressure of the management, a political position is formulated, which in fact amounts to a decision. At that meeting of the *aktiv*, the chairman of the workers' council is assigned the duty of getting it formally accepted by the workers' council; the secretary of the League of Communists fixes political support; the trade-union chairman sends it through the trade unions, the chairman of the Youth Organization does what he can. . . . In that way the entire self-management and political structure is officially mobilized to support the decisions of a group which from a sociological standpoint is outside the system and from the legal point of view, forbidden, but which exercises huge powers. . . ."[14]

An American geologist employed in one of the joint enterprises exploring off-shore oil asked to attend the meetings of his basic work unit to report back on how the self-management system worked. He informed his company that it functioned well as a downward system of communication, enabling the management to convey and explain their instructions to the work-force—but seemed to lack any facility by which the worker could send his grievances or ideas upward to the management.

Did Edvard Kardelj ever recognize the fiasco over which he presided? Looking back at the record of the three phases of his *magnum opus* I had initially had the impression of a man so blinkered by doctrine that he would never see what was really happening. Such an image fitted his wife Pepica, an uneducated Party member whom he met and married when they were in the same communist youth cell. Today, well in her seventies, Pepica continues to defend the Kardelj heritage and is still active in the Slovene communist party sternly repressing any liberalizing inclinations. She must be a lonely woman. Kardelj's only legitimate son had developed a strong antipathy towards his parents' style of life, had tried to make himself a university career, took to drink and, before he was thirty years old, had committed suicide.

It seems that Kardelj himself, in the last years of his life, had come to perceive the corruption, incompetence and greed of the people to whom his one-party system had delivered the country. They were those whom Milovan Djilas had identified as "the new class", and according to Dr Eugene Pušić, Professor of sociology at

Zagreb, by that time, Kardelj's and Djilas's views were very similar. Pušić had been a Party member since before the war, though it was only in the 1980s, by chance of circumstances, that he came to know Kardelj.

The occasion was an international conference on self-management which Pušić had organized. All the papers were written by academics but a proletarian image was needed and it had therefore been decided to have the meeting chaired by the head of the Yugoslav trade union movement. Just before it was due to start, Pušić had been urgently summoned to Belgrade. He took the overnight train and found himself in the marble-pillared union headquarters, confronted by men in what were supposed to be peak positions in Yugoslavia's "worker state", but sitting crestfallen and manifestly frightened. The previous day they had learnt that Kardelj, second in power only to Tito, had taken exception to the conference programme, and they needed Pušić to persuade him that no harm was meant. The professor was guided through intricate corridors to Kardelj's private office and, in no time at all, the ice was broken and the two men were sharing beer and sandwiches. Pušić was able to reassure Kardelj that the conference would enhance his reputation and they remained friends.

The paper which had most offended Kardelj was written by a Slovene and Kardelj poured out his grievances against Slovene intellectuals who, he complained, treated him as a jumped-up schoolmaster and a tool of Belgrade. (This was typical of Yugoslav inter-ethnic jealousies: I had been assured by a Serb professor that Kardelj had invented his entire system exclusively for the benefit of the Slovenes.) Kardelj's distrust for his intellectual compatriots was not entirely new. In his reminiscences he had recalled that Stalin had warned him against the untrustworthiness of Slovene intellectuals and that his subsequent experience had shown him that Stalin had a point.[15]

Increasingly aware in his later life that power was in the hands of a corrupt and irresponsible minority, Kardelj began examining ways in which some elements of opposition and accountability could be introduced into the system.

In the first edition of a new work on self-management, published in 1977, he suggested that conflicts of interest were inevitable in all societies, and the Yugoslav Communist Party should sometimes be ready to find itself in a minority and to adjust its policies accordingly. The idea so shocked the Party veterans that they appealed to Tito himself, and Kardelj, having stuck his neck out, sharply pulled it in again. The following year a corrected edition of the work was published: this made it clear that Kardelj was not suggesting that any individual could know better than the Party. All he had meant was that there might be differences between self-managed units; as these were all safely under Party control, the objections were withdrawn.

Conveniently, Edvard Kardelj died the following year, and could be rehabilitated as an incarnation of self-management. On television, Tito paid a personal tribute to "my closest associate" and the Central Committee declared that Kardelj's work had been "built into the foundations of socialist consciousness and creativeness". Overlooking the final slip-up, the Committee declared that "for more than five decades, Comrade Kardelj confirmed the revolutionary and humanist character of the fight for socialism and for human happiness. For a long time to come, this vision of the future, of a great morning, will illuminate the Party in our struggle for achievements and aims of our revolution."[16] In 1984 it was announced that Kardelj's collected works would be published in 50 volumes over the next ten years.

The lamentations of the Central Committee were parroted by Titoists in the West. In an obituary of Kardelj in the Journal of London's British–Yugoslav Society, Phyllis Auty expressed veneration for "a man who worked unremittingly all his life for his political ideas". She regretted that he had not had time to finish his autobiography (in the uncompleted version, Kardelj alleges British-Nazi collaboration against the Partisans in 1942) but argued: "It was more important for Yugoslavia that he could do his duty as a man of action and an exponent of the theory of Yugoslavia's new socialism."[17] Yugoslavia might be better off if Kardelj had stuck to school-teaching.

The final phase of Kardelj's system coincided with the abundance of petrodollars.[18] By the time he and Tito died the Yugoslavs were living at eleven per cent above their national earnings, with foreign credits making up the difference. The fall when the money ran out, however, was much greater than eleven per cent, as by now the eight parts of the Yugoslav Federation had all developed export-dependent and largely autarchic industries and there had also been a sharp increase in interest-rates on hard currency loans. Between the years 1980 and 1984 real personal incomes were declared to have dropped on average by 30 per cent. A Slovene sociologist calculated that between 1982 and 1984 the number of hours of work required to buy cooking-oil or a pair of children's shoes had doubled. Figures for Yugoslavia's decline varied according to sources. According to the popular magazine *Danas*, 1 October 1983, the Yugoslav average income, reckoned in dollars or deutschmarks, had halved over six years. For many people, of course, life was less bleak than the statistics suggested: earnings in the grey or black sector do not show up in official charts. Though temporary difficulties were eased by foreign credits the Yugoslav economists, meeting at their annual conference in Opatija in November 1983, claimed that, in the long run, the hard currency loans, by postponing the necessary retrenchment and reform, had made things worse. Some of the investment did however have lasting value: many highways, bridges, irrigated fields and orchards and modern industrial plants could not have been built without Western capital and, even if Yugoslavia defaults, they cannot be taken away. The benefits for the West were more dubious. In Britain's case, orders from Yugoslavia in the 1970s did create additional jobs in its declining heavy industry but these were mainly paid for by the British tax-payer (in the form of long-term, unrepayable credits) and from his point of view, the money could have been more productively spent on Britain's own ageing infrastructure.

But political priorities came first: after Tito's death, the IMF, the guiding light of Western governments and banks, gave Yugoslavia a three-year stand-by credit of 2.3 billion dollars: an unconditional sum bigger than anything previously offered to a developing country. It was intended to tide Yugoslavia over what was expected to be a painful three-year period of deflation: in fact it coincided with a time when prices were rising annually, from 30 to 60 per cent. The IMF error is easily explained: its staff were mostly trained in classical business schools and took a long time to understand why the orthodox policies of higher rates of interest and restrictive monetary policies failed to stabilize prices. They were unaware that in Yugoslavia, when credits dry up, the socialized firms stop paying their debts to each other. Dr Spasoje Medenica, a Federal Minister, calculated that the internal debt (including the outstanding bills, the overruns of investment costs and the credit obligations to the National Bank arising from the devaluation of the *dinar*) amounted in 1983, to 2,000 billion *dinars*: a figure representing one half of Yugoslavia's national income. According to Branko Ćolanović, the Chairman of Jugobanka of Belgrade in 1983, "Yugoslav enterprises are indebted to the banks and the banks to each other, and everyone is indebted to everyone

else. We are excessively preoccupied with foreign currency and
have neglected dinar insolvency." In these circumstances the
persistent IMF clamour for "a positive rate of interest" i.e. one
that is higher than the current rate of inflation, has predictably
fallen on deaf ears.

To prevent a financial breakdown, massive rescue operations
worth several billion dollars each had to be put together in 1983
and again in 1984, by international institutions, capitalist governments and commercial banks, under the sponsorship of the US
administration, relieving the Yugoslavs of the immediate obligation to repay the capital. But further help would certainly be
required to enable the Yugoslavs even to continue paying the
interest rate on existing obligations.

"Stabilization" ever since 1956 has been a *leitmotiv* of Yugoslav
official speeches always around the corner. After a journey
through the country in 1983, I wrote to ask the IMF how they
justified their continued endorsement of such manifestly unsuc-
cessful policies. "Measures to enhance efficiency will continue to
constitute essential elements in future IMF programmes with
Yugoslavia", replied Mr Duncan Ripley, Division Chief for
Central Europe. "And in this connexion, we are looking carefully
at the recommendations of the Krajger Stabilization Commission."

This Commission had assembled many of Yugoslavia's leading
specialists (though some of the best refused to serve) and, in the
summer of 1983, issued a number of recommendations favouring
increased competition and more reliance on market criteria. It was
shrugged off by the experts who said that the solutions had been
known for twenty years. As the Commission's chairman, Sergej
Krajger, commented: "Every single reform we recommend needs
a market. But the operation of the market would only destroy the
powers of the ruling body. And this is the Rubicon which those in
office do not wish to cross."[19] They have not crossed it yet.

Since 1968 the Yugoslavs have permitted partnerships between
their own and capitalist firms hoping to profit from hard currency
and know-how. But the rules have been highly restrictive and
though in 1984 there were plans to relax them, Western firms were
unlikely to feel secure in a country where multinational corporations are part of the official demonology.

Struggling to meet their obligations and to preserve their credit-
worthiness, the Yugoslav officials are driving their factories "to
export at any cost". Dumping in the technical meaning of the word

is banned but, as in all Communist countries, there is no way of establishing fair prices. When the Yugoslavs offered a French company ships at one-third of the international price—a sum which would barely cover the costs of the raw materials, it was the French trade unions which vetoed the deal.

Avoiding the complications of joint enterprises and the rules and regulations of self-management, some businessmen simply buy whole production-lines in Yugoslav factories. In Dubrovnik I met a young executive from a Yorkshire textile firm which had ceased to produce its own ready-made clothes, these being available in Yugoslavia at less than half the British price. Their man in Dubrovnik dealt with six factories, scattered over Yugoslavia, some efficient, others less so. The company took no risks: they had retained the right to reject any delivery which failed to arrive on time or to meet required standards. All their man had to do was to negotiate satisfactory prices: these the Yugoslavs varied according to the client and the Yorkshireman was proud of having got better terms than his Arab and American competitors.

The Russians also buy up the entire output of some of the factories, and one small cloth-manufacturer in a port near Dubrovnik was engaged exclusively, when I was there, in making overcoats for the Soviet army. In the trade figures this form of export is not listed separately but it is clear that both for the Russians and West Europeans Yugoslavia is now a reservoir of cheap labour.

In examining how, after the initial industrial leap (characteristic, as we saw, of the first phase of development), Yugoslavia has now sunk back into this semi-colonial condition, we need to reassess the system itself. For, within the foreseeable future, Yugoslavia will remain up to its neck in debt, and as a Federal Minister, Mr Živorad Kovačević, told the Assembly, on 27 November 1984: "One thing is clear, if we do not free ourselves from this excessive indebtedness, there will be no further economic independence, or indeed any independence at all, for our country."

A great deal of work has been and is being done, in Yugoslavia and abroad, on better and more honest ways of implementing the self-management system. The time has come to ask whether the principle itself is not so incompatible with the basic rules of commonsense and the norms of human behaviour that it never could have worked in the first place. This is not, of course, the popular view; nor indeed, inside Yugoslavia may such dangerous thoughts be expressed. Generations of Yugoslavs have been brought up to believe that self-management is inherently virtuous —like kindness to animals in England—and that it would be wicked to reject. Many of them, of course, know better, but dare not publicly say so. Further, self-management enjoys very widespread sympathy and support in the West. Many industrial countries are seeking and failing to find new ways to associate their workers more directly in their enterprises and are sympathetic to the Yugoslav Communists, who seem to be trying. Western leaders visiting Belgrade often pay public homage to self-management principles. Thus in 1977, Conservative leader Mrs Margaret Thatcher made herself very welcome in Belgrade (at least in the official circles in which she moved) by saying that the Yugoslav system compared favourably with the socialism then being practised in Britain by the Labour Prime Minister James Callaghan. And when Mr Roy Jenkins, then Chairman of the EEC, was seeking to improve relations with Yugoslavia in the uncertain times just after Tito's death, he used his official visit to speak reverentially of Yugoslavia's "unique form of socialism": unique it was, but not in the way he meant.

The fundamental error of the concept was that it relied on a non-existent work ethic. Kardelj and his disciples believed that man, having been alienated from the fruits of his labour, could be reconciled to life if the means of production were no longer in the hands of capitalist exploiters. If he had been brought up on Genesis instead of on Karl Marx, he would have known that man works "by the sweat of his brow" to live and does not live to work. Political zealots, creative artists and talented professionals may indeed find fulfilment in their work, but the ordinary run of people are less interested in what they produce than in what they consume and, as human beings, more concerned about what goes on outside the factory and outside working-hours.[20]

This is especially true in Yugoslavia, where people identify not with their work unit—or in Kardelj's language, their Basic Organization of Associated Labour—but rather with their family, their clan and perhaps also their native village. "Of all the areas of human interaction," wrote the anthropologist, Dr Andrej Simić of the University of California, after four years of field work in Yugoslav towns and villages, "family and kinship are the most compelling." He sees the survival of this tradition as something of a social blight: "I would like to suggest that the cultivation of social ties with kin and non-kin alike, can be said to constitute a

Yugoslav national vice. The interest of interpersonal relations is an all-absorbing one, which frequently goes so far as to inhibit the rationalization of the country's administrative and economic foundations."

Perhaps it does, but Simić might also have pointed to the positive benefits provided by the solidarity of the clan. This may be indeed a principal reason why newly urbanized Yugoslavia is almost entirely free of the shanty-towns and *bidonvilles* which disfigure the cities in most developing countries. If a Yugoslav peasant comes to town, he generally joins someone else from his family or his neighbourhood who got there before him. Hygiene and amenities may suffer and several generations including in-laws may be difficult to live with. But he does find not only a home but also a living and welcoming community. Further, the plan underpins Yugoslavia's highly inadequate social security, and most of the unemployed, now edging towards a million, live at home off their families.

Even if Kardelj were right and workers did derive pride and self-respect from being managers, this does not mean that they would be any good at it. On the contrary, as every company executive in the West knows, the manager of a modern enterprise requires a rare combination of stamina, energy and skills, which is why the best business schools can be highly selective and their graduates command almost any salary. As Professor Harold Lydall writes: "An ordinary worker can no more take responsibility for management decisions than he can carry out a surgical operation, write a symphony or play in a champion football team."[21]

Not that Kardelj, with his school-masterish impatience with shirkers and slackers, ever overestimated the capacity of ordinary men and women. On the contrary, he clung right through his life to the conviction of Marx and Lenin that an uneducated labourer is inherently incapable of perceiving his own best interests and should therefore do as he is told. Over and over again, in his writings Kardelj condemns as "infantile" the "theory of spontaneity": that is the belief that workers should be free to do as they liked. In his last work *Socialism and Democracy*, he calls again for "energetic action" against holders of the foolish opinion "that the working man self-manager can make competent decisions and secure his social progress by relying on his spontaneous and pragmatic reaction to everything around him."[22]

In theory the self-managed firms were supposed to function as

independently-run businesses, providing the benefits of competition without the inequalities of capitalism. But if the workers were
really going to depend on what they produced, they would be more
interested in *good* management than in *self*-management. Under
existing rules the employee has the right and obligation to see
endless documents and accounts (and the Rank Xerox copying-
machines are worked more intensively in Yugoslavia than anywhere else) but records of meetings show that the only part of the
management in which they are actively interested has been jobs,
welfare and pay.

Yugoslavia's relative poverty, compared to conditions in other
Mediterranean countries, is sometimes attributed by Yugoslavs
themselves to national character: the absence of any industrial
tradition; the well-entrenched custom of bakshish or the long-
established preference for clerical over manual labour. This
however is belied by the high reputation Yugoslav workers enjoy
in Western Europe. It is only in their own country, where nothing
belongs to anybody and no one is responsible for anything, that
they tend to withhold labour or to redirect their energies into
non-socialized activities.

An executive from the US firm Dow Chemicals, working in a
joint petrochemical enterprise in Croatia, recalled installing a
factory in a new site, which included a large lake. In mid-morning
the American asked why nobody was working: the answer was
obvious, it was a beautiful day and the men had gone fishing.

The enterprises themselves tend to be mini-welfare states. I
have visited factories which had been ordered by their local
commune to take on a fixed quota of additional labour every year.
This applied regardless of whether the manpower was needed and
in some cases where, for the lack of raw materials, the firms were
running at only half capacity. The Slovene economist, Professor
Aleksandar Bajt, has claimed that Yugoslav firms could rid
themselves of one-third of their personnel without any damage to
their production.

It would be wrong, of course, to deduce from this that all the
self-managed enterprises, through the length and breadth of
Yugoslavia, are failures. On the contrary, there have been cases
where a talented management, working in close harmony with the
Party bosses, have managed to recruit a competent work-force and
produced spectacular results. The Bosnian heavy engineering firm
of Energo-Invest has won contracts in developing countries
against sharp competition from Western bidders and the furni-

ture-producing Slovenia firm of Gorenje has carved itself a substantial share in the highly competitive Western markets.

The famous textile firm "First of May" in Eastern Serbia is a model of which its own workers are manifestly proud. Service on the premises includes crêches, hairdressers and a gymnasium, as well as a little museum, showing the factory in pre-war capitalist days when it was no more than a miserable little workshop, with haggard-looking labourers. Outside office-hours the staff have been encouraged to engage in constructive activities and have created themselves a fine garden, with fountains and band-stand, a sports stadium and an Olympic-size swimming pool. When I was there in 1979 the "First of May" had already received visits from 87 foreign delegations, including one headed by the Mayor of Glasgow. When a Soviet group arrived, I was told, they refused to believe that the workers themselves had volunteered their labour and stayed convinced they were being shown a Potemkin village.

In seeking out examples of success in the socialized sector, I was sent by a Professor of Economics at the Belgrade University to visit a bright former student, now an entrepreneur and Party boss, Dušan Pašić. Pašić had indeed successfully transformed the previously backward Serbian township of Milanovac into a profitable agro-industrial complex. I found a successful company town, and Pašić a local boy who made good. After studying economics in Belgrade and joining the Party, he had set up a conglomerate employing several thousand. Most had land of their own in the neighbourhood and were pleased to work cheaply in their free time, particularly for the most profitable of his ventures, the manufacture of a local brand of *eau de vie*.

For those coming from outside, Pašić provided housing on credit and whether they liked it or not, his workers were paid according to performance. All his materials were locally produced and 60 per cent of his output was exported to hard currency markets. When we met in the summer of 1983 he had just returned from a trip to England to sell locally made toys.

But as the Belgrade professor had warned me, Pašić was the exception: in most cases the investors were party functionaries who did not stay to preside over the venture which they financed. And—as a minimum of commonsense would have enabled Kardelj to perceive—waste and extravagance were inevitable consequences of a system where those in charge of investment had neither the prospect of gain nor risks associated with failure. As Prime Minister Milka Planinc said in a TV interview on 29

November 1984: "In a healthy economy, if someone can't sell, he either reduces prices or goes under. This has not started happening here. . . ."

A description of how the investment process works in Yugoslavia today was given to me by a leading Croat economist, often called in to advise the Croat Central Committee. As long as a project was under construction, he said, the man in charge was the dispenser of jobs, contracts and foreign currency, and enjoyed god-like stature. But, once it went into production the venture was socialized and the Kardelj self-management rules were applied: workers assumed the right to hire and fire, the enterprise had to finance both local and federal spending and the local bureaucrats could be counted on to strangle every initiative.

Thus whereas private entrepreneurs would want the construction and equipping of the premises to be as short and cheap as possible, the Party-appointed investor would have an interest in making it as large, expensive and above all long-lasting as possible. Further, a senior manager, operating in the Yugosalv system, would aim to leave the project the moment production went on stream. He would then be free to seek a new project or to take advantage of the system of "horizontal rotation", entitling him to be town-mayor, bank manager or Party secretary, at whatever his appropriate rank.

Despite the exceptions, most self-managed enterprises, as Dr Ljubo Sirc has pointed out, failed to earn enough even to finance the renewal of the existing fixed capital.[23] And an overwhelming majority of them relied on borrowed money not just as in the West for their capital investment but also for their daily operating costs. According to one Assembly delegate Momćilo Tomić, as much as 86 per cent of the working capital in Yugoslav industry has been on credit. Tomić informed the National Assembly that some 6,300 socially owned firms (out of a total of around 26,000) were at that time unable to meet their immediate obligations.[24]

As a loss-making venture, the story of the rise and fall of the Macedonian nickel works, FENI, is exceptional only in the scale of the costs, of which over 80 per cent were in hard currency. Operations started in 1956, when reserves of nickel were discovered in the Macedonian mountains (though it turned out that only an infinitesimal proportion of ore contained sufficient nickel to be worth exploiting). The local bosses disliked living too far from town and the forge was therefore built 50 kilometres away, in a choice residential area near some of Macedonia's finest vineyards.

Six years later, the Belgrade Institute of Economics recommended that the project be cancelled: the ore's nickel content was too low, transport too expensive and energy too dear. A Macedonian civil engineer promised to eat his doctor's diploma if the business proved a success. Notwithstanding these warnings, a forge with a capacity of 21,000 tons a year was built and by 1984 was producing 2,733 tons. The Macedonian authorities calculated that the losses to the community incurred by constructing and operating the nickel-works would be larger than those sustained by the unforgettable 1963 earthquake at Skopje, in which much of the city had been destroyed. But the local people went on resisting a closure and a compromise was reached: the mine and forge, at least temporarily would suspend production. The machine-room, hotel and computer department would carry on.

Yugoslavia has survived such catastrophes partly because a good deal of economic activity remains in private hands. Just how much is hard to calculate. In farming, 85 per cent of the land is still privately owned, though it is the socialized fifteen per cent which received almost all the new investment and allocations of foreign currency. In Communist countries agriculture has always been the step-child and in Yugoslavia, as a result of the long postwar period of depressed prices, the countryside has been drained of labour and ten per cent of the arable land, including some very fertile regions in Vojvodina, are no longer being ploughed. Most of the fertile regions of the Danube and Sava valleys would be ideally suited for family farms, extending over a few hundred acres, but, ever since the Communists took over, for ideological reasons a ceiling of ten hectares has been placed on private holdings (though many farmers make private arrangements with their neighbours and cultivate far more). Kardelj's faith lived after him. In February 1984, some 200 of his disciples chose farming as the topic of their annual conference on "The Thoughts and Revolutionary Work of Edvard Kardelj": the first condition for raising output they resolved would be to socialize more land.

In urban activities, according to the official 1981 census, there were 200,000 privately owned firms, employing an additional 100,000 workers. The figure is obviously far too low leaving out all those who prefer not to register their activities, and most economists agree that, in reality, half the income earned by working people comes from activities undertaken outside the jobs they hold in the socialized sector.[25]

A suggestion that private enterprise was becoming so important to the economy that it was bound to carve itself a corresponding political status, was put to me in 1980 by a Croat sociologist, Professor Dušan Bilandžić (who ironically noted that the man who repaired his TV earned more than he did and that some private farmers whom he knew were making fortunes). Some Western diplomats also argue that, little by little, private initiative will erode the Communist monopoly and change Yugoslavia into an open and plural society. A speaker at a party meeting in Serbia in June 1984 conceded that there were some two million Yugoslavs engaged in private activities and warned that these might be expected to exercise an undesirably right-wing influence.[26]

In practice, however, private firms are still publicly attacked as social parasites and only individuals with sufficient hard currency or connexions in high places can hope for a permit to set themselves up in business. Once they are launched however the absence of competition enables them to benefit from virtually monopolistic conditions; huge fortunes are made out of restaurants, hairdressing salons and bakeries. As there is no possibility of investing the gains productively, the new millionaires put their money into yachts, palaces and sometimes into monumental tombs for themselves and their families, and conspicuous consumption has given the private sector a bad name.

But, as in other Communist countries, individually owned businesses exist only on sufferance, depending on political favours. To get the necessary materials or hard currency they are almost always compelled to involve themselves in black-market transactions. And, as the President of the Council for legal questions in Croatia pointed out: "From the constitutional point of view, the idea of private ownership is not recognized."[27]

A former mayor of Belgrade, Milojoko Drulović, once told me that at the top echelons, the Party has frequently recommended a less restrictive attitude towards private enterprise, recognizing that it is an essential prerequisite of providing services of which the Yugoslavs are otherwise deprived. But, he added, unfortunately if the entrepreneur is too successful the local cadres, activated either by dread of competition or by envy, may very probably tax him out of existence.

A case could be made for tolerating inefficiency on the Feni level and forcing society to pay the costs of low productivity if this served the interest of a more equal and humane society. But with inflation built into the system, Yugoslavia is now divided not only into eight rival autarchies but also into two social categories, with an increasingly clear dividing-line between the haves and have-nots. On the one side, those who keep their bank accounts in hard currency are getting richer; on the other, those who depend for their living on the ever-depreciating dinar are getting poorer. This growing gap has nothing to do with qualifications or performance: the rich may include unskilled manual workers and the poor, highly trained teachers or other specialists unable to sell their particular skills on the hard-currency market.

Most of the savings of the several hundred thousand Yugoslavs employed in the West remain in Western banks (estimates of the total vary between 12 and 22 billion dollars). To induce them to bring their money home, the Yugoslav officials allow them to keep their repatriated accounts in hard currency, on which they receive alluring rates of interest. These are paid to them in dinars calculated according to the going exchange-rates. Many other Yugoslavs, though they have never been employed in the West at all, have found ways of accumulating dollars or deutschmarks and will repatriate them only if, besides favourable rates of interest, they are promised that there will be no investigation into the (almost certainly illegal) ways by which the money was acquired. In 1984 one and a half million bank accounts in Yugoslavia were in hard currency and, despite the régime's Marxist principles, many people lived quite cosily on the yield of their unearned income. The really rich (and there are now Yugoslavs who fit into this category) are inclined to invest the money they bring home principally in real estate in desirable residential areas, notably in the big cities or seaside resorts, and several hundred thousand dollars can secretly exchange hands for a crude cottage with a pocket handkerchief garden.

In contemporary Yugoslavia those with resourcefulness, technical skills and/or hard currency—provided they do not suffer from a surfeit of intellectual integrity—can make themselves comfortable and forget that Kardelj ever existed. The real victims of the concoction that Kardelj called self-management are the working men and women on whose behalf the system was invented.

Conclusion

PICKLED FALSEHOODS

WHY PICK ON Yugoslavia? During the years I have been engaged in this reassessment the question has been thrown at me many times, inside and outside Yugoslavia, often by people who fully accept the validity of my theses and who, by either their writing or conversation, have helped me on my way.

After all, they have said, it is not only Yugoslavia but all countries with a history (some without) which cherish their national mythology and allow themselves to romanticize reality. Tito's Stalinist formation is beyond dispute, but as his apologists remind us, during the last war he did lead the fiercest and most effective of all the resistance forces in occupied Europe. And though, as he later conceded himself, he was engaged in fighting a civil war, in the course of it, particularly in 1943, he did make a significant contribution to the Allied war effort.

A Yugoslav friend of mine from Rijeka read the draft of my chapters on the Partisans and said they saddened her. She had no reason to love the régime, under which she had led a difficult life, and all three of her gifted children (to her secret pride) had rejected the Communist Party, so depriving themselves of chances of reaching the top of their professions. Yet in her youth she had broken with her family, gone up into the mountains to join the Partisans and, though she agreed with my analysis, she regretted now being deprived of a youthful illusion that she had been part of the great army which liberated Yugoslavia. And though Tito unquestionably deceived Churchill and Roosevelt about his plans, they did not do too well themselves in living up to wartime pledges. Britain went to war with a promise to liberate Poland.

On foreign policy, Tito demonstrably aimed to make Belgrade the centre of a communized Balkan peninsula and there is ample reason for believing this led to his split with Stalin. But the three gruesome years of Yugoslavia's postwar history have long been forgotten and those who pleaded for Tito during the war now justify themselves for having argued that, if treated well, he could be prised from Moscow. Further, though in more recent years the non-aligned movement has been discredited, it can be argued that for Yugoslavia, participation was at least one notch better than full-scale adherence to the Soviet military bloc—assumed, perhaps too easily, to be the only alternative.

On the domestic side, no one who has spent any time in Yugoslavia will deny that the Communists have failed to solve their nationalities' question, but it has also to be admitted that irredentist minorities have presented similarly intractable problems for the British in Northern Ireland, the French in Brittany and Corsica, and the Spanish in the Basque country. Finally, though the Yugoslav version of self-management has been shown to provide neither prosperity nor social justice, the Yugoslav Communists did at least try to humanize the status of industrial workers: a task unrealized by any developed country.

All these have been strong arguments in favour of overlooking the system's shortcomings and for treating Yugoslavia as no more than a poorly run country, though commendable as a holiday-resort for its climate, scenic beauties, historical treasures and—at least at the time of writing—a favourable rate of exchange. My decision instead to embark on a basic reassessment was not provoked, as some exasperated officials have suggested, by any personal animosity. On the contrary, Yugoslavia has fascinated and intrigued me since the first time I went there. And it was some of the sceptical young Yugoslavs I met during my travels who were the most emphatic in urging me to expose the contrast between life as it is lived in Yugoslavia today and the way Titoism is presented to the outside world—insisting also that I admit the share of the Western world both in sustaining the Titoist creed and in contributing to the country's present distress.

Five years after the old man's death, the régime clings like a limpet to his glorious legend and still today the cult of the dead personality is by far the most conspicuous feature in Yugoslav political life. And indeed a great deal can and has been said about his outstanding gifts: his charisma, his good looks, his organizational flair, which enabled him to transform ragged guerrillas into a regular army; his diplomatic skill which gave Yugoslavia an international importance out of all proportion to its political power; his physical stamina allowing him, well into his eighties, to lead an active life and travel all over the world; his *joie de vivre* making him an amiable host and, above all, his political astuteness which enabled him to retain undisputed, indeed undisputable power for over 40 years and go to his grave mourned by many —though by no means all—of his countrymen as a great father-figure without whom life would never be the same.

Almost all successful politicians learn to say one thing while doing another, but it was Tito's virtuosity as an impostor that signalled him out among his contemporaries—and indeed can have few historical parallels. We have followed him in this book, from the outset of his political career, when he was tried before a royalist court and in his defence plea (faithfully reported in the contemporary newspapers) appealing to the liberal conscience of the world against "a police state"—though he knew that it was a milk-and-water régime in comparison with the Bolshevik model with which he intended to replace it.

We have seen him concealing from the outside world, including from some of its craftiest politicians, his pursuit of revolutionary aims and hiding the internecine horrors of civil war, under the camouflage trappings of a patriotic struggle for national liberation. In the post-war period, while the killings, persecution and mass murders of Yugoslav anti-Communists were at their peak, Tito managed to preserve good relations with Westerners who, had they been of Yugoslav nationality, would have had no hope of survival, and the US Ambassador to Belgrade felt able to tell President Truman that he and Tito were "good friends". And it was in the year of Tito's Stalinist show-trials against his pro-British opponents that Fitzroy Maclean reported to the Foreign Office that, having cleared up any misunderstandings, he had gone merry-making with the Marshal.

After the war, having been too ambitious to remain a vassal of Stalin, Tito had been thrown out of the Communist bloc and, had it not been for the assertiveness of Truman's foreign policy, it seems probable that the Russians would have occupied his country. Instead of making common cause with the defenders of non-Sovietized Europe, Tito helped to create and propagate the "non-aligned movement". This grouping came to include the most bloodthirsty and aggressive tyrannies of the postwar world, but nothing prevented Tito from representing it, repeatedly and persuasively, as "the conscience of mankind".

Posing as the champion of Yugoslav unity, Tito preserved the monopoly of power by splitting up the country into eight economic autarchies, engaged in constant struggles against each other. Further the alien and archaic Marxist–Leninist creed which Tito inflicted on Yugoslavia left the people spiritually starved, and many educated Yugoslavs believe that this vacuum may well have been filled by the now discernible regression of many of their compatriots into the most primitive form of ethnic chauvinism: the variant which treats rival groups as though they were less than human. Finally it was Tito who decked Kardelj's abstruse concept of self-management in the raiments of a worker-state and sold it as an example to the outside world.

One of the non-Yugoslavs who best encapsulated the Titoist case as something potentially desirable for his own country was Tony Benn, the most prominent member of the left-wing faction of the British Labour Party.

> World interest in Yugoslavia derived from the fact that she set herself the task of attempting to transform a classic communist dictatorship of the proletariat into a real social democracy. . . . Those who dislike the centralized communist dictatorships of the East and who are not satisfied by the tendencies towards technocratic monopoly control of society which are emerging in the capitalist West [among whom Benn plainly counted himself], are bound to be interested in a developing country that is seeking to democratize its socialism and is ready to be self-critical.

The above is an extract from an introduction by Benn to a book on self-management by a leading Communist politician, Milojko Drulović, and published in English in 1978.[1] The author conceded that self-management was proving difficult to operate and that too many decisions were being taken not only by the allegedly self-managing workers but by organs of government. Since his time, this kind of criticism has risen to a cacophony, giving an outward impression that Yugoslavia is a genuinely open society.

This, however, is misleading. Objection may be expressed on administrative or tactical issues but there has never been any relaxation of the prohibition against questioning any of the fundamentalist premises of the Tito creed: first his own reputation, treated as sacrosanct (with a special Federal Commission to defend it and the threat of criminal prosecution against anyone who, even in private conversations, made jokes at his expense). Also, the tripod on which he rested his power, the Party cadres, the secret police and the army. And finally, the fundamental Trinity on which Titoism is based: the Partisan epic, the principle of non-alignment and the Kardelj version of self-management.

Ironically, it was Benn and his left-wing colleagues who were the first on the British political scene to protest against the trials which took place in the winter of 1984/5 of six Belgrade intellectuals. One of these, Milan Nikolić, had been wrongly accused of responsibility for an article in the *New Left Review*, the journal of the Labour Left.

The case of the Belgrade Six began with the intrusion of the secret police into a private meeting of university graduates, who over the previous seven years had been holding discussion meetings, roughly on the same lines as the Czech and Polish "flying universities". On 20 April 1984, a group of these met to hear the veteran dissident Milovan Djilas speak on the question of Yugoslav nationalities: the police broke in and took in 28 for questioning, including Djilas. Seven of them were held and, according to subsequent medical evidence, subjected to various degrees of physical violence. One of them, 32-year-old Radomir Radović, was twice brought into the police cells and manhandled. When his corpse was later found it was generally assumed that he died either from third-degree treatment while being interrogated or else had been tortured into giving incriminating evidence, which could have driven him to suicide: a police practice which Belgrade lawyers say is not unknown. The six others retaliated against the way they were being treated by going on hunger-strike, so provoking an international outcry which may be the reason why the Yugoslav police released them pending their trial. They were later charged with "activities hostile to the state" but as the long indictment revealed, the criminal offences amounted to no more than expressions of disagreement with official doctrine and public policy.[2]

In all societies incidental miscarriages of justice occur and many Western diplomats did their best to shrug off the trials of the Six as an unfortunate lapse in an otherwise civilized country. It is certainly true that as the locality was Belgrade and the prisoners had been on well-publicized hunger-strike, the trials got far more than the publicity which is usually accorded to political cases. What does need to be recognized however is that arbitrary police action and a subservient judiciary, demonstrated on this occasion, are by no means exceptional and that lawlessness is a feature which Yugoslavia shares with all other Communist one-party systems, in which all power derives from a single source.

One of the abiding myths about Titoism is that it is purely pragmatic: accommodated by its protagonists to suit Yugoslav requirements. On the contrary, it is highly ideological and among its most important and durable features has been the collectivization of the economy. Private enterprise exists only on sufferance and virtually all the means of production are socially owned: and, as we have seen, consequently at the disposal of the political apparatus.

Few have written more perceptively about the consequences of such a concentration of power than the Canadian economist, Dan Usher. In his book *The Economic Prerequisite of Democracy*,[3] he does not even mention Yugoslavia, but he effectively demonstrates that government by consent depends on a system of property which exists outside political control. In developing this thesis he points to the basic reason why, contrary to many high hopes, the Yugoslav system has not and cannot evolve towards democracy, as that word is understood in the West.

Accepting the socialist (and Yugoslav) thesis that, as a way of distributing wealth, capitalism is inherently unfair, Usher, unlike the Radical Right, does not recommend unfettered *laissez-faire*. On the contrary, though he accepts that, in our times, capitalism is the only possible form of ownership which is independent of political control, he argues that a government working within a capitalist framework can only make itself acceptable to the people—in other words meet the requirements of democracy—if it can satisfy existing expectations of social justice: these include adequate provision for welfare and employment.

In Usher's view, it is when the political leaders acquire direct control over the distribution of wealth, as they have done in Yugoslavia since 1945, and so decide who will be poor and who will be rich, that government by consent ceases to operate. Society then splits into irreconcilable factions and the energies which should go into creating wealth are diverted instead into lobbying and manipulating for political influence: precisely the features of present-day Yugoslavia.

Had the Yugoslav self-management system been allowed to develop into a genuine cooperative movement, in which independent groups of workers owned and could dispose of their own firms, the economy might have operated outside the control of the political machine. In the autumn of 1984 in Ljubljana I asked a well-known Professor of Economics whether such a cooperative system might not indeed be one way of breaking the present bureaucratic stranglehold about which everybody—including himself—was constantly complaining. "Impossible!" he exclaimed. "If the workers really owned the firms they would sell off their shares and then we shouldn't have socialism any more."

And so in Yugoslavia as in the rest of the Communist world

evolution towards democracy was stunted because no power base was tolerated outside the control of the political apparatus.

The Yugoslav constitution, unlike its Soviet counterpart, does recognize the principle of "the rule of law": but the phrase means very little as long as the Party retains the right to interpret the law and to use it for party purposes. The practical methods by which the Party controls the judiciary were unexpectedly set forward in the journal of the Yugoslav trade unions, *RAD*, in May 1983:

> Legality and free sentencing by judges comes to an end when officials and committees decide whether and when a judge will receive an apartment; whether he will be promoted, when he will be reappointed. The judge, confronted by such politically powerful person or group, has to choose: either he will comply with their will or else he will protect the law and his dignity, knowing in advance that any chance of success in protecting either is often only symbolic and minimal.

Besides the lawlessness which all Communist countries have in common, an extra component has been added by Kardelj's practice of using the statute-book, to try to force society into the approved mould: and the more recalcitrant the worker, the more interventionist the laws. On the economic side, an elderly professor told me in 1983 that even at the height of the Stalinist era, which he remembered very well, government organs had not interfered so much in the country's economic life. Furthermore, all the laws have to be multiplied by nine: one for the Federation and one for each of the eight federal units, each having a legal code of its own, requiring separate enactments.

Corruptissima res publica, plurimae leges. This dictum of Tacitus against the corrupting consequences of excessive legislation served as a preface to an article on the subject by the young lawyer, Kosta Čavoški, published in *Gledišta* in Belgrade in 1972. As his own career was to show, Čavoški argued that the rights granted in principle were withheld in practice. Though the piece is analytical rather than polemical, it earned him a suspended prison sentence which the authorities must mistakenly have supposed would be sufficient to silence him.

Sporadically, the authorized press does let reality peep out: on 19 July 1984, the newspaper *Borba* commented: "We have never had more laws and never more cases of the violation of laws. This is what we call normative idealism: the belief that progress and new human relationships can be enforced by changes in legal texts.''

Within such a framework the constitutional provisions guaranteeing the freedom of the press are meaningless. Though there is no official censor, all journalists need to exercise self-censorship if they are to avoid breaching Article 133 of the Yugoslav penal code, first promulgated in April 1946 and never amended, which makes it a criminal offence to engage in "propaganda against the state". Anything published or broadcast can, of course, be declared propaganda and the interpretation of what is "hostile to the state" is left to the judges and to the Party men who control them.

How far are ordinary Yugoslavs really inconvenienced by the absence of an independent judiciary or of a free press? As in the Soviet bloc, the people have got used to separating their conformist public life from a private life the Party cannot control. The writer Mihajlo Mihajlov, tried in 1966 for trying to launch an independent magazine, referred in his defence plea (which the court refused to hear) to "the schizophrenia of the body politic". He was using the term he said not in mockery or in rage, but in its clinical meaning: "that is simply to describe a disease which manifests itself with the disintegration of the human personality and the splitting of man's consciousness. I used this metaphor intentionally, to characterize the disease of our body politic: the separation of the public consciousness (and in our society this is represented by the press, radio etc.) and social consciousness, which is present only in personal contacts between people."[4]

Most Yugoslavs keep clear of the security police, and some of my Yugoslav friends, as well as Western diplomats who dislike stirring things up, argued that it would be excessive to describe present-day Yugoslavia as a police-state. On the last day of my five-week final visit the police itself clinched the argument. The purpose of the journey had been to discuss the draft of this book—knowing it would be controversial and contested—with as many informed Yugoslavs as possible; hints, in Ljubljana and Zagreb as well as Belgrade, indicated that the police were on my tracks.

In Zagreb a little black notebook had mysteriously disappeared from my hotel bedroom, and could have been of interest only to the secret police. It contained the addresses and telephone numbers of all my Yugoslav connexions. They would find a curious medley of hard-line Communists (who, I like to think, may now figure on some lists of suspects) along with homes and offices of Western diplomats, of many academic and journalistic friends, and of the families of dissidents whom, at their own request, I often called on during my visits to Yugoslavia. As they are under permanent police supervision my concern for them was known and the notebook would reveal nothing new.

My fall from official grace was confirmed by the fact that a number of people previously helpful, this time kept their distance. Three of them in Zagreb who, as I knew, privately agreed with my assessment, had made appointments to see me and then failed to turn up. I did not blame them: many sensible Yugoslavs believe that they and their families will have to live under the present system for the foreseeable future and the best they can do is to limit the damage. I had got to know such people employed in economics institutes, schools, universities, radio, television and newspapers; they had willingly shared their close-up knowledge of how the system really operates and this book has depended a lot on their help.

On arrival at Belgrade I had called at the offices of Yugoslavia's leading civil rights lawyer Srdja Popović and retrieved the missing addresses and telephone numbers. He was encouraged by the international interest which had been aroused by the trials which seemed to be breaking the long silence about arbitrary police power within the present system. Since the hunger strike, he said, US diplomats had, for the first time, started visiting him in his office, knowing that it was bugged, which he interpreted (rightly I later found out) as evidence that the Americans wanted the Yugoslav authorities to know that they were troubled by the proceedings. The pro-Yugoslav policy of the US administration is always at risk from the human-rights lobby. Popović was able to give me good news of another civil rights lawyer, the Croat Vladimir Šeks of Osijek, who had spent a large part of his life, first as magistrate later as advocate, sparring against the arbitrary excesses of the security police. Having heard the previous year how he had been framed in a case which, even by East European standards, was a travesty of justice, I had travelled to Osijek to meet him. The local police chiefs, who had been gunning against him for some time, finally had managed to get him on charges of slandering Tito, backing Djilas, and wishing Hitler had won the war: all as a result of an evening talk at an inn, and according to the testimony of two police informers. While he was waiting to appeal against the verdict, Šeks had paid a visit to the home of one of the witnesses carrying with him a concealed tape-recorder and asked him now that the trial was over, to say frankly what he had heard him say. The man is now on tape admitting that, on that particular evening, after a football match, he had been far too drunk to remember but that the police had told him what had been said and insisted that his testimony was essential to complete the case against a dangerous enemy.

The tapes and other material damaging to the local authorities had been submitted to the federal court, which had ordered a retrial. The Croat judiciary retaliated by reducing the sentence to eight months: just below the necessary minimum which qualifies a criminal case for a federal appeal. While Šeks was waiting to know whether the international outcry from Amnesty and other groups would save him from prison he went to Belgrade where he appeared as one of the lawyers for the defence in the trial of the six scholars. According to the Belgrade radio he challenged the impartiality of the court and was shouted down by the judge. But before the proceedings against his clients had ended, he received instructions to present himself at the Osijek jail. As this book goes to press he has been interned and has started a hunger-strike as a protest against the illegality of the proceedings.

Popović described the courage of the men arrested after their meeting with Djilas, and the nauseating experience of seeing them force-fed. He was to be debarred from defending them himself, on the pretext that he would be needed as a witness. I asked him to help me meet one of the six and, at a café in the centre of Belgrade where I had been invited by another acquaintance, a bearded young man, looking the part of a revolutionary, came forward and introduced himself as Milan Nikolić. Unperturbed by the plain-clothes policemen who came and sat down at the next table, Nikolić proceeded to tell me his brief life-history. What I found strangest was that the Yugoslav authorities should have picked on a man who had done his graduate studies at Brandeis and MIT, and so could count on the support of two of America's most prestigious universities.

Nikolić, a specialist on village communities, told me that he was a regular reader of the *New Left Review* and had written to the editor, disagreeing with an article suggesting that the problem of Kosovo could be resolved by granting to the Albanian-dominated province the status of a federal republic. Nikolić had argued that more attention should be paid to the deeper economic and social factors. But the police, having found the *New Left Review* in his possession, were now accusing him of seditiously propagating the

separation of Kosovo from Serbia. As I learnt later, the editor of
the *New Left Review* had sent the court evidence that Nikolić not
only had not written the article, but was on record disagreeing
with it. The material had not been acknowledged and the editor
agreed with me that the charge was designed to try to deprive
Nikolić of any sympathy from Serb nationalists. For the Yugoslav
authorities, the loss of support from the Labour Left, potentially
the most Titoist of Britain's political groups, was significantly less
important than the discrediting and splitting up of domestic
opposition by the familiar process of inflaming national feeling.

My last day in Yugoslavia was a Saturday and the Professor of
Linguistics, with whom I was staying, had left for the weekend.
There was still a lot to do. I spent the morning with a member of
the British embassy, discussing among other things, divergent
diplomatic views about the consequence of my book and the risk
that the Yugoslavs would mistakenly suppose it was officially
inspired. I had already visited Djilas to discuss the draft of my
account of his split with Tito and I needed to show the section
on the Stalinist foundation of the régime to my scholarly friend,
Kosta Čavoški, an acknowledged expert on that period. I had
also lunched that day with a well-known Party man, Mihailo
Crnobrnja, the son of a Partisan veteran, one of the wittiest
and—privately—the most outspoken critic of the system, who
lives in a beautiful home near the Ambassador's residence and
is a great favourite at diplomatic parties.

He told me he would soon be leaving as an official guest to the
US and looked forward to staying with his friend Laurence
Eagleburger, former Assistant Secretary of State and, as ex-
Ambassador to Belgrade, the leader of what when I was last in
Washington was known as "the Yugoslav lobby". When we met
the previous year Crnobrnja had been a senior official in one of
Belgrade's leading banks. Now he said he had come to see that
there would be no economic reform without political change and
he had therefore "gone into politics" and was working for the
Belgrade Party's Central Committee: "Yugoslavia is in a transitional stage. Things cannot go on as they are. We have to take the
plunge into a truly competitive market."

But how could his desire for reform be squared with jailing the
Six, who, though they differed between themselves, all believed in
an open and plural society? He said he had done his best to prevent
prosecution of the hunger strikers but things had now gone too far
and the trial was inevitable (it started a few weeks later). He

pointed out that, as everyone knew, in Serbia the leadership was far more liberal than in Croatia or Bosnia (earlier that year a Sarajevo court had condemned another non-conformist intellectual, Vojislav Seselj, to a seven-year sentence, reduced on appeal to four, for the trivial offence of criticizing the party in private letters). I found it difficult to accept Crnobrnja's implication that Belgrade felt threatened by counter-revolutionaries from Bosnia, but it did seem likely that the Communist leaders agreed among themselves that when in trouble they should hang together rather than be hanged separately.

Returning home at 5 p.m., I was making myself a cup of tea before packing to leave Belgrade as booked on the 7 a.m. train the next morning. In someone else's flat I did not know whom to let in, and when the doorbell had rung three times, I shouted through the flimsy front-door for the name of the visitor. A female voice identified the woman who owned the flat and I opened the door, wondering why she had cut short her weekend. I was confronted with two men, one in an ill-cut brown suit and brown tie, the other in jeans and a striped navy vest, accompanied by a plump, heavily made-up female interpreter, whose voice I had heard. In a gesture I associated with TV crime thrillers, both men whipped out their credentials, authenticating their right to search.

"Do you have arms or explosives?" The first question addressed to a small elderly woman quietly making tea sounded curiously incongruous. Still, I was relieved that they did not ask to look into my handbag, where they would have found a cheery letter from my husband, an addict of Westerns, saying "Don't worry darling, keep on shooting from the hip." They asked me what I was doing and in order not to embarrass my non-political friend, the Professor of Linguistics, I showed them my senior citizen's European rail-card and said I was on a visit. It seemed reasonable to expect them to leave; instead they demanded to see my luggage, went into my room and examined every bit of paper they could find.

To avoid the painful business of translating Yugoslav newspapers, I had subscribed for some time to an English-language bulletin, a self-financing venture, under the auspices of the British embassy and which consisted exclusively of extracts from the officially authorized Serbo-Croat newspapers. I had kept the most critical of these for further reference and they included diatribes against bureaucratic incompetence and overmanning, lamentations over the public rejection of Communist ideology and protests against the government's failure to check inflation. The wretched interpreter was made to translate page after page of this material, in the form of often badly translated Marxist jargon, from the English back into Serbo-Croat. She was perspiring and evidently worried about her melting mascara and when she asked permission to smoke I had not the heart to refuse. We were all four huddled into my diminutive bedroom when I suddenly remembered that I had left the kettle on. As I rushed to the door fearing a fire, one of the security men barred my way. They also stopped me from answering my telephone seemingly concerned that I might escape.

By the time we were into our third hour, I reminded them of my rights under international law to see my consul, which they said would not be allowed until they had finished their work. Soon afterwards they collected what they wanted and asked me to sign a paper affirming that I was carrying hostile propaganda (I had no propaganda of any kind) and that I had been in contact with "enemy elements". I declined on the grounds that the document was self-incriminating and told them that, though many of my friends criticized the government, I had never met any enemies of Yugoslavia.

In a flourish of authority, the man in brown said that as I had refused I would be summarily expelled and he opened my passport which he had taken from me and banged down the expulsion order. Unfortunately for his dignity, the clerk had forgotten to put any ink on to the stamp, the page of the passport stayed clean and he had to scurry back to base to get replenishments. While he was away I continued to argue with his jean-wearing junior about the difference between critics and enemies and got him to admit that we would have to agree to differ. Before leaving he shook hands with me whereas the man in brown never recovered his equanimity, and skulked out carrying with him five of my little notebooks (unreadable to anyone but myself—and not always to me), a carbon copy of the draft of part of my book (the original was in London) and 71 pages of translated extracts from the Yugoslav press.

Sitting opposite me in my first-class carriage when I left Belgrade the next morning was an old Party member and ex-Partisan, already well into his slivovitz, who soon started railing against Yugoslavia's present rulers for ruining the country. Finding him sympathetic, I showed him the incriminating document which, perhaps inadvertently, the security men had left behind, complete with the record that I had refused to sign. He chortled as he read it aloud to the compartment, commenting that, just as he thought, the Yugoslav rulers were behaving like cornered animals.

A British defender of Titoism, who read my account of the incident in *The Times* on 10 October 1984, commented that the veteran's freedom to talk openly against authority shows that, despite all that I had said about the trials, Yugoslavia was a free society. What in reality it suggested however was not that the government was liberal or tolerant but rather that it was incapable of exercising authority. The political leaders, conscious that they were losing control, were inclined to strike out with arbitrary acts of repression: in my case of singular ineptitude; in the case of young Radomir Radović (whether he was murdered or driven to suicide) of vicious brutality.

Perhaps their disarray was justified; the creed on which the system rested was now being overtly challenged and despite 40 years of monopolizing education and the media, the leadership confronted an opposition which had never been more strident or more contemptuous. Leading the party faithful was the Croat Communist leader, Štipe Šuvar, who as Minister of Education had recently promoted an educational reform, first in Croatia and now spreading across the whole federation, which considerably expanded the time and energies reserved for political indoctrination and which demoted the humanities; irate Yugoslav lecturers compared it to the Chinese Cultural Revolution.

Eighteen months before my police encounter, Šuvar had publicly protested against "efforts to destroy our Yugoslav society" and "to provoke the social democratization of Yugoslavia and its transformation into a marginal country of liberal democracy". Speaking of what he called "the anti-Communist hysteria" of the Croat middle class, he had complained of "the enormous and contagious popularity of any book, film, exhibition, magazine, round-table conference, play or so-called political theatre, just as long as any of these contain an anti-Communist or anti-socialist message."[5] Šuvar had made himself notorious that year by issuing an internal party directive of 235 pages listing the writers considered to be ideologically objectionable. His critics had pounced on the document, had it printed and circulated, some party members resigned in protest and intellectuals from all over the country declared it worthy of the Spanish Inquisition. As a rampart defending the Marxist–Leninist creed, the party was manifestly crumbling: one leader deplored public meetings being held at

which Lenin himself was being described as "a bandit" while
Party members present kept silent.[6]

It is impossible to say how far the open disavowal of Communism is the cause and how much the consequence of the marked
revival of religious practice, now evident all over Yugoslavia, in
the Catholic, Orthodox and Moslem communities alike. The
régime has tried to hit back and, at the beginning of 1984, a priest
in Croatia was sentenced to 50 days in jail for publishing the text of
a prayer "To God and to all Croat Saints", which pleaded "for our
parish and for all our people, that they may not be overcome by the
plague of the theory and the practice of materialism . . ."[7] Ivan
Lalić, the chairman of the Croat Committee for relations with
religious communities, later protested that believers in materialism (a philosophy which has been compulsory in all educational
courses for several decades) were now subject to "a witch-
hunt".[8]

The collapse of the Marxist–Leninist ideology has not meant
that there is any visible opposition ready to take over (if there had
been, they would all be in jail). Nor for the mass of Yugoslavs has
the balance of the Titoist record been entirely negative: there are
no Soviet troops on their soil and unlike the Russians, they do not
have to queue for basic foodstuffs—although all over Yugoslavia,
such items as flour, cooking oil, detergents and coffee frequently
disappear on to the black market.

The dissidents remain a small minority and many of the Yugoslavs who privately share their views are afraid that any upheaval
could make things worse. As in the rest of Eastern Europe, people
have adjusted to an unfree society, knowing that among other
needs their jobs, housing, prospects for their children's education
and their right to travel depend on Party favours, and behaving
accordingly. When life gets more difficult, as it has in recent years,
they express their frustrations by evasion. In 1984, when real
wages fell for the third year in succession no one took to the streets
but about half the citizens of Belgrade and Zagreb were reported
to have stopped paying their electricity bills and their rents: a
number far too great to penalize.

For the Communist leaders the real problem was whether or not
the precipitate decline in living standards could be halted. By the
end of 1984 inflation was inching towards 80 per cent and, in
output per head, Yugoslavia trailed behind even the other Communist countries, with the exception of Albania and, marginally,
Romania. Some of those at the top hoped that further tinkering

with the system and continued Western backing could head off social upheavals; others were less sure.

Whichever way things went, Western financial support would be crucial. Rescue operations for Yugoslavia are now an accepted feature of international life. In diplomatic jargon there is never any "interference in Yugoslav internal affairs", which means in practice only that by refinancing and rescheduling loans the West continues with its interference but shrinks from confronting the political consequences.

Good relations with the Yugoslav régime are considered an end in themselves. Shortly after my own misadventure, which followed closely after the indictment against the six Belgrade intellectuals, the British government threw a party in honour of the Foreign Minister of Yugoslavia, Raif Dizdarević, then on an official visit. The Tanjug agency reported a festive *soirée*, in which the British Foreign Secretary, Sir Geoffrey Howe, had said that Anglo-Yugoslav relations were so good that they should be an example to the world and promised the United Kingdom's support in helping the Yugoslavs deal with their debts.[9] When, as a British tax-payer, I objected to financing these jollifications, I was told that if Sir Geoffrey had absented himself the Yugoslavs might have been offended. The Foreign Office declined to confirm Tanjug's account of what had been said but Sir Geoffrey described his meeting with his Yugoslav opposite number as "cordial".

Why should the British take the lead in helping the Yugoslavs when the system itself deprived them of accountable entrepreneurs or effective competition: two traits held by most British politicians to be pre-conditions of a sound economy? The official reason was that the British had invested in Yugoslavia almost a billion dollars, more than the other Western countries, and would therefore stand to lose most if the Yugoslavs defaulted. The British government of the early 1980s had been particularly tight-fisted in refusing to bail out the countless British firms which, often through no fault of their own, had been unable to meet their debts; yet ministers could see nothing odd in their demand that British tax-payers should be asked to finance the rolling-back of Yugoslav obligations. Indeed they expressed themselves gratified with the record of the Planinc government which in 1984 had squeezed the Yugoslav consumer hard enough to enable the country to meet the interest—though not the principal—on all its international loans.

What London—and Washington and Paris—seemed unaware

of was the success which the Communist leaders were having in getting the Yugoslav public to believe that the burdens they were shouldering and which, as we saw, weighed most heavily on the poorest parts of the community, were the fault not of their own improvident leadership but of the greed of the capitalist world—a view which, as I discovered during my travels, was shared even by some of the fiercest critics of the present régime.

All in all, the record shows that the support which the West has given the Yugoslav Communist régime, year in, year out, in word and in deed, has gained it neither popular esteem, nor an effective Yugoslav government nor a solvent Yugoslav economy. And so as Lenin once asked: *What's to be done?* Some critics of the present policy suggest going to the other extreme: arguing that instead of bailing out the Western banks responsible for the bad loans, Western governments and institutions should pull out of Yugoslavia altogether: the régime would thus be unable to meet its obligations, be declared bankrupt and be left to sink into the mire of Communist making.

The usual response of politicians and diplomats to this drastic course is that, deprived of Western support, Belgrade would turn to Moscow. No one has explained why the Russians would risk bailing out the Yugoslavs or taking over the debts and discontents of a now raucously anti-Communist populace—particularly as any use of violence to subdue or Sovietize Yugoslavia would have the unacceptable side-effect of disrupting East–West relations, thus interfering with trade and preventing the technology transfers which the Soviet Union requires.

But there is another reason for excluding the cut-and-run policy: the West has played a central role in installing and sustaining the present system: it is neither fair nor sensible for us to forget that the Yugoslavs are fellow-Europeans and that we cannot be indifferent to their future. Inevitably, we cannot avoid continued business with Yugoslav officials as long as we accept some responsibility for Yugoslavia's present disarray. Such intrusion, however, would be to meet Yugoslav needs, not our own, and could be equally well achieved without fanfare. Nor do we have to accept the present régime's statistics or its pledges for the future. Indeed, in negotiating financial arrangements Western governments already work on three sets of figures: those from official sources, those from the IMF and those prepared by commercial banks.

As for new investment, the World Bank, in obtaining the right to allocate a quarter of a billion dollars specifically for developing private farms, has already shown the way; it might be possible to finance other forms of individual enterprise. As a Croat economist, Dr Slaven Letica, has suggested, the best service that Western banks could render to Yugoslavia would be to apply to Yugoslav enterprises the same severe criteria they apply to their domestic clients: never invest in a project unless there are proven prospects of a sound return.

But the necessary reassessment has a political as well as a financial dimension. The Yugoslav press and radio constantly report receptions and banquets given in honour of Yugoslav official delegations by, among others the Western parliamentarians in Strasbourg, the European High Commission in Brussels and almost all Western governments; each occasion is marked by speeches and toasts glorifying Tito and paying homage to Yugoslavia's external and internal achievements. To invert the familiar aphorism: the approbation paid by Western democracies to Titoist Communism is the tribute virtue pays to vice.

As the philosopher Leszek Kolakowski, the leading authority on Marxism–Leninism, said: "Mendacity is the immortal soul of Communism. The gap between reality and façade is now so enormous that the lie has become a normal and natural way of life."[10] One reason why Yugoslavia, in its present, post-Titoist phase, is so stimulating is that there are men and women, young and old, who, at considerable risk to themselves, are refusing to go on living this lie. Such people have the right to expect sympathy and support not just from private individuals in the West but also from their elected governments. This does not mean trying to upset the balance of power in Europe by incorporating Yugoslavia into the Western defence complex nor is there any evidence that that is what any Yugoslavs want. The Russians have the right to be assured that the West will respect Yugoslavia's military neutrality as scrupulously as they have done Austria's.

In so far as the West in general, and the British in particular have contributed to the Partisan mythology, they have an extra obligation to desist from further contributions to the screen separating the Yugoslav people from their own past. Yet instead everything is being done to sustain and to prolong for posterity the Communist monopoly of the historical record. For several years, under the auspices of the British National Committee for the History of the Second World War organized by the Imperial War Museum in London, there have been sessions of an "Anglo-

Yugoslav colloquium", chaired by Sir William Deakin, meeting in private and by invitation only. The Yugoslav view is represented exclusively by the officially authorized historians and many of these, like their British opposite numbers, have come to believe their own legend: perceiving Tito and the other Partisan commanders as fellow-fighters in the Allied war effort rather than as a politically motivated minority, using the Second World War as an occasion for acquiring a Communist monopoly of power in the new Yugoslavia.

Participants in the 1984 colloquium agreed that this meeting had been "great fun" and that the visiting Yugoslavs had been in particularly good form. After the gathering some of those involved were surprised to be told that in Yugoslavia today it is a criminal offence to challenge the orthodox Partisan account of the last war and that this is indeed one of the charges against Miodrag Milić, who at the time of the London meeting was being tried alongside five other intellectuals in Belgrade. According to the criminal indictment, Milić had written that 44 years ago Tito had shown himself "not equal to the task of assessing the momentum of the uprising and the need for a higher form of organization and tactics". In searching Milić's home, the police had found and confiscated a three-volume manuscript history of the Yugoslav civil war.

The official suppression of reinterpretations of history cannot fail to raise doubts about the objectivity and sincerity of the Yugoslav historians who take the orthodox view. It was therefore to the principle of academic freedom that I appealed when I wrote to the Secretary of the Imperial War Museum and got his agreement to pass on to the chairman a request that the colloquium be alerted to the international implications of the Belgrade trial. I suggested that the Yugoslavs present be told that they could not expect further invitations to seminars intended to seek the truth until they publicly condemned penal action being taken against those of their compatriots who hold differing views of the historical record. Though my appeal was given prominence in *The Times Higher Education Supplement* of 30 November 1984, the chairman chose not to act on it. When future historians are allowed access to the Imperial War Museum's secret archives all they will find is the Partisan version of wartime operations: a perpetuation of the misconceptions about the Yugoslav civil war.

The now elderly men and women who helped the Yugoslav Communists to win the civil war (this book has identified the principal ones) can hardly be expected to abjure their past. It would be too much to hope that they would have the courage of Milovan Djilas who, during the trials of the six Belgrade intellectuals, wrote in *Le Monde* that, to the degree that through his revolutionary past he shared responsibility for the creation of the present Yugoslavia, he wishes to convey "to all, and first of all to the six men in the dock, the expression of my solidarity and my apologies."[11]

Yet it is surely time that Westerners visiting or working in Belgrade, should cease to treat as social outcasts Yugoslavs who, like themselves, believe in a plural society and the rule of law. They ought to be eager to meet not only Milovan and Stefica Djilas, who can help them understand Yugoslavia's past, but also the many younger Yugoslavs, who have also turned their backs on the régime's fundamentally anti-Western and totalitarian ideology.

We would be breaking no international law by conveying to the present Yugoslav leaders that if they go on indicting and prosecuting people, because of unorthodox views or because these have dared revise the official version of Yugoslav history, they disqualify themselves from international respect: no more banquets and no more international seminars.

The doctrinal absolutism of the Communist Party should be no less objectionable to us than it is to its Yugoslav critics; after 40 years of Western support and subsidy for their repressors, democratically-minded Yugoslavs deserve a different treatment. The policy of confounding our friends and comforting our enemies needs to be reversed.

NOTES AND REFERENCES

Introduction: Tito and Seven Myths

1 S. K. Pavlowitch, *Historical Background of the Nationality Question.* Lecture to the Institute of European Defence and Strategic Studies, London 1984.
2 M. Mackintosh, "*Military Considerations of Soviet–East European Relation.*" From *Soviet–East European Dilemmas*, ed. by K. Dawisha and Philip Hanson. London 1981.
3 M. Djilas. Interviewed by George Urban in *Stalinism*, London 1982.
4 D. Ćosić, *In Times of Death*. Translated by Muriel Heppell, New York 1982.
5 D. Rusinow, *The Yugoslav Experiment*, New York and London 1977.
6 V. Maček, *In the Struggle for Freedom*, New York 1957.
7 R. Shaplen, "Tito's Legacy". *The New Yorker*, February 1984.
8 *The Constitution of the S.F.R.Y. 1974.* Basic principles, paragraph 1. Published in English, New York 1976.

Chapter 1   Tito the Latter-Day Patriot

1 M. Djilas, *Tito: the story from the inside*, New York and London 1980.
2 V. Dedijer, *Additional notes for a biography of J. B. Tito*, Volume 1, Rijeka 1981.
3 M. Djilas, *Rise and Fall*, New York and London 1985.
4 E. Hoxha, *The Titoists*, Tirana 1982.
5 V. Dedijer, *ibid.*
6 P. Auty, *Tito: a biography*, London 1970.
7 F. Maclean, *Tito: a pictorial biography*, New York and London 1980.
8 P. Auty, *ibid.*
9 F. Maclean, *ibid.*
10 V. Dedijer, *ibid.*
11 F. Maclean, *ibid.*
12 P. Auty, *ibid.*
13 F. Maclean, *ibid.*
14 M. Djilas, *Tito: the Story from the Inside*, New York and London, 1980.
15 F. Maclean, *ibid.*
16 M. Djilas, *Memoirs of a Revolutionary*, New York and London, 1973.
17 F. Maclean, *ibid.*
18 D. Pešić, *The Yugoslav Communists and the National Question: 1919 to 1935*, Belgrade 1983.
19 F. Maclean, *ibid.*

20 J. Rootham, *Miss Fire*, London 1946.
21 S. Clissold, *Yugoslav Soviet Relations: 1948–1975*, London, 1975.
22 M. Djilas, *ibid.*
23 V. Dedijer, *ibid.*
24 V. Dedijer, *ibid.*
25 V. Cenčić, *Enigma Copinić*, Belgrade, 1983.
26 V. Dedijer, *ibid.*
27 M. Djilas, *Wartime*, New York and London, 1977.

Chapter 2   The Legend of the Liberation

 1 *The Journal of the British Yugoslav Society*, Summer 1984.
 2 N. Bethell, *The Great Betrayal*, London 1984.
 3 Salvatore Loi, *Operations of Italian units during the occupation of Yugoslavia: 1941–1943*, Rome 1978.
 4 P. N. Hehn, *The German struggle against the Yugoslav guerillas in World War Two*. Boulder and NY 1979.
 5 M. Howard, Letter to *The Times*, 7 June 1983.
 6 *Politika Ekspres*, Belgrade, 20 and 27 March 1983.
 7 S. Clissold, *ibid.*
 8 S. Clissold, *ibid.*
 9 Branko Lazitch, *Tito and the Yugoslav Revolution 1937–1949*, Paris 1957.
10 Branko Lazitch, *ibid.*
11 Sir Alexander Glen, interviewed in London November 1984.
12 J. Goebbels, *Diaries 1939–1941*, London 1982.
13 V. Maček, *ibid.*
14 N. Balfour and S. Mackay, *Paul, Prince Regent of Yugoslavia*, London 1981.
15 Field Marshal Lord Wilson of Libya, *Eight Years Overseas*, London 1950.
16 Velimir Terzić, *Memoirs*, Belgrade 1980.
17 M. Van Crefeld, *The Balkan Clue: Hitler's Strategy 1940–1941*, Cambridge 1973.
18 Dedijer, *ibid.*
19 L. Karchmar, 'Draža Mihailović. The rise of the Chetniks 1941 –1942', PhD, Stanford 1973.
20 M. Djilas, *Memoirs of a Revolutionary*, London and NY 1973.
21 Z. Vučković, *War Memoirs*, volume 2, cited in *Naša Reč*, London 1984.
22 S. Clissold, *ibid.*
23 M. Wheeler, *Britain and the War for Yugoslavia 1940–1943*, Boulder 1980.
24 L. Karchmar, *ibid.*
25 V. Dedijer, *ibid.*
26 W. Hudson, interviewed in London November 1983.
27 M. R. D. Foot, *Resistance: An Analysis of European Resistance to Nazism 1942–1945*, London 1976.

28 L. Karchmar, *ibid.*
29 L. Karchmar, *ibid.*
30 S. Clissold, *ibid.*
31 S. Clissold, *ibid.*
32 J. Wüscht, "Population Losses in Yugoslavia in World War Two", published in *Forum*, Bonn, Brussels and NY 1963.
33 C. Malaparte, *Kaputt*, London 1952.
34 P. N. Hehn, *ibid.*
35 L. Karchmar, *ibid.*
36 V. Maček, *ibid.*
37 V. Dedijer, *ibid.*
38 V. Drašković, *The Knife*, Belgrade 1982.
39 L. Rayner, *Women in a Village: An Englishwoman's Experience and Impressions of Life in Yugoslavia under Occupation*, London 1957.
40 Salvatore Loi, *ibid.*
41 P. E. Boughey, interviewed in London 1976.
42 R. West, Letter to *The Times Literary Supplement*, 21 April 1972.
43 W. Roberts: *Tito, Mihailovic and the Allies 1941–1945*, NY 1973.
44 The 1942 Meyszner Report. English version published in *South Slav Review*, London 1982.
45 P. N. Hehn, *ibid.*
46 P. N. Hehn, *ibid.*
47 Robert Wade interview October 1982.
48 T. Ford, "Pawns and pawnbrokers: OSS and the Yugoslav resistance during the Second World War", Michigan Ill. DPhil.
49 V. Dedijer, *ibid.*
50 W. Roberts, *ibid.*
51 M. Djilas, *Wartime*, London and NY 1977.
52 V. Dedijer, *ibid.*
53 P. N. Hehn, *ibid.*

Chapter 3   How Churchill was Hoodwinked

1 W. Churchill, *The Second World War*, Volume V, London 1954.
2 General Semić-Daki, *The Best have Fallen*, Volume 3, Ljubljana 1971.
3 E. Kardelj, *The Struggle for the Recognition and Independence for Yugoslavia, 1944–1947*, Belgrade 1980.
4 M. Howard, *Mediterranean Strategy*, London 1966.
5 A. Seaton, *The German Army 1933–1945*, London 1982.
6 A. Boyle, *The Climate of Treason*, London 1980.
7 A. Glen interviewed, November 1984.
8 H. Seton Watson, *The Kim Philby Affair*, London 1968.
9 L. Adamic, *Dinner at the White House*, NY 1946.
10 B. Davidson, *Special Operations Europe*, London 1980.
11 V. Velebit, introduction to Dušan Biber's *Top Secret*, Ljubljana 1981.

12 A. Powell, *Faces in My Time*, London 1980.
13 D. Martin, *Ally Betrayed*, NY 1946.
14 F. Hinsley, *History of British Intelligence in the Second World War*, Volume 3, London 1984.
15 W. Hudson interviewed, London February 1984.
16 P. Auty and R. Clogg (eds), *British Policy towards Wartime Resistance in Yugoslavia and Greece*, London 1975.
17 F. Hinsley, *ibid.*
18 P. Kemp, *No Colour or Crest*, London 1958.
19 M. Stenton, "British Propaganda and Political Warfare 1940–1944", PhD thesis, Cambridge, 1979.
20 S. Pavlowitch, "Neither heroes nor traitors: suggestions for a reappraisal of the Yugoslav resistance," in *War and Society*, ed. by B. Bond and I. Roy, London 1975.
21 A. Seaton, *The Russo-German War*, London 1971.
22 P. N. Hehn, *ibid.*
23 D. Muir, *Dudley Clarke. Master of Deception*, London 1981.
24 T. Ford, *ibid.*
25 W. Hudson *ibid.*
26 PRO/FO/R/371/376 609. 24 June 1943.
27 M. Stenton, *ibid.*
28 F. W. D. Deakin, *The Embattled Mountain*, London 1971.
29 M. Stenton, *ibid.*
30 M. Stenton, *ibid.*
31 D. Martin, *Patriot or Traitor: The Case of General Mihailovich*, Stanford 1978.
32 T. Ford, *ibid.*
33 F. Hinsley, *ibid.*
34 T. Ford, *ibid.*
35 G. Rendel, *The sword and the Olive*, London 1957.
36 W. Churchill, *ibid.*
37 W. Churchill, *ibid.*
38 PRO/FO/371/37/615 3154. November 1943.
39 S. D. Bosnitch, "The significance of the Soviet military intervention in Yugoslavia 1944–1945" published in *The Review of the Study Centre for Yugoslav Affairs*, No. 8, 1968.
40 *The Diaries of Evelyn Waugh*, ed. M. Davie, London 1976.
41 P. Auty and R. Clogg, *ibid.*
42 J. Erickson, *The Road to Berlin*, London 1984.
43 F. Maclean, *Eastern Approaches*, London 1949.
44 PRO/FO/R/3688/2/G 3 January 1944 and PRO/FO/R/132/8/092 8 Dec 1943.
45 P. Auty and R. Clogg, *ibid.*
46 M. Wheeler, *Crowning the Revolution*, at Symposium, London 1982.
47 PRO/FO/R/1388/2/G 6 January 1944.
48 PRO/FO/R/2571/8/G92 9 January 1944.

49 PRO/FO/R/414/8/G92 6 February 1944.
50 J. R. Beevor, *SOE Recollections and Reflexions*, London 1981.
51 *Acts and documents of the Holy See relating to the Second World War*, January 1944–May 1945, The Vatican.
52 F. W. D. Deakin, *Churchill and Tito. Meeting at Caserta*, Symposium, London 1982.
53 W. Churchill, *ibid.*
54 US Foreign Relations, Volume IV, Washington DC 1944.
55 T. Ford, *ibid.*
56 S. D. Bosnitch, *ibid.*
57 US Foreign Relations, *ibid.*
58 V. Kljaković, *Tito's Talks with Stalin September 1944*, Symposium, London 1982.
59 W. Churchill, *ibid.*
60 S. D. Bosnitch, *ibid.*
61 L. Karchmar, *ibid.*
62 T. Ford, *ibid.*
63 D. Martin, *ibid.*
64 V. Dedijer, *ibid.*
65 M. Djilas, *Vlast*, London 1984.
66 PRO/FO/R/3124/11/92 28 January 1944.
67 A. Glen, *ibid.*
68 S. Barnes, *Anthony Crosland*, London 1982.
69 D. Lloyd Owen, *Providence their Guide. A Personal Account 1940–1945*, London 1980.
70 D. Hamilton Hill, *SOE Assignment*, London 1975.
71 Field Marshal Wilson, *ibid.*
72 S. D. Bosnitch, *ibid.*
73 B. Novak, *Trieste 1941–1945*, Chicago 1970.
74 W. Churchill, *ibid.*
75 B. Novak, *ibid.*
76 N. Basta, *The War Ended Seven Days Later*, Belgrade 1983.
77 N. Tolstoy, "The Klagenfurt conspiracy" *Encounter*, May 1983 London.
78 *War Diary of the 38th Irish Infantry Brigade*, republished by *The Journal of Croatian Studies* 1977/1978.
79 PRO WO 170/4982 May 1945.
80 S. Barnes, *ibid.*
81 H. Macmillan, *The Tides of Fortune*, London 1975.
82 M. Djilas interviewed by G. Urban in *Stalinism*, London 1982.
83 Yugoslav information sheet 14 May 1946 *Today in Yugoslavia* by a British officer later identified as G. Waddams.
84 Lord Aldington (formerly Brigadier T. Low) interviewed, London December 1983.
85 V. Ivanović, *LX: Memoirs of a Yugoslav*, London 1975.
86 V. Dedijer, *ibid.*

Chapter 4   *Tito's Rupture and Reconciliation with Moscow*

1 M. Djilas, *Tito: The Story from the Inside*, London 1982.
2 US F R 13 December, Volume 1V 1944 Washington DC.
3 PRO/FO/R/628/130 G92 8 January 1945.
4 US F R 23 Jan Volume V 1945.
5 US FR 13 February Volume V 1945.
6 I. Jukić, *The Fall of Yugoslavia*, NY 1974.
7 US FR 12 April Volume V 1945.
8 G. Bilainkin, *Tito*, 1949.
9 PRO/FO/R/371/48832 26 July 1945.
10 US F R 31 August 1945 Volume V Washington DC.
11 *Yugoslav Information Sheet*, Bromley, Kent 1946.
12 S. Alexander, *ibid.*
13 J. Korbel, *Tito's Communism*, Denver Col. 1951.
14 M. Djilas, *Vlast*, New York 1984.
15 This and all other references to the statements of Yugoslav politicians during the post-war elimination of the opposition taken from V. Koštunica and K. Čavoški, *Party Pluralism and Monism*, Belgrade 1983.
16 F. Maclean, *Disputed Barricades*, London 1957.
17 PRO/FO/R/1309/1430/92 September 1947. Republished in *The South Slav Review*, 1984.
18 J. Peel, liaison officer in Moscow, unpublished report written in 1983.
19 S. Clissold, *Yugoslavia and the Soviet Union 1939–1973*, London 1975.
20 M. Djilas, *Vlast*, New York 1984.
21 A. Ulam, *Tito and the Cominform*, New York 1952.
22 Ivan Supek, *Hebrang: A Docu-novel*, Chicago 1984.
23 D. Larson, *US Foreign Policy towards Yugoslavia 1943–1963*, NY 1965.
24 V. Koštunica and K. Čavoški, *ibid.*
25 D. Larson, *ibid.*
26 Bela Kiraly interviewed by M. Charlton, *Encounter*, July 1983.
27 M. Djilas in conversation with the author, October 1984.
28 *Foreign Relations*, February 1949, Volume V, Washington DC.
29 D. Larson, *ibid.*
30 Dean Acheson, *Present at the creation*, New York 1969.
31 J. Tomašević, in *At the brink of war and peace*, ed. by Wayne Vucinich, Stanford 1983.
32 *Khrushchev Remembers*, London 1974.
33 A. Bullock, *Ernest Bevin*, Volume 3, London 1983.
34 D. Wilson, *Tito's Yugoslavia*, Cambridge 1979.
35 E. Waugh, *Anthology*, London 1984.
36 *The Economist*, 18 February 1984.
37 L. Sirc, unpublished autobiography.
38 M. Djilas, *Tito: The Story from the Inside*, London 1982.
39 D. Wilson, *ibid.*
40 S. Clissold, *Djilas: The Progress of a Revolutionary*, London 1983.

41 M. Djilas, *Land without Justice*, New York and London 1973.
42 S. Clissold, *ibid.*
43 L. Sirc, *ibid.*
44 S. Clissold, *ibid.*
45 S. Clissold, *Yugoslavia and the Soviet Union*, London 1975.
46 F. Maclean, *Disputed Barricades*, London 1957.

Chapter 5   Non-Aligned against the West

1 P. Johnson, *A History of the Modern World*, London 1983.
2 E. Kardelj, *Reminiscences*, London 1982.
3 S. Clissold, *ibid.*
4 S. Clissold, *ibid.*
5 *Khrushchev Remembers, ibid.*
6 D. Larson, *U.S. Foreign Policy towards Yugoslavia 1943–1963*, Washington 1979.
7 R. Stephens, *Nasser: a political biography*, London 1971.
8 A. Rubinstein, *Yugoslavia and the Non-Aligned World*, Princeton 1970.
9 V. Mićunović, *Moscow Diary*, London 1980.
10 S. Clissold, *ibid.*
11 D. Zagoria, *The Sino-Soviet Conflict 1956–1961*, Princeton NJ 1962.
12 "Yugoslavia's struggle: the Programme of the League of Communists of Yugoslavia", English version published in NY 1958.
13 S. Clissold: unless otherwise indicated all the texts on Soviet Yugoslav relations are taken from his collection: London 1975.
14 G. Kennan, *Memoirs 1950–63*, 1973.
15 G. Kennan, *ibid.*
16 N. Khrushchev, *ibid.*
17 P. Johnson, *ibid.*
18 B. Suvorov, *The Liberators*, London 1982.
19 M. Heikal, *Nasser: The Cairo Documents*, London 1972.
20 L. Sirc, "A new look at Tito and non-alignment", *Journal of Soviet and political studies*, 13 June 1977 London.
21 *Komunist*, 22 March 1973 Belgrade.
22 M. Vego, *Yugoslavia and Soviet Policy of Force in the Mediterranean since 1961*, Washington DC 1981.
23 L. Sirc, *ibid.*
24 M. Vego, *ibid.*
25 W. Scott Thompson (ed.), *The Third World*, San Francisco 1983.
26 W. Brandt and A. Sampson (eds), *Programme for Survival*, London 1980.
27 J. B. Tito, "Sixty years of revolutionary struggle of the League of Communists", address delivered to the special meeting of the Central Committee 19 April 1979 Belgrade.

28 The tracts include the following:
Zdravko Mičić, *The Movement and policy of non-alignment*, M. Marović, *Divisive attempts in the non-aligned movement*, M. Ćušić, *The freedom and integrity of the non-aligned countries*, S. Stanić, *Non-alignment and the New International Economic Order*, all published in Belgrade 1979.

29 ADN International, Service East. Berlin 21 March 1982.

30 J. Pilon, "Shattered illusions: the US and the UN", in *Survey*, London December 1983.

31 E. Kardelj, *Historical Routes of Non-alignment*, Belgrade 1975.

32 A. Golytsin, *New Lies for Old*, London 1984.

33 Tanjug News agency, 14 March 1983.

34 Grenada Radio 8 January 1983.

35 P. Johnson, *ibid*.

36 *New Times*, Moscow, 14 April 1983.

Chapter 6   Neither Brotherhood nor Unity

1 M. Djilas, *Wartime*, London and New York 1977.

2 E. Hoxha, *The Titoists*, Tirana 1982.

3 M. Djilas, *Vlast*, New York 1984.

4 L. Sirc, Unpublished autobiography.

5 M. Djilas, *ibid*.

6 I. Lapenna, lecture at the Symposium London School of Economics April 1984.

7 *Osmica*, 22 March 1984 Belgrade.

8 B. Horvat, interviewed in *Nin* 8 June 1984.

9 B. Horvat, *ibid*.

10 M. Djurić, interviewed in *Borba* 11 April 1983.

11 S. Alexander, *Church and State in Yugoslav since 1945*, Cambridge 1979.

12 B. Frankolic, "Language policy and language planning in Yugoslavia with special reference to Coatia and Macedonia", *Lingua* Volume 5 No 1, Amsterdam May 1980.

13 I. Supek, *Hebrang*, Docu-novel, Chicago 1984.

14 The full story of the 1968–1972 national and liberal upheavals are told in D. Rusinov, *The Yugoslav experiment 1948*, Berkeley 1977; A. Carter, *Democratic reforms in Yugoslavia*, London 1982; and S. Burg, *Conflict and cohesion*, Princeton NJ 1983.

15 M. Veselica, *The Croatian National Question: Yugoslavia's Achilles Heel*. London 1980.

16 B. Petrovich, *A History of Modern Serbia*, New York and London 1976.

17 A. Carter, *ibid*.

18 B. Pahor and A. Rebula, *Edvard Kocbek: A Witness of our Time*, Trieste 1975.

19 S. Barović, "The Yugoslav national question, the Kosovo issue" DPhil. thesis, Yale 1974.

20 A. Pipa and S. Repishli, *Studies on Kosovo*, East European Monographs, New York 1984.
21 S. Pavlowitch and Elez Biberj, "The Albanian problem: Two views", *Conflict studies*, No. 137/8 London 1982.
22 D. Ćosić interviewed by the author Belgrade September 1983.
23 Petrovich, *ibid*.
24 *Times of Death*, New York 1982.
25 S. Alexander, *ibid*.
26 "Report on the trial of Moslem Intellectuals in Serajevo", in *South Star Journal*, 1983.
27 A. Zulfikarpašić, interviewed in Poruk Stockholm 1983.

Chapter 7   The Holy Grail of Self-Management

1 M. Djilas, *The Imperfect Society*, London 1969.
2 E. Kardelj, *Reminiscences*, London 1982.
3 F. W. D. Deakin, *The Embattled Mountain*, London 1971.
4 S. Clissold, *ibid*.
5 E. Kardelj, *Specialist Thought and Practice, Selections from Some of his Works*, Belgrade April–May 1979.
6 J. Moore, *Growth with Self-Management*, Stanford 1980.
7 S. Brittan, *The Role and Limits of Government*, London 1983.
8 L. Tadić, "Les habits neufs du President Tito", *Autogestion*, Paris 1976.
9 A. Carter, *ibid*.
10 H. Lydall, *ibid*.
11 L. Tyson, *The Yugoslav Economic System and its Performance in the 1970s*, Berkeley 1982.
12 H. Lydall, *ibid*.
13 Djureković, interviewed in London June 1983.
14 N. Jovanov interviewed *Nin* 20 August 1978.
15 E. Kardelj, *ibid*.
16 J. B. Tito, "Four Decades of Close and Undisturbed Cooperation", TV broadcast, 10 February 1979 and reproduced in *Socialist Thought and Practice*, a Yugoslav monthly, April–May 1979.
17 P. Auty in *The Journal of the British Yugoslav Association*, 1983 London.
18 L. Tyson, *ibid*.
19 *Danas*, Zagreb 2 August 1983.
20 A. Simić, contribution to *The Anthropological Quarterly*, California April 1977.
21 H. Lydall, *ibid*.
22 E. Kardelj, *Socialism and Democracy*, London 1978.
23 L. Sirc, *The Yugoslav Economy under Self-Management*, London 1979.
24 *Borba* 3 January 1984.

25 C. A. Zebot, *Yugoslav Self-Management on Trial. Problems of Communism.* August 1982 London.
26 *Novosti*, 5 September 1983 Belgrade.
27 *Novosti*, 3 June 1984, Belgrade.

Conclusion: Pickled Falsehoods

1 M. Drulović, *Self-Management on Trial*, London 1978.
2 Indictment with comment published in the *South Slav Journal*, London 1984.
3 D. Usher, *The Economic Prerequisite of Democracy*, Oxford 1981.
4 M. Mihajlov, *Russian Themes*, New York 1968.
5 S. Šuvar, speech reported in *Politika*, 16 March 1984 Belgrade.
6 Dušan Dragosavac, member of the Presidency, interviewed on Radio Belgrade, 26 July 1984.
7 The Vatican Radio, 17 December 1983.
8 Ivan Lalić speaking on Radio Belgrade, 4 May 1984.
9 Tanjug News Agency, 11 November 1984.
10 Leszek Kolakowski, interviewed on the BBC by M. Charlton, 17 January 1983.
11 *Le Monde* 15 November 1984.

SELECT BIBLIOGRAPHY

Dean Acheson *Present at the Creation* Hamish Hamilton, London 1970

Stella Alexander *Church and State in Yugoslavia Since 1945* Cambridge University Press, Cambridge, England 1979

Phyllis Auty *Tito: A Biography* Longman, New York 1970

Phyllis Auty and Richard Clogg (eds.) *British Policy Towards Wartime Resistance in Yugoslavia and Greece* Barnes & Noble/Harper & Row, New York 1975

Neil Balfour and Sally Mackay *Paul of Yugoslavia* Hamish Hamilton, London 1980

Elizabeth Barker *British Policy in South-East Europe in the Second World War* Barnes & Noble/Harper & Row, New York 1976

J. R. Beevor *Special Operations Executive* Bodley Head, London 1980

Andrew Boyle *The Climate of Treason* Hutchinson, London 1980

Stephen Burg *Conflict and Cohesion* Princeton University Press, Princeton, N.J. 1983

April Carter *Democratic Reforms in Yugoslavia* Frances Pinter, London 1982

Sir Winston Churchill *The Second World War*, 6 vols. Cassell, London 1948–1953

Stephen Clissold *Whirlwind: An Account of Marshal Tito's Rise to Power* Cresset Press, London 1949

——— *Milovan Djilas: The Progress of a Revolutionary* Temple Smith, London 1983

Stephen Clissold (ed.) *Yugoslavia and the Soviet Union 1939–1973*, documentary survey published for the Royal Institute of International Affairs by Oxford University Press, London 1975

Dobrica Ćosić *Times of Death*, translated by Muriel Heppell, Harcourt Brace Jovanovich, New York and London 1982

Susan Crosland *Tony Crosland* Cape, London 1982

Basil Davidson *Special Operations Europe: Scenes from the Anti-Nazi War* Gollancz, London 1980

F. W. D. Deakin *The Embattled Mountain* Oxford University Press, London 1971

Vladimir Dedijer *Tito Speaks: His Self-portrait and Struggle with Stalin* Weidenfeld & Nicolson, London 1953

——— *Further Contributions to a Biography of Josip Broz Tito* Rijeka 1981

Milovan Djilas *Land Without Justice* Harcourt Brace Jovanovich, New York 1958

——— *Conversations with Stalin* Harcourt Brace Jovanovich, New York 1962

——— *The Imperfect Society* Harcourt Brace Jovanovich, New York 1969

———— *Memoirs of a Revolutionary*   Harcourt Brace Jovanovich, New York
      1973
———— *The New Class*   Praeger Publishers, New York 1974
———— *Wartime*   Harcourt Brace Jovanovich, New York 1977
———— *Tito: The Story from the Inside*   Harcourt Brace Jovanovich, New
      York 1981
———— "Conversation with George Urban," in *Stalinism*, edited by
      George Urban   Temple Smith, London 1982
———— *Rise and Fall*   Harcourt Brace Jovanovich, New York 1985
Milojko DRULOVIĆ   *Self-management on Trial*, with a foreword by Tony
      Benn,   Spokesman Books, London 1978
John EHRMAN   *Grand Strategy: History of the Second World War*, Volumes 5
      and 6   HMSO, London 1956
John ERICKSON   *The Road to Berlin*   Weidenfeld & Nicolson, London
      1984
M. R. D. FOOT   *Resistance: An analysis of European Resistance to Nazism
      1942–1945*   Eyre Methuen, London 1976
Thomas K. FORD   "Pawns and Pawnbrokers: OSS and Yugoslav Re-
      sistance During the Second World War,"   Ph.D. dissertation
      for University of Mississippi, University, Miss. 1980
Alexander GLEN   *Foothold Against the Whirlwind*   Hutchinson, London
      1975
Joseph GOEBBELS   *Diaries 1939–1941*   Pan Books, London 1982
David HAMILTON HILL   *SOE Assignment*   William Kimber, London
      1975
Paul N. HEHN (ed.)   *The German Struggle Against the Yugoslav Guerrillas in
      World War Two: German Counterinsurgency in Yugoslavia 1941–
      1943*   East European Monographs, Boulder and New York
      1979
F. H. HINSLEY   *British Intelligence in the Second World War: Its Influence on
      Strategic Operations*   HMSO, London 1984
Michael HOWARD   *The Mediterranean Strategy in the Second World War*
      Weidenfeld & Nicolson, London 1966
Michael HOWARD   *Grand Strategy: History of the Second World War*,
      Volume 4   HMSO, London 1972
Enver HOXHA   *The Titoists*   Ndermarja e Botimeve Ushtarake, Tirana
      1982
Vane IVANOVIĆ   *LX: Memoirs of a Yugoslav*   Harcourt Brace Jovanovich,
      New York and London 1977
Robert JACKSON   *The Non-Aligned, the UN and the Superpowers*   Praeger
      Publishers, New York 1984 for the Council of Foreign Re-
      lations
Paul JOHNSON   *A History of the Modern World from 1917 to the 1980s*
      Weidenfeld & Nicolson, London 1983
Ilija JUKIĆ   *The Fall of Yugoslavia*   Harcourt Brace Jovanovich, New
      York 1974
Lucien KARCHMAR   "Draža Mihailović and the Rise of the Ćetnik
      Movement,"   D. Phil. dissertation, Stanford University,
      Stanford, Cal. 1973

Edvard KARDELJ   *Democracy and Socialism*, translated by Margot and
    Boško Milosavljević,   The Summerfield Press, London 1978
——— *Reminiscences: Struggle for Recognition and Independence*, translated by
    David Norris,   Blond & Briggs, London 1982
Peter KEMP   *No Colour or Crest*   Cassell, London 1958
George KENNAN   *Memoirs 1950–1963*   Hutchinson, London 1973
Nikita KHRUSHCHEV   *Khrushchev Remembers: The Last Testament*, trans-
    lated by S. Talbot,   André Deutsch, London 1974
Milan KUNDERA   *The Book of Laughter and Forgetting*   Penguin, London
    1983
David L. LARSON   *United States Foreign Policy Towards Yugoslavia 1943–*
    1963   University Press of America, Washington, D.C. 1965
Branko LAZITCH   *Tito et la révolution Yugoslave, 1937–1949*   Fasquelle,
    Paris 1957
Harold LYDALL   *Yugoslav Socialism: Theory and Practice*   Clarendon
    Press, Oxford 1984
Vladko MĂCEK   *In the Struggle for Freedom*   Robert Speller & Sons, New
    York 1957
David MARTIN (ed.)   *Patriot or Traitor? The Case of General Mihailovich*
    Hoover Institutional Archival Documentaries, Stanford Uni-
    versity, Stanford, Cal. 1978
Vojtech MASTNY   *Russia's Road to the Cold War*   Columbia University
    Press, New York 1979
Veljko MIĆUNOVIĆ   *Moscow Diary*, translated by David Floyd,   Chatto
    & Windus, London 1980
Mihajlo MIHAJLOV   *Russian Themes*, translated by Marija Mihailov,
    Farrar, Straus & Giroux, New York 1968
John MOORE   *Growth with Self-Management: Yugoslav Industrialisation*
    1952–1975   Hoover Institution Press, Stanford University,
    Stanford, Cal. 1980
David MUIR   *Practice to Deceive*   William Kimber, London 1977
——— *Master of Deception*, William Kimber, London 1980
Fitzroy MACLEAN   *Eastern Approaches*   Cape, London 1949
——— *Disputed Barricades: The Life and Time of Josip Broz Tito, Marshal of*
    Yugoslavia   Cape, London 1957
——— *Tito*: A Pictorial Biography   Macmillan, London 1980
David Lloyd OWEN   *Providence Their Guide: Long-Range Desert Group*
    1940–1945   Harrap, London 1980
Stevan K. PAVLOWITCH   *Yugoslavia*   Ernest Benn, London 1971
——— "Neither Heroes nor Traitors: Suggestions for a Reappraisal of
    the Yugoslav Resistance," in *War & Society*, edited by Brian
    Bond and Ian Roy, Croom Helm, London 1975
B. PETROVICH   *A History of Modern Serbia*   Harcourt Brace Jovanovich,
    New York 1976
Anthony POWELL   *Faces in My Time*   Heinemann, London 1980
Louise RAYNER   *Women in a Village: An Englishwoman's Experience and*
    Impressions of Life in Yugoslavia Under German Occupation   Heine-
    mann, London 1957
George RENDEL   *The Sword and the Olive*   John Murray, London 1957

Walter ROBERTS   *Tito, Mihailović and the Allies 1941–1945*   Rutgers University Press, New Brunswick, N.J. 1973

Jasper ROOTHAM   *Miss Fire: The Chronicle of a British Mission to Mihailovich 1943–1944*   Chatto & Windus, London 1946

A. RUBINSTEIN   *Yugoslavia and the Non-Aligned World*   Princeton University Press, Princeton, N.J. 1970

Dennison RUSINOW   *The Yugoslav Experiment 1948–1974*   University of California Press, Berkeley, Cal. 1977

Albert SEATON   *The German Army 1933–1945*   Weidenfeld & Nicolson, London 1982

Fred SINGLETON and Bernard CARTER   *The Economy of Yugoslavia*   Croom Helm, London 1982

Ljubo SIRC   *The Yugoslav Economy Under Self-Management*   Macmillan, London 1979

David STAFFORD   *Britain and the European Resistance 1940–1945: A Survey of SOE with Documents*   Macmillan, London 1980

M. STENTON   "British Propaganda and Political Warfare: 1940–1944"   Ph.D. thesis, Cambridge University, Cambridge, England 1979

Ivan SUPEK   *Hebrang: A Docu-novel*, translated by N. N. Gill,   Markaton Press, Chicago, Ill. 1984

Viktor SUVOROV   *The Liberators*   Hamish Hamilton, London 1982

Scott THOMPSON (ed.)   *The Third World: Premises of US Policy*   Institute for Contemporary Studies, San Francisco, Cal. 1983

Laura TYSON   *The Yugoslav Economic System and Its Performance in the 1970s*   University of California Press, Berkeley, Cal. 1982

Adam ULAM   *Tito and the Cominform*   Harvard University Press, Cambridge, Mass. 1952

Dan USHER   *The Economic Prerequisite of Democracy*   Basil Blackwell, Oxford 1981

M. VAN CREVELD   *Hitler's Strategy 1940–1941: The Balkan Clue*   Cambridge University Press, Cambridge, England 1973

Milan VEGO   *Yugoslavia and Soviet Policy in the Mediterranean Since 1961*   Center for Naval Analyses, Washington, D.C. 1981

Wayne VUCINICH (ed.)   *At the Brink of War and Peace*   Stanford University Press, Stanford, Cal. 1983

F. C. WADDAMS   *Today in Yugoslavia: By a British Officer*, published in the Yugoslav Information Sheet, London 1946

Evelyn WAUGH   *Diaries*, edited by Michael Davie,   Weidenfeld & Nicolson, London 1976

Mark C. WHEELER   *Britain and the War for Yugoslavia 1940–1943*   East European Monographs, no. 64, Boulder and New York 1980

Duncan WILSON   *Tito's Yugoslavia*   Cambridge University Press, Cambridge, England 1979

Field Marshal Lord WILSON of Libya   *Eight Years Overseas*   Hutchinson, London 1950

Donald ZAGORIA   *The Sino-Soviet Conflict 1956–1961*   Princeton University Press, Princeton, N.J. 1962

INDEX

Acheson, Dean, 150, 151
Adamic, Louis, 89
Afghanistan, 181, 187
Agriculture, 243
Aid: from Tito to Third World, 177; to
    Tito from Russia, 176; to Tito
    from West, 18, 27, 99, 100, 103,
    149–51, 169, 189, 235, 161–2; to
    Third World from West, 180
Albania, 143, 192; and Kosovo,
    209–14
Aldington, Lord, 125, 126
Alexander I, 41, 44, 48, 49, 50
Alexander, Field-Marshal, 85, 101,
    122, 125
Algeria, 176
Allcock, John B., 24
Allies, 56; attitude to Chetniks, 87, 91,
    93, 98–9, 116, 119; attitude to
    Partisans, 84–5, 87–93, 95, 97,
    104; as class enemies of Tito, 159;
    See also Britain, USA
Angelarije, Archbishop, 214
Angola, 177
Anti-Communism in Yugoslavia, 19,
    41–5, 48–52; *See also* Chetniks
Arafat, Yasser, 172
Armstrong, Brigadier, 91, 99
Association of War Veterans, 67
Astor, David, 151
Atrocities, 72, 74, 77, 117–19, 127,
    146, 190
Auty, Phyllis, 37, 81, 234
Axis Pact, 63
Ayatollah Khomeini, 215–16

Ba Congress, 107
Bailey, Colonel, 101
Bajt, Prof. Aleksandar, 240
Bakali, Mahmud, 210, 211, 212
Bakarić, Stjepan, 43
Bakarić, Vladimir, 43, 195, 203
Bandung Conference, 163, 168
Banks, Yugoslav, 229

Barbarossa, 56, 60, 65
Barker, Elizabeth, 105
Basta, Milan, 123
Bebler, Alex, 144
Belgrade, 46, 58, 65, 121, 131, 132
Belgrade Six trial, 250, 254–5, 264
Beloff, Nora; trouble with Yugoslav
    police, 253, 257–8
Benn, Tony, 249
Bethell, Lord, 57
Bevan, Aneuran, 154, 156
Bevin, Ernest, 151
Bilandžić, Prof. Dušan, 243
Blunt, Anthony, 89
Borba, 33, 61, 134, 155, 198, 229, 252
Bosnia-Herzegovina, 37, 74, 192, 193,
    196, 209, 215–17, 231
Boughey, Peter, 78
Boyle, Andrew, 87, 88
Brandt, Willie, 180, 202
Brezhnev, Leonid, 21, 169, 181, 203–4
Brezhnev Doctrine, The, 174–5
Brioni, 162, 163, 166, 171, 182, 203
Britain: Yugoslavs in, 18; press
    attitude to Yugoslavia in, 23;
    Tito's pre-war attitude towards,
    61–2; landing in Greece, 65;
    Intelligence Service, 87;
    admiration for USSR;
    repatriation of Croat refugees,
    124–7; Tito in, 151 *See also* Allies,
    SOE
British A Force, 67, 95
British-Yugoslav Society, 57
Brittan, Samuel, 226
Broz, Josip *See* Tito
Bukovsky, Vladimir, 23
Bulgaria, 143, 185, 214
Burgess, Guy, 78, 89
Byelusnova, Pelagea, 39, 40

Cadogan, Sir Alexander, 105–6
Cairo SOE, 89–93, 96, 104
Canadian Communist Party, 96

Carinthia, 123–4
Castro, Fidel, 186
Čavoški, Kosta, 136–7, 140, 252, 256
Censorship, 253
Central Investment Fund, 195
Chad, 177
Chetniks: origin of name, 67; Tito takes stand against, 67–8; resistance to Germans, 69–70; war with Croatia, 75–7; accusations of collaboration, 77–9, 81; war with Partisans, 73–7, 99, 115; and Italian defeat, 85; Western prejudice against, 87, 91, 93, 98–9, 116; denunciation as traitors, 111; rescue by British, 119–20; See also Mihailović, Draža
China, 166, 167, 185
Churchill, Randolph, 101, 105, 108
Churchill, Winston, 20, 30, 64, 68, 84, 89, 93, 95, 96, 100–1, 104–7, 114–15, 129, 151; meeting with Tito, 109–10
Civil war in Yugoslavia, 73–7, 104, 117
Clark, Colonel, 62
Clissold, Stephen, 153–5
Colanović, Branko, 235
Collectivization, 147
Čolaković, Rodoljub, 146
Comecon, 182
Cominform, 143–4, 145
Comintern, 42, 49, 66, 142, 143
Communism in Yugoslavia: pre-war, 22–3, 41–2, 61–2; post-war, 131–5, 147, 152, 157, 166–7, 195, 263; See also Partisans
Concentration camps, 134, 146, 202
Conferences in Bandung, 163, 168; in Brioni, 163; in Stolica, 70; in Teheran, 104
Constitution, Yugoslav, 193–5
Consumerism, 226–7
Čopić, Vladimir, 35, 54
Ćosić, Dobrica, 20, 214
Crnobrnja, Mihailo, 256–7
Croat Peasant Party, 22, 64, 97, 137, 138
    See also Vladko Maček
Croat refugee repatriation, 124–7

Croatia, 32, 76, 192, 193, 201, 202–3, 231, economy of, 206; See also Ustashas
Crosland, Anthony, 119–20, 124, 125
Cunningham, Admiral Sir John, 88
Czechoslovakia, 173–6

Danas, 234–5
Dapčević, Peko, 156
Dapčević-Kućar, Savka, 203, 204
Davidson, Basil, 89, 96
Deakin, Capt. William, 20, 83, 95, 96–9, 127, 137, 151, 221, 264
Dedijer, Vladimir, 31, 41, 54, 55, 70, 73, 82, 127, 157
Demokratija, 137–8
Dictatorship of the proletariat, 15
Dizdarević, Raif, 261
Djemsembayev, Hadj Isaj, 39
Djilas, Aleksa, 25
Djilas, Milovan on modern communism, 19; on Tito, 31, 33, 36, 45–6, 68, 143; meeting Tito, 52; in delegation to Germans, 81, 82; on Partisans, 111, 131; on Kocbek, 117; on Domobranci, 126; on concentration camps, 134; on Grol, 138; and Cominform, 144; his career, 153–8, 207, 218, 265; on Bosnia, 192; his arrest, 250
Djordjević, Professor, 194
Djureković (defector), 231
Domobranci, 125–6
Donovan, General, 99–100
Drašković, Milorad, 41
Drašković, Vuk, 76
Drulović, Milojko, 244, 249
Dubček, 174–5
Dulles, Alan, 162
Dulles, John Foster, 162
Duško (prisoner), 156

Eagleburger, Lawrence, 15, 256
Economist, The, 151
Economy, Yugoslav, 197–200, 234–6
Eden, Antony, 105, 106, 130
EEC, 183
Egypt, 163, 171–3, 177
Elections in Yugoslavia, 138
Energo-Invest, 240

Ennals, John, 57
Ethiopia, 177

Federalism, 193
Fifth Offensive, 83
Filaković, Imre, 138–9
First of May (textile firm), 240–1
Fisher, Archbishop of Canterbury, 151
Five Year Plan, 147, 149
Floyd, David, 54
Floyd, Sir Henry, 121
Foot, M. R. O., 71
Franz Ferdinand, Archduke, 38
"Friends of Yugoslavia", 15
Frontier skirmishes with Soviets, 148

Gačić, Radica, 59
Gaj, Ljudevit, 203
Gavrilović, Milan, 65
Gehlen, Reinhardt, 79
German communism, 50–1
German invasion of Russia, 60
German occupation of Yugoslavia, 57–83, 94–5
German treaty with Yugoslavia, 63
Gledišta, 252
Glen, Alexander, 62, 87–8, 119
Goebbels, 63, 64
Goli Otok, 146
Golytsin, 185
Goodman, Prof. A. E., 179
Gorenje, 240
Gorkić, Milan, 50, 53, 54
Gornji Grad, 49
Gornji Milanovac, 68
Greece, 65, 102, 142, 143, 172
Greene, Graham, 87
Grenada, 186–7
Grol, Milan, 131–2, 137–8, 139
Guardian, 23
Guinea, 177, 188

Hackett, General Sir John, 17
Haile Selassie, 163
Hajić, Judge Rozah, 216
Hebrang, Andrija, 145–6, 150, 203
Hinsley, F. H., 91, 92, 99
Hitler, Adolf, 50, 51, 64, 80
Horvat, Branko, 197
Howard, Michael, 59, 85

Howe, Sir Geoffrey, 261
Hoxha, Enver, 36, 82, 143, 192
Hoxha, Mehmet, 210
Hudson, Bill, 70, 72, 91, 92, 96, 98
Hungary, invasion of, 165–6
Hydro-electric projects, 198

INA, 231
India, 177
Iraq, 176–7
Italian occupation of Yugoslavia, 58, 78, 94
Italian surrender, 85, 94
Ivanović, Vane, 127

Jackson, Richard, 184
Jajce Assembly, 103, 104, 105
Jasenovac concentration camp, 202
Jenkins, Roy, 238
Johnson, Paul, 188
Jovanov, Prof. Neca, 231
Jovanović, Arso, 120
Jovanović, Prof Dragljub, 139–40
Jovanović, Iso, 82

Kaplan, Robert, 57
Karchmar, Lucien, 71, 116
Kardelj, Edvard: as theorist, 30; and Tito, 33, 52, 143, 218; and Comintern, 49; and Stalin, 55; his wartime reminiscences, 73, 84, 159–60, 219; and Partisans, 75, 122; and Maček, 76, 97; as Tito's deputy, 132; his ideology, 141; and Cominform, 144; on Czech crisis, 175; his writings, 184; and centralist policy, 193, 195; and self-management, 219, 223–34, 239; his career, 220–3
Kardelj, Pepica, 232
Kavčič, Stane, 208
Keble, C. M., 89
Keightley, General, 125, 126
Kennan, George, 169–72
Khrushchev, Nikita, 147, 150, 157, 162, 164–8, 171–2, 223
Kidrič, Boris, 45, 49, 52, 193, 218
Kiraly, General Bela, 148
Kissinger, Henry, 36
Kljaković, Vjomir, 113
Klugmann, James, 88, 89, 96, 135

Kocbek, Edvard, 117–18, 208–9
Kolakowski, Leszek, 263
Komunist, 176
Kopinič, Josip, 54
Korbel, Josef, 138
Kosovo, 26, 192, 193, 209–14
Koštunica, Vojislav, 136–7
Kovaćević, Zivord, 237
Krajger stabilization commission, 236
Kraljevica shipyard strike, 42
Kundera, Milan, 16

Lalić, Ivan, 260
Language, 202–3, 208, 211
Lapenna, Ivo, 194
Law of Associated Labour, 227
Lepoglava jail, 45, 47
Letica, Dr Slaven, 263
Libya, 176–7
Little Entente, 50
Ljotić, Dimitrije, 72, 138
Ljubišić, General, 212
Ljubljana, 58; 'liberation' of, 132
Lloyd-Owen, General, 120
Low, Brigadier, 125, 126
Loznica, 71
Luther, Rudolf, 83
Lydall, Prof. Harold, 24, 239

McCarthy, Senator, 160
MacDowell, Robert, 113
Macedonia, 209, 214; nickel works in, 242–3
Maček, Vladko, 22, 63, 66, 76, 97, 117, 137
Maclean, Donald, 88
Maclean, Brigadier Fitzroy, 20, 47, 95, 99, 101–5, 106, 111–12, 121, 129, 141–2, 151, 248
Macmillan, Harold, 101, 110, 112–13, 122, 125–6
Malaparte, Curzio, 74
Mali, 177
Maribor jail, 45, 47
Marjanović, Jovan, 73
Marshall, Secretary of State, 149
Martin, David, 80
Marxism in Yugoslavia, see Communism in Yugoslavia
Matica Hrvatska, 203, 204
Matl, Josef, 72

Medenica, Dr Spasoje, 235
Meyszner, Police Chief, 79
Mićunović, Veljko, 31, 165
Mihailović, Colonel Draža: and Alexander Glen, 62; his career, 66–73; meetings with Tito, 69, 71; and Chetniks, 75; and Italians, 78–80; continued resistance, 80–1; trial and execution, 81, 116; discrediting of, 91–2, 97; Allied prejudice against, 98–9, 100–1, 105; and King Peter, 106; and the Ba congress, 107; Tito's attitude towards, 115; See also Chetniks
Mihajlov, Mihajlo, 201, 253
Miklavčič, France, 209
Milić, Miodrag, 264
Minić, Milos, 139
Molotov, 144, 145
Montenegro, 191, 193
Moore, Dr John, 224
Moslems, 94, 215–17
Most Favoured Nation Treaty, 170–1
Muggeridge, Malcolm, 87
Muir, David, 95
Murphy, Robert, 110, 112
Murray, General Horatius, 119
Mussolini, 56, 80
Musulin, George, 107

Nagoda, Dr, 140, 141
Naš Rod, 221
Nasser, Gamal Abdel, 163, 171–3
National Liberation Front, 113, 140, 147
NATO, 152, 186
Nedić, General, 69, 79, 115, 138
Nehru, Pandit, 163
Neutrality, 162
New International Economic Order, 179–80, 210
New Left Review, 250, 255–6
New York Times, 23
New Yorker, 24, 36
Nicaragua, 187
Nickel works in Macedonia, 242–3
Nigeria, 177
Nikolić, Milan, 250, 255–6
Non-alignment, 159, 163–4, 168–9, 178–84
Nova Misao, 156

Nova Revija, 209
Nuclear tests, 168

Obrenović, Prince Michael, 175, 206
Observer, The, 23, 151
Office of Strategic Services, 99, 120
Operation *Schwatz*, 83
Orwell, George, 166
OZNA, 130, 132–5, 140

Palestine Liberation Organisation, 172
Paraga, Dobroslav, 205
Partisans, 20, 41, 75, 190; glamorous image, 57; limitations, 58–9; heroism, 59–60; and Chetniks, 69–71, 76, 80–1, 82, 99; offer to collaborate, 81; German attacks on, 82–3, 94, 108; combat effectiveness, 85–6, 94; British support for, 84, 87–93, 95, 97, 104; control of surrendering Italians, 86; dishonesty, 98, 102; Balkan airforce support, 107–8; rejection of Allied presence, 120–2; seizure of Trieste, 122–3; claim on Carinthia, 123–4; after the war, 130–1
Pašić, Dušan, 241
Patterson, US Ambassador, 132, 133
Paul, Prince, 18, 60, 62–3
Pauperization, 15
Pavelić, Ante, 49, 74, 117, 137
Pavlowitch, Stevan, 16
Peter I, 206
Peter II, 63–4, 92, 100, 103, 105–6, 108, 111, 130
Phelps, Arthur, 75
Philby, Kim, 89
Pijade, Mosa, 45, 47, 55, 192
Planinc, Milka, 189, 241
Polak, Samuel, 40
Poland, 60, 113
Political prisoners, 45, 47–8
  See also Belgrade Six, Concentration camps
Political Warfare Executive, 97
Politika, 198, 199, 219
Polka *see* Pelagea Byelusnova, 39
Popović, Koča, 81
Popović, Srdja, 201, 254, 255

Powell, Anthony, 90
Požega, 71–2
Pravoslavlje, 202
Praxis, 226
Price, Colonel Robin, 125
Princip, Gavrilo, 38
Priština, Kosovo, 210, 211, 212, 213
Private enterprise, 243–4
Proleter, 49
Proxmire, William, 170
Purić, Premier, 90
Pušić, Dr Eugene, 232–3

Qadhafi, Colonel, 177, 182

Radić, Stjepan, 43
Radio Free Europe, 23
Radović, Radomir, 250, 259
Ranković, Aleksandar, 52, 82, 139, 195–6
Ravna Gora, 70
Rayner, Louise, 77
Reagan, President, 187, 189
Religious persecution, 103, 118, 135, 151, 202
Rendell, Sir George, 100
Rendulić, General Lothar, 75
Repatriation of Croat refugees, 124–7
Ribar, Lola, 53
Ribičič, Mitja, 59, 186
Roberts, Walter, 79
Romania, 186
Roosevelt, Eleanor, 89
Roosevelt, President, 100, 104
Rootham, Jasper, 51–2, 93
Rubinstein, A., 164
Rusinow, Dennison, 20

Sabić, Stevo, 42
Sadat, Anwar, 176
Sarajevo, 38
SAWPY, 224
School of Yugoslav Studies (Bradford), 24–5
Scott, Brigadier T. D., 124–5
Seaton, A., 94
Šeks, Vladimir, 254
Self-management, 218–45
Semić-Daki, General Stane, 84

Serbia: losses in World War I, 38; in the 1920s, 41; hostilities with Partisans, 72–3, 110–11; rebellion against Germans, 72; and Ustashas, 74–5; soviet invasion of, 112; in Federation, 190–2, 193, 201; language of, 202–3; in 1970s, 206–8; nationalism of, 212–4

Shaplen, Robert, 24

Silbermann, Lawrence, 180

Simić, Dr Andrej, 238

Singleton, Fred, 24

Sirc, Dr Ljubo, 25, 98, 135, 140, 152, 156, 242

Slovene Liberation Front, 221

Slovenia, 32, 41, 118, 192, 193, 194, 201–2, 208–9

Smederevo railway workshop strike 42

Social services, 230, 239

Socialist Utopianism, 23–4

SOE, 70, 78, 88, 99, 120; Cairo SOE, 89–93, 96, 104

Solzhenitsyn, Alexander, 23

Somalia, 177

Sovereignty, 196–7

Spanish Civil War, 53

Špiljak, Mika, 187, 189, 228

Srebrić, Borislav, 183

Stabilization, 236

Stalin, 21, 46, 48, 50, 52, 55, 68, 73, 111, 142–9, 155

Stenton, M. M., 98

Stephenson, George, 106

Stepinac, Cardinal, 39, 136, 203

Stewart, Colonel, 98

Štipe Šuvar, Stipe, 228, 259

Students, 53, 204

Šubašić, Ivan, 108–10, 130

Suvorov, Boris, 172

Syria, 177

Tanzania, 177

Tempo, Svetozar Vukmanović, 150

Terzić, General Vladimir, 64

Tetovo, Macedonia, 214

Thatcher, Margaret, 189, 238

Third Word aid from Tito, 177; aid from West, 180

Tikhonov, Nikolai, 188

Tito (Josip Broz): his achievement, 29, 247–8; his childhood and youth, 31; his character, 21, 31, 34, 42, 46, 162, 178, 220; his popular image, 29, 130, 247; his ideology, 30, 45, 250; Western bias in favour of, 25, 84, 87–93, 95, 97; his death, 35; his appearance, 35, 110; his clothes, 35–7, 109; his early career, 36–7; his military career, 37–8; his first marriage, 39–40; at Polak's mill, 40–2; his second marriage, 40–1; as trade union organiser, 42–3; as communist revolutionary, 42–3, 48–50; imprisonment, 43, 44–5, 47; adoption of code-name Tito, 48; and Stalin, 52, 55, 68, 73, 111, 142–9, 155; in Moscow, 54, 142, 168; as General Secretary of Yugoslav Communist Party, 55–6, 66; and Chetniks, 67; relations with Russia, 68, 176; meetings with Mihailović, 69, 71; hostility towards Allies, 84–5, 120–2; impression made on Deakin, 97; repudiation of Yugoslav monarchy, 103; British endorsement as leader, 107; at Vis, 108–9, 111, 137; meeting with Churchill, 109–10; expansionist ambitions, 142–3; his popularity, 146; in London, 151; choice between East and West, 152–3, 160–2; and Djilas, 154–7; as model to other leaders, 178; 1972 directive to Party cadres, 207, 227; and self-management, 219; See also Partisans

Tito, Jovanka, 31, 41

Todorović, Mijalko, 174

Tolbukhin, Marshal, 59

Tolstoy, Count Nicolai, 127

Tomić, Momćilo, 242

Trieste, 122–3

Tripalo, Mika, 203, 204–5

Truman, President, 116, 133, 143, 150

Ulam, Adam, 145

Unemployment in Yugoslavia, 15
United Nations, 160, 183–4
UNRRA, 121, 134, 135
USA: attitude to Yugoslavia, 21,
148–51; Office of Strategic
Services, 99, 120; Yugoslav
emigrants in, 21, 170
Usher, Dan, 251
USSR, 21; German invasion of, 56, 60,
65; friendship pact with
Yugoslavia, 65; invasion of
Yugoslavia by, 114, 115–16;
break with Yugoslavia, 142–8;
reconciliation, 157, 165; use of
Yugoslav airspace/ports, 173,
176–8; trade with Yugoslavia,
182
Ustashas of Croatia, 49, 50, 66, 74–5,
82, 86, 124, 136, 137, 202
Užice, 71

Vego, Milan, 177
Velebit, Vlatko, 81, 88, 89–90, 106
Veselica, Marko, 205
Vidmar, Josef, 209
Vis, 108–9, 111, 137
Vojvodina, 192, 193
Volunteer postwar labour, 131
von Weichs, Field-Marshal, 59, 86
Vučković, Zvonimir, 68

Waddams, Frank, 126, 133–5
Wade, Robert, 80
Warsaw Pact, 159, 173
Washington Post, 23
Watson, Hugh Seton, 89
Waugh, Evelyn, 103, 120, 151
Weil, Major Richard, 95–6
West, Rebecca, 62, 78
Wheeler, Mark, 20
Williams, Marcia, 154
Wilson, General Maitland, 64, 121
Wisshaupt, General, 73

Worrel, Colonel Denys, 124

Yalta, 129, 140
Yugoslav Official Gazette, 63
Yugoslavia: unemployment in, 15;
history, 16, 26; population, 16, 74;
strategic importance, 16; tourism,
17; overseas aid to, 18, 27, 99,
100, 103, 149–51;
anti-communism in, 19, 41–5,
48–52; political prisoners in, 45,
47–8, 134, 146; communism in,
22–3, 41–2, 61–2, 131–5, 147,
152, 157, 166–7, 195, 263; pact
with USSR, 65; German
occupation of, 57–9, 64–83,
121–2; treaty with Germany, 63;
Italian occupation of, 58, 78; civil
war in, 73–7, 104, 117; discussions
on postwar future, 104; Russian
invasion of, 114, 115–16;
expulsion from Soviet bloc, 129,
142–8; aid from West, 18, 27, 99,
100, 103, 149–51, 169, 189, 235,
261–2; elections, 138;
reconciliation with Russia, 157;
non-alignment, 159, 163–4,
168–9, 178–84; recent relations
with Russia, 172, 176–8, 182,
185–6; constitution, 193–5;
economy, 197–200, 234–6

Zagoria, Prof., 166, 167
Zagorje province, 32–3
Zagreb, 58, 206; liberation of, 132;
metal workers' union, 42–3;
public rally in, 204; university,
204
Zaječar, 71
Zinoviev, 23
Zujović, Sreten, 82
Zulfikarpašić, Adil, 216